Reconsidering *Roots*

Reconsidering *Roots*

RACE, POLITICS, AND MEMORY

EDITED BY Erica L. Ball
AND Kellie Carter Jackson

The University of Georgia Press

ATHENS

Parts of chapter 6 originally appeared in "What's Your Name?: Race, Roots, and Popular Memory," by C. Richard King, in *African Americans on Television: Race-ing for Ratings*, ed. David J. Leonard and Lisa Guerrero, 114–140 (Santa Barbara, Calif.: Praeger, 2013).

© 2017 by the University of Georgia Press
Athens, Georgia 30602
www.ugapress.org
All rights reserved
Set in 10/13 Kepler Std by Graphic Composition, Inc.

Most University of Georgia Press titles are
available from popular e-book vendors.

Printed digitally

Library of Congress Control Number: 2017934778

ISBN: 9780820350837 (hardcover: alk. paper)
ISBN: 9780820350820 (paperback: alk. paper)
ISBN: 9780820350844 (ebook)

For those
who preserve our history
and tell our stories

It can be said that we know the rest of the story—how it turned out, so to speak, but frankly, I don't think that we do know the rest of the story. It *hasn't* turned out yet, which is the rage and pain and danger of this country.

—James Baldwin, "How One Black Man Came to Be an American: A Review of *Roots*," *New York Times*, September 26, 1976

CONTENTS

FOREWORD

HENRY LOUIS GATES JR.

Roots: The Saga of an America Family, which aired on eight consecutive nights in the winter of 1977 on ABC, created a singular American moment that is unimaginable to those growing up in an era in which we can binge-watch all sorts of black programming, from *Scandal* and *Empire*, and *Black-ish* and *How to Get Away with Murder*, to *The People versus O. J. Simpson, Underground*, and even our own three seasons of *Finding Your Roots*.

Alex Haley's *Roots*, when it premiered, achieved a feat nobody could ever even have imagined before it aired: the series attracted an astonishing 85 percent of U.S. households, which tuned in at least to parts of the journey unfolding within the long genealogical history of a single black family—the Haleys—from Kunta Kinte and his harrowing enslavement across the Middle Passage from West Africa to Colonial Virginia before the American Revolution, to the uncertain aftermath of the Civil War and the efforts of Kinte's grandson "Chicken" George to purchase land as a freedman in Tennessee. *Roots* was epic. Haley's book was a runaway bestseller following its release in 1976 and earned the author a special Pulitzer Prize, while the television series adapted from it garnered a stunning thirty-seven Emmy nominations. *Roots* wasn't just part of the pop culture conversation in 1977. It *was* the conversation.

Roots presented readers and viewers with a new kind of black royalty, timed to meet the rising "black-is-beautiful" generation that had emerged from the tumultuous era of civil rights and Black Power freer of mind and more positive of racial self-image, and with greater opportunities for advancement, than any generation of African Americans before it. At the same time, by way of its vivid characters and plot, drawn from stories passed down within the Haley family and stories imaginatively invented by Haley, *Roots* jolted the American general public out of their long, repressive slumber over the history of slavery (just as historians such as John W. Blassingame had done in *The Slave Community*, published just five years before). *Roots* made it clear in human terms that slavery was not only real, it was violent, it went on over generations and generations, and it left far deeper, far more painful scars than the *Gone with the Wind* template had let on, but its victims, its objects, ultimately triumphed over this most heinous of human institutions, nevertheless, in the most noble and heroic ways, ways that could be the stuff of great storytelling, whether histories such as Blassingame's or novels such as *Roots*.

xi

Roots achieved something quite complex and paradoxical: on the one hand, it exposed historic and lasting wounds; but at the same time that it revealed scars, it was revealing the coexistence of injury, healing, and transcendence. After all, the slaves did, in the most meaningful sense, not just *endure* but *prevail*, since we, Haley's novel attested, the descendants of slaves, were here to testify both about those antecedents *and* the institution that shaped every aspect of their lives. Telling the story of slavery, as a descendant of slaves, was a defeat for the whole purpose of enslavement: eternal bondage, eternal social death, eternal silence in the republic of letters. *Roots* also helped to instill the belief in African Americans that there was an unshakable majesty within the black family itself, whose functionality, it must be remembered, had been called into serious question only a decade earlier by *The Moynihan Report* and its focus on cyclical, impoverished, single-parent households. Here, instead, was the linear story of a continuous family running through the heart of U.S. history, a family that found a way to stay together through the stories they told and retold against the most formidable odds, making their way *up from the silencing non-discourses of the slave regime* and into the publishing houses of narrative.

Roots' power, and its most important legacy, I believe, was in the way it used the narrative arc of a single black family to challenge audiences to face their history while inspiring African Americans in particular to search for personal connections to a past that had long been silenced by that history and, for the first time, to see themselves as part of a longer journey with roots deeper than slavery on this side of the Atlantic, in specific places with specific names on the other side of the Atlantic, in Africa. In accepting this invitation, *Roots'* audience bore witness to Black America's suffering and survival over centuries—how human beings had withstood the debasement of chattel slavery while forging a culture that centrally helped to define and shape *American* cultural forms from the beginnings, really, of "American culture." In this sense, Alex Haley's *Roots* was the most American of American stories, a story of resiliency and rise released in the glow of the nation's bicentennial, a coincidence which we often forget. Haley's gifts as a storyteller and as a shaper of this new narrative were prodigious; they also were not surprising. After all, he had, famously, shaped and written the extraordinary life Malcolm X had dictated to him, published to great acclaim as *The Autobiography of Malcolm X: As Told to Alex Haley*. For many in my generation, that hybrid book was an instant classic, and it remains one for my students at Harvard to this very day.

When *Roots* premiered on ABC more than a decade later in 1977, I was working on my dissertation at the University of Cambridge and teaching in the English Department and the Afro-American Studies Program at Yale. I was only four years out of college myself, a revolutionary time in the country when the first critical mass of affirmative-action students integrated histori-cally white institutions and demanded that their history be taught as a field on par with every other American history, so that the truth of our past could be known and disseminated. *Roots* was a different kind of teacher, staging a different kind of pedagogy inside U.S. living rooms, registering—I still find this difficult to believe—the biggest audience ever for a television show up to that time. As a cultural phenomenon in print and on screen, it worked its way deep into the public and private cultural imagination, liberating black families to pursue answers to who they were and from where they had come, to attempt to trace their African roots, to travel to the continent to make a connection, and to take a hard look at the past with persistence and open eyes, and with more openness and, yes, with more courage, than perhaps ever before.

Part of that hard look extended to Haley's own research. As genealogists weighed in, we soon learned that not all of the *Roots* story could be called nonfiction, that Haley's research had leaned on stories passed down within his family that could not be verified against the paper trail, some of which contradicted what he had written, including the connections he had drawn among the pre–Civil War ancestors so many of us had come to love.[1] As the controversy over *Roots* dragged on into the early 1980s, it was easy for critics to become mired in debates over the proper label to assign to Haley's work. Was it history? Was it fiction? Or was it a blending of the two: *faction*? Did this matter or did it disqualify Haley from entering the ranks of the greats? Had we been sold a bill of goods, or was *Roots* true enough to remain worthy of our admiration and trust? Along the way, many of my peers in the academy lost sight of Haley's formidable talents, his staggering imaginative powers, and what *Roots* had meant to so many as a touchstone of their lives, as the black text that had touched the Zeitgeist more directly and completely than had any black text before it, and certainly any text since *Uncle Tom's Cabin*, published a century and a quarter before.

While sympathetic with my colleagues' concerns, on a personal level I do not hesitate to say that *Roots* was a crucial encouragement to my own efforts to continue exploring, first, my own, and much later, other people's ancestral roots, an intellectual odyssey which for me had begun long before—in fact, when I was nine years old, growing up in the hills of eastern West Virginia, on the very day we buried my father's father, in July 1960. A touchstone for me personally, *Roots* showed me what was possible beyond the stories passed down at my parents' kitchen table, at Big Mom's house on Thanksgiving, and at Gates and Coleman family reunions. As my own interest in genealogy de-veloped over time, the tools of my trade became the historical paper trail and the endlessly fascinating science of ancestral DNA tracing. Forty years later, technology has revolutionized this work, making the historical paper trail more accessible than ever through the digitization of census records, tax and military records, slave schedules, and wills, while DNA science is now able to approximate where, and to what degree across Sub-Saharan Africa, a person's recent African ancestry (since, say, the last five hundred years) originates, from Senegambia to Madagascar—discoveries that Haley could, literally, only have imagined when he was writing in the 1970s.

Working on the third season of my genealogy series for PBS, *Finding Your Roots*, reminded me of the magical powers of Haley's storytelling art when, in the course of my interview with comedy legend Keenen Ivory Wayans, he told me that, in the absence of facts, he had grown up imagining his original African American ancestor as a proverbial Kunta Kinte, a black man who would rather chop off his foot than endure one more day as a slave.[2] As it happened, I had to break the news to Keenen that he actually descended from a South Carolina slave named Ben Pleasant who had chosen to remain with his master (John Manning, the future governor of the state) even when presented the chance to be free by abolitionists who had rescued him while he was traveling with Manning in Canada. It was remarkable to watch Keenen, one of the funniest comedians at work today, process this information in real time, grasping the agonizing complexities of individual decisions, which, in his ancestor's case, had been bound up in the meaning of home and the pain that freedom might have brought in being separated from his still-enslaved family and friends, raising levels of complexity about slavery and freedom that we don't generally ponder.

Until evidentiary-based genealogy shows came onto the scene, *Roots* was the stand-in for countless African Americans' family trees. From Kunta Kinte to Kizzy to Chicken George, *Roots* provided flesh and bone to the elusive ancestors that black people, including Alex Haley himself, conjured in the absence of proof denied by slavery. Thus, there is no accurate way to measure the ripple effect *Roots* had on families that, well into the twentieth century, had been taught, as Arthur Schomburg once wrote, that "the Negro has been a man without a history because he has been considered a man without a worthy culture."[3] In other words, *Roots* wasn't just a publishing or television phenomenon; it was a gateway to new worlds, genealogical, geographical, cultural, and psychological worlds.

For this reason, I am pleased that a rising generation of scholars more likely to know LeVar Burton as the genial and book-loving host of PBS's *Reading Rainbow* than as the original Kunta Kinte is now interested in giving *Roots* a fresh, and rigorous, scholarly treatment, one that befits its importance as a cultural multiplier while also wrestling with the critiques leveled against it. "I do not believe it is something I have done by myself," Haley remarked about his creation in his keynote address at the 1977 Opportunity Fair of the Greater Washington Business Center. "I believe that I have only been a channel, a conduit that has been used at this particular time to tell the story of a people."[4] That story takes a giant leap forward with this edited volume, *Reconsidering Roots*, and I am proud of my enterprising colleagues, Kellie Carter Jackson, and her coeditor, Erica L. Ball, as well as of the array of talented contributors they have assembled, for filling this void. In doing so, they are making it possible for readers to engage *Roots* in a comprehensive way so that they can grapple both with the heated debates it sparked in the world of letters among historians, literary critics, and genealogists and with its larger significance to the African American—and to the American—saga.

Alex Haley's *Roots: The Saga of an American Family* fundamentally altered the way black families thought about their history while forcing the wider public to examine *American* history—our history, real and imagined—as never before. *Roots*, which so forcefully told our story, is now a part of that story itself, and it is time to read and interrogate that story in all of its facets.

Cambridge, Massachusetts
Winter 2016

NOTES

1. For a thorough analysis of the genealogical accuracy of *Roots*, see Gary B. and Elizabeth Shown Mills, "*Roots* and the New 'Faction': A Legitimate Tool for Clio?," *Virginia Magazine of History and Biography* 89, no. 1 (January 1981): 3–26.

2. *Finding Your Roots*, season 3, episode 3, PBS, aired January 19, 2016.

3. Arthur Schomburg, "The Negro Digs Up His Past," *Survey Graphic* 6 (March 1925).

4. Alex Haley quoted in Joseph D. Whitaker, "Alex Haley Says *Roots* Helped Dispel Myths," *Washington Post*, February 24, 1977.

ACKNOWLEDGMENTS

The work of the historian is usually a solitary endeavor. But this project has been just the opposite. It took shape over many phone calls, emails, and the occasional mealtime conversation at conferences in New York, Washington, D.C., Boston, and Los Angeles. In the years since we first began working on *Reconsidering Roots*, we have benefited from the assistance of multiple departments, organizations, institutions, and individuals. Although it would be impossible for us to mention everyone who supported *Reconsidering Roots* the past four years by name, we would like to acknowledge those who contributed to this volume most directly.

First, it has been a privilege to collaborate with such a talented group of scholars. Their thoughtful interpretations of *Roots* and their enthusiasm for this project remained a source of inspiration for us. In addition, we are grateful to Matthew F. Delmont for his support as well as his own efforts to bring *Roots* back into the academy for discussion. Many thanks to Alejandro de la Fuente and Sara Bruya at *Transition Magazine* for giving us the opportunity to extend our conversations about Alex Haley and *Roots* outside of this collection. As members of the Dark Room for Race and Visual Culture, we have also benefited greatly from their interdisciplinary scholarship and solidarity and the fearless leadership of Kimberly Juanita Brown.

Our respective universities have also been extremely helpful to us. Kellie would like to thank her colleagues at Harvard University during her time as a Harvard College fellow, and her colleagues at Hunter College for travel support as well as encouragement. Her students both at Harvard and Hunter have compelled her to think in new and nuanced ways about how we understand slavery through film and what is at stake. Erica would like to thank the collegial faculty and students in the Departments of African American Studies and American Studies at California State University, Fullerton (CSUF). A spring 2014 sabbatical provided Erica with the time necessary to begin working on this project, and Erica's conference travel expenses were funded by a generous CSUF General Faculty Research grant. Special thanks go to Shelley Herbert, who served as a CSUF graduate assistant during the spring 2016 semester, and to American Studies graduate students Jamal Batts and the late Courtney Brown for their countless insightful observations about African American expressive culture.

Working with the University of Georgia Press has been a terrific experience. Claire Potter and Renee Romano have believed in this collection from the very beginning. Mick Gunside-Duffy, Walter Biggins, John Joerschke, Jon Davies, and Bethany Snead have helped us negotiate all the stages of this process, and Deborah Oliver skillfully copyedited the final version of the manuscript. We remain indebted. Many thanks to Kim Gilmore and her team from the History Channel for an invitation to an early screening of the 2016 *Roots* remake at the Tribeca Film Festival, as well as to Hazel Gurland-Pooler for her amazing efforts to make history accessible, authentic, and accurate.

We would also like to thank our families. Eugene and Carolyn Ball sustained Erica with their unconditional love and shipments of homemade sour cream pound cake and organic grapefruit from the backyard. As always, Stephanie Ann Ball and Tom Sitzler remained a source of good cheer and enthusiasm for all things. Abby continues to be the very best dog in the world, and Brian Michael Norton continues to be everything, always.

Nathaniel Jackson has been the greatest champion Kellie could ever ask for. You will always be home base. William Charles Carter Jackson, thank you for being so pleasant and forgiving during all the moments she had to be away. Kellie's parents, William and Norvella Carter, and sisters, Camille Carter, Mia Oberlton, China Jenkins, Crystal Rose, Valerie McNeil, and Victoria Jones, continue to serve as her foundational support system and her best friends from birth.

Finally, we would like to thank each other. It has been over seven years since we (virtually) met, and over five years since we had the opportunity to meet face to face. Our interests in the history and representation of slavery and abolition brought us together, but our penchant for encouraging each other and our desire to perfect the world around us have sustained us. In many ways, our countless discussions on *Roots* became a reunion of sorts. Every Skype, phone call, or conference gave us the opportunity to reconnect and replenish our emotional and intellectual beings. While Alex Haley's *Roots* investigates our enduring ties of family, we hope this collection will also honor our friendship and the scholarship that compels us to continue to consider nd reconsider the roots of African American history, culture, struggles, and 'umphs.

Reconsidering *Roots*

Reconsidering *Roots*

ERICA L. BALL AND
KELLIE CARTER JACKSON

On January 23, 1977, something extraordinary began to happen in the United States. On that evening and for the seven consecutive nights that would follow, Americans of all backgrounds turned the dials on their television sets to their local ABC affiliate station, made themselves comfortable, and settled in to enjoy an eight-part television miniseries called *Roots*. The television event would be the first of its kind: a multipart melodrama with episodes aired over the course of days rather than weeks. It was also a series inspired by a black man—journalist Alex Haley—a writer who put the experiences of enslaved people of African descent at the center rather than the periphery of a story chronicling the experiences of generations of a black American family from the mid-eighteenth century through the aftermath of the Civil War.

Based on Haley's book, *Roots: The Saga of an American Family*, the television miniseries chronicled the life of Kunta Kinte of the Mandinka people and followed his descendants over generations from slavery to freedom in the aftermath of the Civil War. Viewers were treated to scenes of Kunta Kinte's boyhood years in his idyllic eighteenth-century West African village of Juffure (in modern Gambia), where the entire village worked together in harmony for the good of the community. Strong and dignified fathers served as role models, wives and mothers cared for home and family, elders dispensed wisdom, and charismatic grandmothers handed out love and discipline in equal parts. Audiences were subsequently horrified when fifteen-year-old Kunta Kinte was kidnapped during a hunting expedition, forcibly marched to the coast, chained and shipped across the Atlantic in the dark hold of a slave ship, auctioned off in Annapolis, Maryland, and finally forced to reckon with his new condition as a chattel slave on a plantation in Virginia. Over the course of the week, increasing numbers of Americans watched, intrigued by the personal dramas that characterized Kunta Kinte's resistance, acculturation, and ultimately, his incorporation into the slave community through his friendship with Fiddler, his marriage to Bell and the birth of their daughter, Kizzy. Viewers stayed with the family saga as generations of Kunta Kinte's progeny grew to adulthood; they shared in the heartbreak when Kizzy was sold to a North Carolina planter, and they later rooted for her son, Chicken George, as he saved his winnings as his owner's prize cockfighter, hoping to someday purchase his and his mother's freedom. Over the course of the series, viewers saw that each of Kinte's descendants honored his memory by taking the time to tell the next generation about the ancestor they called "the African." And as the program came to an end on the eighth night, viewers watched Kunta Kinte's newly emancipated great-grandsons Tom and Louis leave their North Carolina slave quarters behind and, led by their father Chicken George, head out for their own family homesteads and freedom in Tennessee. The finale concludes with the voice-over of Alex Haley announcing that these were the experiences of his ancestors, passed down to him in stories told by elderly relatives and substantiated through his years of painstaking genealogical research.

Although ABC executives had feared that the ratings for *Roots* would be low (indeed, they reportedly chose to air the series on back-to-back nights to mitigate the expected ratings damage), by the end of the broadcast more than 130 million Americans—nearly half the nation's population—had seen at least one episode. When the *Roots* finale aired on January 30, 1977, an estimated 90 million viewers tuned in, making it what was then the most-watched program in television history. With television in over 85 percent of U.S. homes and video cassette recorders not yet on the market, Americans canceled meetings and social events in order to stay home to participate in this collective cultural event. Even pop star Barry Manilow of "Looks Like We Made It" fame reportedly wished he could cancel his Sunday evening concert in order to see the conclusion. Bars and restaurants, meanwhile, kept their television sets tuned to ABC so that patrons wouldn't miss a moment.[1]

The extraordinary interest in the television miniseries, in turn, propelled massive sales of Haley's book, which had been published only a few months earlier in September 1976. Blending historical fiction, literary journalism, and memoir, *Roots: The Saga of an American Family* would sell over 1.5 million copies in its first seven months in stores.[2] Marketed as nonfiction rather than historical fiction, it remained on the New York Times Best Seller list alongside titles like Saul Bellow's *To Jerusalem and Back* and John W. Dean's *Blind Ambition* (an account of Watergate) for an astounding forty-six weeks and held the number one spot for more than twenty-two weeks.[3] By the time of Haley's death in 1992, 4 million paperback copies had sold.[4] It would eventually be translated into nearly thirty languages. Haley, meanwhile, became one of the most celebrated authors in the world, a folk hero who had set a new bar for African American literary achievement. To this day, *Roots* has sold more copies than any other African American writer's narrative.[5]

Roots also quickly expanded into a larger cultural phenomenon. In an age long before internet outlets like etsy and ebay, entrepreneurs began capitalizing on the nation's obsession with *Roots* by designing and selling "Mandinka Maiden" T-shirts, plaques referencing the show, Root Tracing Kits, and even "Roots music."[6] African Americans began naming their children after characters from *Roots*. In New York City alone, twenty newborns were named Kunta Kinte or Kizzy within days of the program's broadcast.[7] Haley noted, "I know of at least 12 newborns named for him, and in San Francisco the mother of twins named one baby Kunta and the other Kinte."[8] Black Americans placed *Roots* alongside the Bible on the family coffee table. Americans of all backgrounds rushed to their local historical societies in an attempt to create their own personal meaningful heritage.[9] Meanwhile, high schools and colleges across the country began using *Roots* as a learning tool, with close to three hundred adopting the book for their courses.[10] A harbinger of early twenty-first-century college classes that used acclaimed television series to teach courses such as "*The Wire* and Urban Inequality" or "Consumerism and Social Change in *Mad Men* America," episodes of *Roots* became the springboard for lectures and discussions on U.S. slavery.[11] For these reasons, Vernon Jordan, president of the Urban League, called *Roots* "the single most spectacular educational experience in race relations in America."[12]

Roots, or "Haley's Comet" as *Time Magazine* called it in a February 1977 cover story, was a rare cultural phenomenon, a literary and television event that captured the U.S. imagination in ways never seen before or since.[13] But why was *Roots* so successful? Why were so many Americans drawn to the series? Why did Alex Haley's family story become such an extraordinary cultural phenomenon? How did it immediately reframe "the dominant culture's" interpretation of slavery and ultimately recast what film scholar Linda Williams calls the ongoing U.S. "melodrama of black and white"?[14]

In some respects, the success of the television series (which is how the vast majority of Americans were first introduced to *Roots*) can be attributed to the novelty of the miniseries format. Relatively new in the 1970s, U.S. miniseries and multi-episode dramas were scheduled to air one episode a week. By broadcasting the series on consecutive nights, ABC established a new precedent. And each successive night generated momentum in the ratings. In what could be considered an early experience with binge watching for Americans, this format made *Roots* more of a collective, nationwide sensation than a typical television drama. Much like the Super Bowl—the only type of broadcast with the potential to rake in such high market share—*Roots* became a collective event for Americans, an experience that was not to be missed. Indeed, executives apparently referred to the ratings bonanza as "Super Bowl every night."[15]

The distinguished cast of actors contributed to the popularity of *Roots*. Actors such as Leslie Uggams, Cicely Tyson, Ben Vereen, Lorne Greene, Louis Gossett Jr., John Amos, Sandy Duncan, Edward Asner, Chuck Connors, Robert Reed, and O. J. Simpson were household names in the 1970s. Americans knew performers like Uggams, Tyson, and Vereen as glamorous Broadway and variety show entertainers, whereas Asner, Amos, Reed, Connors, and Greene were familiar stars of popular sitcoms and dramas like *The Mary Tyler Moore Show, The Brady Bunch*, and *Bonanza*. Both Connors and Simpson were popular professional-athletes-turned-actors—instantly recognizable to a range of Americans. So although they were now cast in unusual roles as slaves, slaveholders, and beneficiaries of the system, the performers were familiar to U.S. viewers. The most notable exception was LeVar Burton, a talented University of Southern California theater student who was first introduced to audiences in the lead role of Kunta Kinte. The charismatic Burton would go on to become a fixture in U.S. television for his later roles on *Star Trek: The Next Generation* as Lieutenant Commander Geordi La Forge and as the host of an extraordinarily popular PBS children's show, *Reading Rainbow*.

But it was not just the format, casting, and production of *Roots* that was revolutionary. *Roots* served as a vehicle to introduce mass U.S. audiences to the historical experiences of the enslaved. As literary scholar Timothy Ryan notes in his reading of the 1976 text, "*Roots* vividly dramatizes the series of traumatic shocks that make up the process of enslavement: capture, transport, and introduction to the New World." Taking place over large portions of episodes 1 and 2 of the miniseries, "the book's protracted and graphic depiction of the horrors of the Middle Passage has yet to be surpassed in fiction, and its subsequent presentation of a defamiliarized and alien America from Kunta's disoriented perspective remains extremely powerful."[16] Moreover, as the tale continued, the focus remained on the experiences of the enslaved, exploring the various ways people of African descent resisted the system, dissembled when they interacted with whites, and constantly longed for their freedom.

These images and plotlines in *Roots* were a startling revelation to viewers, regardless of race; most Americans were accustomed to very different depictions of black Americans and slavery on screen. Before *Roots* appeared, the most iconic popular stories set in the slaveholding South were *Uncle Tom's Cabin, The Birth of a Nation*, and *Gone with the Wind*. All originally novels with wildly popular stage or screen (or both) adaptations, the plots, characters, and iconic scenes from these three sentimental tales were so deeply woven into the fabric of U.S. culture that popular depictions of the pre–Civil War

South inevitably contained key stock characters and melodramatic tropes: a pure, virtuous white girl who dies an untimely death, a belle who becomes the object of a dashing cavalier's affection, and a romance played out against the backdrop of a gracious plantation estate filled with black "servants" who invariably love their kind masters and mistresses more than their own freedom. Such portrayals were palatable for U.S. audiences, easy-to-digest versions of what were then prevailing scholarly arguments about agrarian ideals and the mildness and inefficiency of the "peculiar institution." These celebrations of the antebellum South and its so-called Lost Cause, as historians like David Blight and film scholars like Linda Williams remind us, performed prodigious ideological work, serving as the collective public memory justifying the nation's pernicious race-based caste system. And they remained phenomenally popular over the course of the twentieth century. Indeed, just a year before *Roots*, the network broadcast of *Gone with the Wind* "broke all previous records for audience share."[17]

But in *Roots*, these stock characters and plotlines either failed to appear, or, if they did, they were soon reconfigured and redefined into new ideological material. In *Roots*, Africa was a real place—a civilized place. And as James Baldwin explains in his *New York Times* review, although "the American setting is as familiar as the back of one's hand. . . . as Haley's story unfolds, the landscape begins to be terrifying, unutterably strange and bleak, a cloud hanging over it day and night."[18] In this southern landscape, black Americans were not happy with their lot as slaves. Enslaved men were not simply cheerful servants of white masters and black women were not the "mammies" and "jezebels" of popular lore. Rather, enslaved African Americans were mothers, fathers, sisters, brothers, children—members of families and communities who did their best under the most repressive circumstances, affirming and protecting their families and resisting the institution to the best of their abilities.

Roots, then, in no uncertain terms, was an unexpected paradigm shift in U.S. popular culture.[19] Throughout *Roots*, "African American characters were both the heroes and the victims," while "whites were mostly portrayed as villains, a few of whom, were, at best, conflicted by their participation in the evils of slavery."[20] Perhaps in an effort to continue breaking paradigms, Haley insisted that the lead characters, particularly Kunta Kinte, be played by darker-skinned actors, even as lighter-skinned actors play secondary characters.[21] (This might explain why a darker-skinned "Chicken George" played by Ben Vereen could somehow be classified as a "mulatto," with Kizzy as his mother and Tom as his white father.) In the process, *Roots* also defied conventional wisdom about what—or perhaps *who*—white U.S. audiences would and would not watch on U.S. television. And for many white Americans, it was their first opportunity to consider, and even identify with, the perspective of the enslaved, thus offering them new ways to think about slavery as both an institution and an experience. As film historian Linda Williams puts it, "the strikingly original phenomenon of *Roots* as both book and film was that for the first time blacks and whites together would powerfully identify with the pathos and action of an African-American-authored work about African-American heroes."[22] Thus, the radically new content of the story invited an unprecedented opportunity for the entire country to engage in discussion, commentary, and self-reflection.

This national conversation was especially important in 1976 and 1977. Still reeling from the community actions, legislative changes, political realignments, assassinations, and urban uprisings of the 1960s and early 1970s, many Americans longed for something that could explain the upheaval of the previous decade. Disillusioned by the Watergate scandal and U.S. defeat in the Vietnam War, they also longed to turn the page on the Nixon era. In the midst of these developments, Americans were asked to reflect on the meaning of the nation itself during the bicentennial celebrations honoring the two hundredth anniversary of the country's birth. And just three days before the *Roots* miniseries aired, Jimmy Carter was sworn in as the thirty-ninth president, the first to hail from the Deep South since the Civil War. This milieu ensured that the *Roots* phenomenon would be as much about the present as it was about the past. For those who hoped that the late 1970s would inaugurate a new, more hopeful era, *Roots* served as a popular metaphor for the legislative gains of the civil rights movement and a promise of a better tomorrow.

In addition to reading *Roots* as a post–civil rights era parable, audiences also responded to the fact that *Roots* was, at the end of the day, about connecting with one's family history. As it turns out, *Roots* appeared at a significant moment for white "ethnic" U.S. viewers who felt themselves cut off from their own family histories when their turn-of-the-twentieth-century grandparents and parents struggled to assimilate into what a bicentennial educational cartoon called "the Great American Melting Pot." These "hyphenated" European Americans, for their part, responded enthusiastically to *Roots*. For these white Americans, *Roots* performed two main functions, not only affirming for the first time the "Americanness" of the descendants of slaves, but also endorsing the ascendant Ellis Island vision of the United States as a nation of European immigrants. To put it another way, insofar as *Roots* incorporated people of African descent into the founding mythology of the nation, *Roots* also validated the idea of pluralist ethnic history, one where immigrants undertook a perilous sea voyage to America, lived in ethnic communities, dealt with persecution at the hands of the Anglo Protestant elite, struggled, persevered, and finally triumphed as true Americans rightfully celebrating the bicentennial alongside Anglo-Saxon Protestant descendants of the *Mayflower*. Indeed, white interest in genealogy exploded in the aftermath of *Roots*. As Matthew Frye Jacobson explains, "in the wake of the broadcast . . . hundreds of thousands of Americans descended on local libraries and archives in search of information, not about slavery or black history, but about themselves and their own ethnic past." He notes that such repositories "across the country experienced a run, not on books about slavery, but rather on materials relating to the genealogical search for roots in myriad 'exotic,' premodern villages—whether in County Cork, Abruzzi, Vilna, or Crete." In other words, "*Roots* was rather nimbly appropriated as a generic saga of migration and assimilation, not an African-American story, nor even an American story, exactly, but a modern one—a story that 'speaks for all of us everywhere.'"[23]

Haley, who along with series producer David Wolper proclaimed that *Roots* was a "universal" family story, welcomed and encouraged this response. In "What *Roots* Means to Me," published in the iconic *Reader's Digest* in 1977, Haley wrote: "With the exception of American Indians, we are a land of immigrants. All of us ancestrally come from somewhere across the ocean. Our roots with our immigrant forebears touch the deepest chords within us. When you look at slave-ship scenes, as horrible as they were, you also have to remember the long lines of immigrant ships, with their passengers huddled in steerage, desperately trying to learn a few words of a language that was to be their adopted tongue forever." As Haley saw it, "the whole business of family quest, which is the wellspring of *Roots*, is a great common denominator, a leveler in which a king is no more than a peasant. It reaches into something subliminal in people, and I have been most astonished that the response of it transcends all lines—color lines, age lines, ethnic lines." And to dispel any doubt that Haley's *Roots* was meant for everyone, the essay was accompanied by a hazy turn-of-the-century photo of an Eastern European immigrant family, gazing toward the Statue of Liberty.[24]

Of course, men and women of African descent certainly did not come to this continent seeking a better life or fleeing religious persecution; theirs was a forced migration. Haley recognized this, saying, "yet, in our nation of immigrants, blacks have been the only unwilling immigrants; the lot of chattel slaves was not comparable to the status of indentured servants."[25] But Haley ultimately believed that African Americans found their own sense of legitimacy by laying claim to a U.S. narrative defined by striving and by dreams of improvement. In this way, he saw his *Roots* as a way to help the nation begin to see descendants of slaves like himself as fully American. Long "excluded as significant subjectivities in mass popular culture" from the national "imagined community," *Roots* insisted that black Americans were Americans, too, and that "the story of a black family, like the stories of the Hawkses, the Rabinowitzes, and the O'Haras, could finally be, as the book's subtitle has it, *The Saga of an American Family*."[26] *Roots* also suggested, as James Baldwin noted in the *New York Times*, that the struggle to remake America must continue. "*Roots* is a study of continuities, of consequences, of how a people perpetuate themselves, how each generation helps to doom, or helps to liberate, the coming one—the action of love, or the effect of the absence of love, in time. It suggests, with great power, how each of us, however unconsciously, can't but be the vehicle of the history which has produced us."[27] For these ideological reasons, *Roots* became "the most astounding cultural event of the American Bicentennial."[28]

For African Americans, however, *Roots* and its creator, Alex Haley, were something deeply personal, long awaited, and profoundly special. For this segment of the population, *Roots* was not a generic *American* story, but rather, a collective, *family* history. As Alex Haley explained in his *Reader's Digest* piece, "Ancestrally, every black person has the same pattern. He or she goes back to an African—who was born and reared in a village like Juffure, was captured and put into some slave ship, processed through some succession of plantations, on up to the Civil War and emancipation. From that day to this, the black human being has struggled for freedom. That is the constant story for every one of us. There are no exceptions!"[29] With *Roots*, black U.S. families were now free to watch a dramatization of their collective history unencumbered by the "white gaze." Uncensored and uninhibited by public audiences, tears, pain, even laughter, could flow from a place of genuine provocation.

This collective history was not new to African Americans in 1976. From as early as the nineteenth century, black Americans had insisted on telling the story of slavery from a black perspective, explaining the nature of the chattel principle, affirming the importance of family and community, honoring black heroes and heroines, and giving voice to the freedom struggle.[30] While scholarship by prominent white historians continued to peddle the mythology of the so-called Lost Cause, work by a diverse and growing group of scholars like W. E. B. Du Bois, Kenneth A. Stampp, John Hope Franklin, Herbert G. Gutman, John W. Blassingame, and Lerone Bennett sought to challenge these interpretations with historical research that took into account the words and perspective of African Americans. *Roots* personalized and dramatized this history. And it appeared that the nation was ready to hear more. In 1976, the same year *Roots: The Saga of an American Family* was published, President Ford proclaimed that Black History Week would be expanded to Black History Month. And now, with *Roots*, this story was introduced to the world. And as one reviewer of the television series put it, in 1977, *Roots* was "Our Own Story—At Last!"[31]

Roots also dramatized truths about what it meant to be black in the United States—not simply during centuries of enslavement, but more recently in the context of Jim Crow, when twentieth-century men and women of African descent were forced by law and custom to navigate the social whims and legalities of white supremacy. The character of Fiddler, for example, whose body was used as an instrument against itself, served as a metaphor for black life in modern white America. Fiddler, played by Louis Gossett Jr., is used for everyone's entertainment but his own. While sitting with Kunta Kinte under a tree discussing the politics of lying over the meaning of Kizzy's name, Fiddler polishes his fiddle with great care. He admires his fiddle: "Pretty ain't it? Shines like a baby's behind." He places the fiddle under his chin and begins to play a song. He sighs long and hard and laments that while Kunta Kinte is concerned about the probability of the master believing his lie, Fiddler assures him, "Probably is as good as it gets for a nigger, Kinte. Now make your peace with that." He then tunes out the anxiety of Kinte, and states that he is "Gonna play me some music. Play me a song I wants to hear. I'm tired of all the time playing white folks' song. I got my own song to play."

Fiddler's songs do not belong to him and, in the televised version of *Roots*, once he is finally able to play his own music, his own song, for his own personal enjoyment, he plays only a few notes before he keels over and dies. (In Haley's book, he dies after his master refuses to accept their earlier agreed-upon amount Fiddler had earned to purchase his freedom.) For Fiddler, freedom comes only through death. It is a stark reminder to audiences of the strong hold of slavery over every avenue of pleasure. The brilliance of the scene is recalled in Steve McQueen's film *12 Years a Slave* (2013) when Solomon Northup breaks his own violin, an instrument of his oppression, a puppet for white pleasure. These are the scenes of subjection which author Saidiya Hartman so eloquently lays out in her work.[32] The notion that slavery becomes a continual performance of staged servitude carries throughout the series, and it was especially poignant to a generation of African Americans who had so recently experienced the pleasure and pain of the civil rights and Black Power movements.

In addition to getting the story of slavery from the perspective of African Americans, black viewers and readers also appreciated Haley's emphasis on the importance of honoring black families and black history. This was not the first time Haley had made this case. In fact, *Roots* can be read as Haley's follow-up to the popular *Autobiography of Malcolm X*, which Haley published in 1965 a few months after the subject's assassination. Malcolm X, whom Haley had interviewed extensively for that book, frequently lectured on the loss of identity that people of African descent experienced upon being brought to the United States and forced to take on a new "slave name." And he explained that this is why the followers of the Nation of Islam used the X in place of a last name, the X symbolizing all of the African family and history that was stolen and lost.

In *Roots*, Haley meditated on this sense of disconnection by translating this collective trauma into the experience of Kunta Kinte, who, after his arrival in Maryland, was beaten into accepting the name Toby, given to him by his new master. As difficult and painful as it was for viewers to watch Kunta Kinte beaten until he accepted Toby as his new name, *Roots* emphasizes that neither his new name nor his status as chattel truly defined his core identity. It is Fiddler who embraces a whipped and wounded "Toby" and declares, "your name is Kunta Kinte." And, on Kinte's death, daughter Kizzy scratches out "Toby" on his gravestone, changing it to read "Kunta Kinte." Moreover, as Haley tells the story, every generation of Haley's ancestors had been taught the story of Kunta Kinte (not Toby) "the African" who first came to America. Even though they bore the last name Palmer by the end of the series, it was "the African" who was their original ancestor. And they dutifully retold his story—their family saga—to their children, who would in turn repeat the story to their own descendants. The lasting naming power of Kinte is a testament to the enduring resilience of identity formation in the space of oppression. As Haley put it, "for black people, Kunta Kinte is the symbolic, mythological ancestor out of Africa, and with him there is a positive, lineal *Roots* identification."[33] Haley resurrected this lost ancestor in a way that "reaffirmed the proud and militant spirit of blackness which defined the Black Power movement."[34] This had profound resonance for black Americans, irrespective of regional differences and class backgrounds. And it served as a springboard for more widespread direct engagement with black history, art, and culture.[35]

Some of the appeal of *Roots* was certainly bound up in the success of Haley himself. As Haley told it, it was through hard work, dogged determination, and luck that he was able to put a name, a cultural affiliation, and an actual village to his original ancestor, thereby reclaiming a stolen history and connecting the past with the present. The final moments of *Roots* dramatize this connection. As slavery came to an end, Kunta Kinte's descendants were ready to defend themselves against the violence of those who would seek to reenslave them. But they were also ready to move forward into new territory, toward the promise of freedom. As the final images of Kunta Kinte's descendants making their way west by wagon train toward Tennessee fade from the screen, photographs of Alex Haley's more recent ancestors appear while a voice-over names each one. The voice belongs to Haley, who strides toward the camera, a link between past and present, a personification of upward mobility, a direct connection to Kunta Kinte, a monument to the gains of the civil rights movement, a perfect message for a nation in the midst of its bicentennial celebration. Haley had done the impossible, reaching beyond the veil of slavery to connect with his ancestors, tracing them all the way back to Africa. He was the living embodiment of their pain, perseverance, and triumph in the post–civil rights era United States.

In this way, Haley and both versions of *Roots* connected the present with the past. And because the story of *Roots* was the story of Haley, the two became virtually indistinguishable. "A public opinion poll conducted after the series aired revealed that Alex Haley, a stocky, fifty-six-year-old writer, had become the third most admired black man in America among Afro-American youth—surpassed only by boxer Muhammad Ali and Motown singer Stevie Wonder."[36] Those writing to *Ebony* in May 1977 in response to a profile of Haley echoed these sentiments. Three black residents of Santa Barbara, California—Arthur and Monica Cowan and Mrs. Willie Mae Smith—together thanked Haley "not only for giving us our *Roots*, but for giving us his autograph," during a visit to Los Angeles where thousands of fans lined up to meet him. They continued: "he is truly an outstanding black man who has the class to share his success with his brothers and sisters." Meanwhile, Mrs. Diann Griffin of Durham, North Carolina, wrote that "not only should *Roots* be purchased to be read but it should actually be in every black home for easy access as a reference book for our forthcoming generation." For Griffin and those like her, Alex Haley had finally presented the world with the truth.[37]

Although television audiences enthusiastically supported *Roots*, it immediately attracted criticism from scholars. For a number of black academics, the *Roots* miniseries diverged from Haley's novel in ways that blunted its radical possibilities and obscured the black point of view. They argued that the series "had become popular among whites because of the alterations and distortions made to please them." As the historian William Van Deburg notes, "critics charged that compromises resulted from a partial substitution of white for black perspectives on the African/Afro-American past. Complaints about everything from the opening statement—that the Haley family history had begun in 'primitive Africa'—to the length and polish of Kizzy's . . . nails."[38] A roundtable of scholars critiqued *Roots* in a 1977 symposium in the *Black Scholar*, arguing that it ultimately reinforced rather than challenged Stanley Elkins's thesis, which argued that enslavement had infantilized and irreparably damaged those who were enslaved.[39] An Ann Arbor, Michigan, woman wrote to *Ebony*, saying, "Although I hate to think it's true, the evidence suggests that once again the black experience has been pimped. If Haley was a close consultant to the filming, then he has much explaining to do to the black community." She explained what troubled her: "over a third of Haley's book explores and explains the culture and lifestyle of the Mandinka people. *Roots* (the novel) reveals that our people were an extremely religious and spiritual people even before the introduction of Christianity into Africa. The film only alludes to this. We are shown in the book that many of our ancestral tribes were made up of very literate people who were able to both read and write Arabic. There is no mention in the movie." Additionally, "that part of our history which would indeed tie us closer to the mother country; to the victims of the atrocities in South Africa and Rhodesia was only hinted at" in the televised version of Haley's book. Ultimately, "I am disappointed in ABC's halfhearted efforts to tell the story of our heritage and in Alex Haley for allowing them the liberties. At the same time, I am glad that it was televised so that my son who is yet unable (but not unwilling) to read 587 pages can participate in still another learning experience of his people's heritage. Such is the paradox of being black in America."[40]

For leftist intellectuals, both black and white, *Roots* was counterrevolutionary. Part of the show's popularity among white viewers was its conservative subtext, the way it privileged faith, family, and "rising above" over revolt, and reduced the singular experience of enslavement into something much more benign and palatable for broader audiences.[41] Some scholars noted that all examples of racism were depicted only in the revolutionary and antebellum eras, making it easy for viewers to believe that racism itself was also a phenomenon of the past. Others argued that, in producing the miniseries, the network manipulated impressionable teenagers into rooting for Chicken George rather than for the likes of Nat Turner, who led the bloodiest slave rebellion in U.S. history.[42] The Palmer-Haleys, meanwhile, appeared to be typical "race uplifters," irritatingly bourgeois bootstrappers in step with Booker T. Washington's accommodationist political philosophy, primarily concerned with personal success. This reading wasn't too far afield given Haley's personal political leanings as a self-professed Republican with a brother (George Haley) serving as a Republican state senator in Kansas.[43] Scholarship by Manning Marable has even found that Haley was working with the FBI while drafting *The Autobiography of Malcolm X* and that he intended to portray Malcolm's life not as a call for radical black action but as a "cautionary tale," regarding it as one of the "tragedies produced by racial segregation."[44] As David Chioni Moore argues, "in its depiction of antebellum America, *Roots* is a house-and-barn slave's story, and speaks little of the slaves in the field; post–Civil War, it becomes a bootstrapper's story, and therefore turns its subjects, in significant ways, into an ethnicity like any other in America."[45]

Additionally, there was the question of whether *Roots* was fact or fiction. For many readers and viewers, *Roots* was not simply historical fiction. It was *Truth*. Kunta Kinte was "the African," the original ancestor to whom Haley was related, and, as he recounted in the final pages of *Roots* and repeated during promotional appearances, Haley had located him through painstaking genealogical research and travel to remote villages in the Gambia. This popular understanding of *Roots* was validated when Haley's book won a special Pulitzer Prize. However, genealogists and historians quickly began critiquing Haley's claim to have traced his lineage back to his African roots. Most famously, genealogists Elizabeth Shown Mills and (neo-Confederate)

Gary B. Mills "attacked Haley's genealogical research by revisiting many of the sources for *Roots*," arguing that "he failed at the typical family challenge of reconciling oral tradition with documentary evidence."[46] In the course of speaking to Gambians about the veracity of *Roots*, Donald Wright interviewed a Gambian tour guide, asking specifically about Haley's story and if the guide truly believed Haley had found his ancestors in Juffure. "He answers honestly," remarked Wright, "'Sometimes, . . .' and he pauses; 'Sometimes, I have doubts about it. But the story has been very good for the Gambia. Very good.'"[47] For his part, Alex Haley played coy about the question of the veracity of his text, calling it "faction"—a combination of fact and fiction.

Then, there was the issue of Haley's plagiarism. The copyright infringement suits that followed the publication of *Roots* confirmed growing doubts about Haley's historical accuracy, research methodology, and intellectual integrity.[48] Although Haley consistently maintained that "he had actually traced his ancestors back to Africa," he never published a promised defense of his sources and methods.[49] And his out-of-court settlement of $650,000 to Harold Courlander confirmed what many saw as intellectual betrayal. He lost all credibility with black academics and scholars who were struggling to develop and give legitimacy to Black studies departments and the study of African Americans at the collegiate level. To many of them, Haley was a hack and a fraud, a man entirely lacking in ethics, and an opportunist who marketed fiction as historical fact and personal, family memory.

The economic motivations of Haley's project also led critics to believe that he was more interested in having a best seller than in contributing to our understanding of the past. Cultural critic and professional provocateur Stanley Crouch offered an especially scathing critique of Haley in 2002, calling *Roots* "one of the biggest con jobs in U.S. literary history." Surprisingly, Crouch did not place all of the blame for the enduring popularity of the book and TV series on black people alone. No, Crouch blamed the bulk of Haley's success on white gatekeepers who he believed restrained their scruples in exchange for large profits. "The most important reason for the durability of the hoax is white folks," claimed Crouch. "Those at Doubleday who published *Roots* had a best seller and were not interested in people knowing it was phony baloney. David Wolper Productions created the most successful miniseries of its time and was not interested. Federal Judge Robert Ward, who presided over the plagiarism case, protected Haley's reputation."[50] For critics like Crouch, white Americans wanted, even needed, to give Haley a pass, as did Black Americans.

Insufficiently political, dogged by controversy, and difficult to clearly categorize, *Roots* remained until about 2015 a text that scholars have been unwilling to engage. To date there are only a handful of articles written on the book or the miniseries.[51] As David Chioni Moore points out, *Roots* has not been *historical* enough to warrant serious sustained attention by professional historians. For specialists in African American history, *Roots* is often simply mentioned as an event of passing significance, while considerably more attention is devoted to the Black Arts Movement and blaxploitation films as significant cultural forces of the late 1960s and 1970s. Literary critics, meanwhile, do not treat Haley's work with the same seriousness that characterizes their analyses of Zora Neale Hurston, Richard Wright, Langston Hughes, James Baldwin, and other writers of the same period. For many literary scholars, *Roots* is simply too middlebrow to warrant sustained scholarly interrogation.[52] Consequently, as Robert Norrell notes, Haley was "all but left out" of the movement to institutionalize African American literature in the academy in the 1980s and 1990s.[53]

This silence on the subject of *Roots* is unfortunate, because popular textual representations of slavery are rife with political meaning. As literary scholar Timothy A. Ryan notes, any popular representation of slavery ultimately "participates in multiple discourses," including "a discourse about the [history] of slavery, a discourse about the culture and identities of those who were enslaved, a discourse about their enslavers, and . . . a discourse about . . . race."[54] Scholars have long demonstrated that popular representations of U.S. slavery from the wildly popular twentieth-century stage adaptations of Harriet Beecher Stowe's *Uncle Tom's Cabin* to D. W. Griffith's anti-Tom polemic and epic celebration of the Ku Klux Klan in *The Birth of a Nation* (1915) to the plantation romance *Gone with the Wind* (1939) have been bound up with everything from the abolitionist movement to the antiblack violence and Jim Crow segregation of the post-Reconstruction New South to the activism of the mid-twentieth-century civil rights movement.[55] The cultural and political significance of these texts transcends their contested literary credentials and historical inaccuracies. And we would argue that this is especially the case with *Roots*.

Beginning from the premise that the significance of the *Roots* phenomenon was both political and cultural, the essays in this interdisciplinary collection reconsider the politics of *Roots*, exploring the ways *Roots* engaged the race and gender politics of the 1970s and 1980s, revised the visual lexicon for subsequent representations of black life in television and film, and impacted political movements abroad. Taken as a whole, all of the chapters here ask us to reconsider the political limitations and possibilities of *Roots* and its lasting significance as a cultural touchstone within and outside of the United States.

We have organized *Reconsidering Roots* into three key sections. Part 1, "Rethinking the Context," focuses on the historical moment in which *Roots* was created. All of the chapters in this section take on three of the concerns that have stymied critics since the publication and broadcast of *Roots*: the contested spaces of memory, ownership, and genealogy.

In chapter 1, "*Roots*, the Legacy of Slavery, and Civil Rights Backlash in 1970s America," Clare Corbould examines the outpouring of letters that viewers sent to newspapers, executive producer David L. Wolper, author Alex Haley, ABC headquarters in New York, and local affiliate television stations. The letters, primarily written by self-identified black and white Americans, ranged from sympathetic, praiseworthy, and pensive, to resentful, belligerent, and hateful. Ultimately, the rhetoric in *Roots* fan letters and hate mail captures the nation's starkly divergent attitudes about race and reconciliation on the eve of the "Reagan Revolution," serving as a preview of the conservative rhetoric of "color blindness" that will come to dominate the political discourse of the 1980s, obscuring African American continuing demands for justice.

In chapter 2, "The Politics of Plagiarism: *Roots*, Margaret Walker, and Alex Haley," Tyler D. Parry examines black novelist, poet, and university professor Margaret Walker's copyright infringement suit against Haley. While many are aware of Haley's settlement of the lawsuit brought by Harold Courlander, few know of Walker's claims that Haley lifted passages from her 1965 novel, *Jubilee*—a popular work of historical fiction that traced the experiences of her ancestors from slavery to freedom in the U.S. South. Focusing on Walker's personal diary entries and correspondence, as well as on trial transcripts and newspapers, Parry explores the sociopolitical landscape of this second plagiarism suit, analyzing the ways that perceptions of race, gender, and regionalism may have contributed to Walker's crushing financial and emotional defeat in the courtroom and the court of black public opinion. Parry argues that Walker's unsuccessful plagiarism suit against Haley helped to enshrine *Roots* as the premier representation of U.S. slavery in popular culture and to secure Haley's position as the leading interpreter of the black experience.

In chapter 3, "'My Furthest-Back Person': Black Genealogy Before and After *Roots*," Francesca Morgan argues that Haley's work accelerated what was then a growing interest in genealogy among African Americans. She demonstrates that Haley drew on a longstanding understanding of African American genealogy as a political endeavor, from the journalist Ida B. Wells recalling her mother Elizabeth writing from Memphis to Virginia for information on her "people," to the civil-rights activist and feminist Pauli Murray managing to persuade a commercial press to publish her own mixed-race family history, *Proud Shoes* (1956); interest in black forebears reached back into the eras of slavery and emancipation. At the same time, Haley's success set the stage for new publications and institutions for black family history. In this way, Morgan demonstrates that Haley's importance for black genealogy is better understood in terms of *Roots'* role as a watershed text than in terms of its genealogical accuracy.

The chapters in part 2, "Rereading *Roots*," examine how the themes of labor, violence, and manhood intersect with the social construction of race and representations of family and slavery. These chapters offer close readings of *Roots* and its 1979 sequel, *Roots: The Next Generations*, analyzing them alongside a range of twentieth- and twenty-first-century films and television shows. Collectively, these chapters tease out the central paradox of *Roots*: that a series can be so revolutionary and profoundly significant in some respects, yet retrograde and problematic in others. Ultimately, this section explores the political possibilities and limitations of *Roots'* representation of the experiences of black and white Americans in U.S. history and memory.

In chapter 4, "Roots of Violence: Race, Power, and Manhood in *Roots*," Delia Mellis considers the ways in which *Roots* represented black and white masculinities and violence—whether actual or threatened. She explores the ways that the black men and women in the series faced forms of physical violence as an expression of white male power and control. Offering a close reading of instances of gendered violence in *Roots*, Mellis asks whether *Roots* was simply making an argument about the utter brutality of the slave system, or was it in fact commodifying, fetishizing, even to some extent reinscribing that brutality. Furthermore, in what ways did these representations of violence reflect the discourses of 1970s black power? Because violence and masculinities have been so central to race relations in U.S. history, Mellis engages *Roots* on such terms in hopes of gaining insight into the persistence of such violence that continues to this day.

In chapter 5, "The Roots of African American Labor Struggles: Reading *Roots* and *Backstairs at the White House* in a 1970s Storytelling Tradition," Elise Chatelain places *Roots* in the context of a larger 1970s television phenomenon: using labor history to narrate the nation's past. Keeping the rise of the new social history in mind, Chatelain offers a comparative analysis of *Roots* and the miniseries *Backstairs at the White House* (1979), exploring their narrative projects as well as their critical reception. Chatelain argues that *Roots* and *Backstairs* both drew on the emerging impulse to tell histories "from the bottom up." And both placed labor exploitation and economic conditions at the center of their stories, making work and family central component of their depictions of collective African American experience.

In chapter 6, "Letting America Off the Hook: *Roots*, *Django Unchained*, and the Divided White Self," C. Richard King and David J. Leonard offer a reading of *Roots* as it relates to whiteness and white supremacy. These authors contend that despite depicting the evils of slavery on-screen, *Roots* failed to fully interrogate or challenge ideologies of white supremacy. They argue that *Roots'* historic accounting of slavery reinscribed longstanding fictions of a "divided white self" by positing whiteness as a simplistic binary of good and evil, and characterizing slavery as fundamentally a southern enterprise rather than a core U.S. practice. King and Leonard extend their analysis into the twenty-first century by juxtaposing *Roots* against Quentin Tarantino's 2012 film, *Django Unchained*. They argue that despite the central critiques of the peculiar institution inherent in both of these stories, both media events ultimately let white Americans "off the hook" by failing to reckon honestly and fully with the fundamental nature of white supremacy.

In chapter 7, "The Black Military Image in *Roots: The Next Generations*," Robert K. Chester looks beyond the original miniseries into the continuing narrative of Haley's ancestors in *Roots: The Next Generations* (*RTNG*). Chester contends that this subsequent miniseries, while even less appreciated by scholars than its predecessor, is nonetheless important for its expression of a radically dissenting vision of World War II and its racialized repercussions in U.S. culture. Reading *RTNG* against other cinematic representations of African American wartime service, Chester argues that *RTNG* tapped into the post–Vietnam War shift in black political consciousness and strenuously rejects the notion that military service provides a pathway to equality for African Americans. A stark contrast to the triumphalist narrative of World War II (and its impact on race relations in the United States), this critique was unprecedented on network television, and a reminder of the complex political possibilities of the *Roots* phenomenon.

The third and final part, "Rerouting *Roots*," takes up David Chioni Moore's challenge to consider "trajectories, paths, interactions, links" and explores the global implications of *Roots* both within and beyond the African Diaspora.[56] The three chapters in this section explore the political impact of *Roots* in the United Kingdom, South Africa, and China. Together they suggest that even though *Roots* may have failed to lead to substantive political change in the United States, when exported to other countries, it was placed in the service of a surprising range of political ends. All three chapters conclude with surveys or interviews with their British, South African, and Chinese subjects, offering insight into the deeply personal and political response *Roots* elicited in the 1970s and 1980s.

In chapter 8, "The Same, but a Step Removed: Aspects of the British Reception of *Roots*," Martin Stollery explores the differences between black and white British responses to *Roots*. He argues that while *Roots* reinforced the prevailing white British perception that slavery was something that happened "over there," black viewers in the United Kingdom responded differently. Agreeing with Alex Haley's declaration that "the story of black people in England is the same but it's a step removed," many Black Britons found that *Roots* fostered a new sense of pride in their own ancestry and a new Afrocentric cultural consciousness. In these ways, mass British audiences diverged from leftists in the United Kingdom, who critiqued the series for its conservative ideological impulses.

In chapter 9, "Re-Rooting *Roots*: The South African Perspective," Norvella P. Carter, Warren Chalklen, and Bhekuyise Zungu move beyond analyses of *Roots* in West Africa to explore the reception of *Roots* in South Africa at a moment of growing antiapartheid activism. While *Roots* was being televised all over the world—from Australia to Canada to Belgium to Japan—apartheid government censorship led to countrywide bans over the broadcast of the miniseries, particularly for black audiences. But despite this ban, South Africans saw the series and listened to the soundtrack. And South African artists would return to the series in their own work twenty years later after apartheid was officially dismantled. This chapter is both the history of *Roots* censorship and a chronicle of the reactions of those South Africans who managed to view the miniseries. The chapter concludes with interviews of South African scholars Bhekuyise Zungu and Warren Chalklen as black and white citizens, respectively, of the country.

In the final chapter, "One Man's Quest: Chiang Ssu-chang, *Roots*, and the Mainlander Homebound Movement in Taiwan," Dominic Meng-Hsuan Yang recounts the tremendous impact *Roots* had on Chiang Ssu-chang, who was only thirteen years old when the retreating Chinese Nationalist army abducted him and his classmates on their way home from school. The Nationalists forced about 13,000 men and boys into the service when they passed through Chiang's community on their escape route to Taiwan 1949–1950. Pressed into service, along with the 13,000 other Chinese men and boys forcibly kidnapped and transported to Taiwan between 1949 and 1950, teenagers like Chiang relied on the Nationalist regime for survival in a new land, and dreamed of returning home every moment they lived. And when *Roots* arrived in Taiwan in the 1980s, the book and the miniseries affected Chiang deeply. According to Chiang's published memoir and a 2014 interview with Yang, Chiang credits the example of Haley's determination to reconnect with his ancestors and the television series' depiction of Kunta Kinte's abduction and enslavement with inspiring him to launch a social movement demanding that he and other retired veterans receive the right to return home. The movement eventually gathered enough momentum to force the island's authorities to lift the ban on travel to Mainland China and became the starting point of contemporary cross-strait relations.

Taken as a whole, these chapters demonstrate that *Roots* must be understood as a complex cultural phenomenon with surprising political range as well as profound limitations. Since it first circulated in print and on screen in the late 1970s, it has been the subject of both fierce denunciation and deep admiration. We hope that the chapters in this book will encourage others to take part in a growing conversation about this transformative event, for there is still much to say about *Roots* in the fields of history, literature, gender, visual culture, and genealogy. The themes of power, identity, struggle, and perseverance remain as compelling as they were when *Roots* first debuted. The rage and pain and danger of this country can be located in our ability to memorialize and celebrate the past without ever fully understanding its significance, its lessons, and its pitfalls. And as James Baldwin reminds us, "We don't know the rest of the story. It hasn't turned out yet."[57] Quite simply, *Roots* requires reappraisal.

NOTES

1. William L. Van Deburg, *Slavery and Race in American Popular Culture* (Madison: University of Wisconsin Press, 1984), 155–157; William E. Huntzicker, "Alex Haley's *Roots*: The Fiction of Fact," in *Memory and Myth: The Civil War in Fiction and Film from "Uncle Tom's Cabin" to "Cold Mountain*," edited by David B. Sachsman, S. Kittrell Rushing, and Roy Morris Jr. (West Lafayette, Ind.: Purdue University Press, 2007), 272; "*Roots* Causes Phenomenal Reaction: Television May Never Be the Same," *Bakersfield Californian*, Jan. 29, 1977, 1–2; "Theater Revenues Decline during *Roots* Telecast," *New York Amsterdam News*, Feb. 26, 1977, D-15.

2. Given the ambiguous generic status of *Roots: The Saga of an American Family*, the contributors to this collection refer to the book in a variety of ways, including as a novel.

3. Robert D. McFadden, "Alex Haley Denies Allegation that Parts of *Roots* Were Copied from Novel Written by Mississippi Teacher," *New York Times*, April 24, 1977, 4. New York Times Bestseller List, Nov. 21, 1976, accessed Jan. 20, 2016, http://www.hawes.com/no1_nf_d.htm.

4. Huntzicker, "Alex Haley's *Roots*," 272.

5. Donald R. Wright, "The Effect of Alex Haley's *Roots* on How Gambians Remember the Atlantic Slave Trade," *History in Africa* 38 (2011): 300.

6. Van Deburg, *Slavery and Race in American Popular Culture*, 155.

7. Robert J. Norrell, *Alex Haley and the Books That Changed a Nation* (New York: Palgrave Macmillan, 2015), 168.

8. Alex Haley, "What *Roots* Means to Me," *Reader's Digest*, May 1977, reprinted in *Alex Haley: The Man Who Traced America's Roots: His Life, His Works* (New York: Reader's Digest Association, 2007), 160.

9. Michelle Hudson, "The Effect of *Roots* and the Bicentennial on Genealogical Interest among Patrons of the Mississippi Department of Archives and History," *Journal of Mississippi History* 53, no. 4 (1991): 321–336.

10. According to Donald Wright, 276 college and university classrooms used the novel. Wright, "Effect of Alex Haley's *Roots* on How Gambians Remember the Atlantic Slave Trade," 300.

11. Eliana Dockterman, "There's Now a College Course about Beyoncé at Rutgers University: It's a Whole New Kind of 'Schoolin' Life," *Time.com*, January 31, 2014, accessed April 27, 2015, http://entertainment.time.com/2014/01/31/theres-now-a-college-course-about-beyonce-at-rutgers-university/.

12. David L. Wolper, with Quincy Troupe, *The Inside Story of TV's "Roots"* (New York: Warner Books, 1978), 251; Scot French, *The Rebellious Slave: Nat Turner in American Memory* (New York: Houghton Mifflin, 2004), 273 n141.

13. "Why *Roots* Hit Home," *Time*, Feb. 14, 1977.

14. Linda Williams, *Playing the Race Card: Melodramas of Black and White from Uncle Tom to O. J. Simpson* (Princeton, N.J.: Princeton University Press, 2001), 239.

15. "Why *Roots* Hit Home."

16. Tim A. Ryan, *Calls and Responses: The American Novel of Slavery since "Gone with the Wind"* (Baton Rouge: Louisiana State University Press, 2008), 118.

17. Williams, *Playing the Race Card*, 239.

18. James Baldwin, "How One Black Man Came to Be an American: A Review of *Roots*," *New York Times*, Sept. 26, 1976, accessed Aug. 11, 2015, https://www.nytimes.com /books/98/03/29/specials/baldwin-roots.html.

19. Herman Gray, "The Politics of Representation in Network Television," in *Channeling Blackness: Studies on Television and Race in America*, edited by Darnell M. Hunt (New York: Oxford University Press, 2005), 160–161.

20. Aniko Bodroghkozy, "Television and the Civil Rights Era," in *African Americans and Popular Culture*, edited by Todd Boyd (Westport, Conn.: Praeger, 2008), 160.

21. Eric Pierson, "The Importance of *Roots*" in *Watching while Black: Centering the Television of Black Audiences*, edited by Beretta E. Smith-Shomade (New Brunswick, N.J.: Rutgers University, 2013), 22.

22. Williams, *Playing the Race Card*, 221.

23. Matthew Frye Jacobson, *Roots Too: White Ethnic Revival in Post–Civil Rights America* (Cambridge, Mass.: Harvard University Press, 2008), 43–44.

24. Haley, "What *Roots* Means to Me," 159–160.

25. Ibid., 160.

26. Williams, *Playing the Race Card*, 221.

27. Baldwin, "How One Black Man Came to Be an American."

28. Wright, "Effect of Alex Haley's *Roots* on How Gambians Remember the Atlantic Slave Trade," 302–303; Willie Lee Rose, *Race and Region in American Historical Fiction: Four Episodes in Popular Culture* (New York: Oxford University Press, 1979), 5.

29. Haley, "What *Roots* Means to Me," 160.

30. See Stephen G. Hall, *A Faithful Account of the Race: African American Historical Writing in Nineteenth Century America* (Chapel Hill: University of North Carolina Press, 2009).

31. L. D. Reddick, "Our Own Story—At Last!," *Freedomways* (1976): 253–255. See also Carole Meritt, "Looking at Afro-American Roots," *Phylon* 38, no. 2 (1977): 211–212.

32. Saidiya V. Hartman, *Scenes of Subjection: Terror, Slavery, and Self-Making in the Nineteenth-Century America* (New York: Oxford University Press, 1997).

33. Haley, "What *Roots* Means to Me," 160.

34. Van Deburg, *Slavery and Race in American Popular Culture*, 145.

35. Gray, "Politics of Representation in Network Television," 61.

36. Van Deburg, *Slavery and Race in American Popular Culture*, 155.

37. *Ebony Magazine*, May 1977, 21–22.

38. Van Deburg, *Slavery and Race in American Popular Culture*, 156.

39. Ryan, *Calls and Responses*, 116.

40. Janice L. Cooke, letter to the editor, *Ebony*, May 1977.

41. Huntzicker, "Alex Haley's *Roots*," 278–279; Williams, *Playing the Race Card*, 221.

42. Scot French, *The Rebellious Slave: Nat Turner in American Memory* (New York: Houghton Mifflin, 2004), 273 n.143.

43. President Bill Clinton also appointed George Haley to be the ambassador to the Gambia during his presidency.

44. Manning Marable, *Malcolm X: A Life of Reinvention* (New York: Viking Press, 2011), 9.

45. David Chioni Moore, "Routes: Alex Haley's *Roots* and the Rhetoric of Genealogy," *Transition* 64 (1994): 7–10.

46. Huntzicker, "Alex Haley's *Roots*," 276; Norrell, *Alex Haley and the Books That Changed a Nation*, 199–201.

47. Wright, "The Effect of Alex Haley's *Roots* on How Gambians Remember the Atlantic Slave Trade," 312. In the same vein, a Gambian told newspaper columnist Stanley Crouch that "Yes, [*Roots*] is a lie, but it is a good lie." Quoted in Stanley Crouch, "The 'Roots' of Huckster Haley's Great Fraud," *Jewish World Review* 5 (Jan. 18, 2002), 57–62.

48. Robert D. McFadden, "Alex Haley Denies Allegation that Parts of *Roots* Were Copied from Novel Written by Mississippi Teacher," *New York Times*, April 24, 1977, 4; Philip Nobile, in "Uncovering Roots," *Village Voice*, Feb. 23, 1993. Stanley Crouch, "The Roots of Alex Haley's Fraud," *New York Daily News*, Jan. 17, 2002, accessed April 27, 2015, http://www.nydailynews.com/archives/opinions/roots-haley-great-fraud-article-1.485673.

49. Williams, *Playing the Race Card*, 237.

50. Crouch, "'Roots' of Huckster Haley's Great Fraud." See also Nobile, "Uncovering Roots." Nobile called Haley's work "criminal."

51. Two new definitive books on the subject are the previously mentioned Robert J. Norrell, *Alex Haley and the Books That Changed a Nation*, and Matthew F. Delmont, *Making "Roots": A Nation Captivated* (Oakland: University of California Press, 2016).

52. Moore, "Routes."

53. Norrell, *Alex Haley and the Books That Changed a Nation*, 224.

54. Ryan, *Calls and Responses*, 77.

55. Van Deburg, *Slavery and Race in American Popular Culture*.

56. Moore, "Routes," 21.

57. James Baldwin, "How One Black Man Came to Be an American: A Review of 'Roots,'" New York Times, Sept. 26, 1976.

PART I

Rethinking
the Context

CHAPTER ONE

Roots, the Legacy of Slavery, and Civil Rights Backlash in 1970s America

CLARE CORBOULD

It is well-known that tens of millions watched the miniseries *Roots* and that the broadcast reignited already impressive sales of the hardcover book. Another way to measure the impact of the series has been far less examined: an outpouring of letters, which viewers sent to executive producer David L. Wolper, author Alex Haley, ABC in New York, local television stations, and to newspapers nationwide. These responses are a treasure, because it is rare to find such a wide cross-section of American people responding to a cultural event, even in an era of mass literacy such as the 1970s. While letters to newspapers mostly came from the kinds of people who might often have put pen to paper on a topical issue, the letters to Wolper and Haley, by contrast, frequently began with a statement about how the author had never before written to respond to a television program. And while some were neatly typed on letterhead, many were handwritten, and a few came from people with halting script who apologized for their rudimentary literacy. These letters came from young and old, from white, black, and "ethnic" Americans, from men and women, city dwellers and farm folk, and from every corner of the United States, as well as from overseas.

The great variety among these letters offers an opportunity to reflect on how so-called ordinary Americans experienced the profound cultural changes of the postwar nation. Some historians in this new millennium see the 1970s as "the pivotal decade" of the post–World War II era, in which conservative politics and a conservative culture found their feet.[1] It marked the nexus between a bright two decades of postwar prosperity and, beginning in the mid-1970s, a long period of economic decline and increased wealth inequality. As Americans struggled with high unemployment and rising costs of living, they lost faith in the government's capacity to assist them. A growing awareness of environmental degradation and overpopulation made individuals even more despondent that the federal government could provide solutions to such enormous, global problems. Losing wars in Southeast Asia shook Americans' faith in U.S. military supremacy and undermined belief in the putative moral force that propelled the use of U.S. military power. Corruption at the highest executive office, the ignominious end to Nixon's presidency, and the chaotic years with Ford and Carter at the helm only increased general skepticism about politicians. Such disarray at the federal and international levels was mirrored at the local level, too, with several cities nearly going broke.

From the 1973 oil crisis onward, then, most Americans shared a sense that the United States was in decline. Some historians have interpreted the period as one in which Americans came to recognize their nation was part of a global, connected world, and that the era of aloofness, isolation, and belief in American exceptionalism had to end. For other historians, the shock of the 1970s produced insularity and a U.S.-affirming culture that was steeped in nostalgia and tradition.[2] Letters about *Roots* showed strains of both tendencies, but also reveal how differently white Americans and African Americans imagined the place of the United States in the world.

The letters also demonstrate that many white Americans thought the civil rights movement was at least partly to blame for what they perceived as a diminishing of U.S. power, and of their own happiness. In both the South and North, continued efforts to move the progress of desegregation along, for example in schools and workplaces, but also to secure jobs, housing, and environments safe from police brutality, meant that far from being over, the civil rights movement, with all its attendant tensions, was alive and well.[3] *Roots*, for these viewers, was yet another affront. They took umbrage at the misuse of resources, which were needed to mount such an extensive costume drama, and by the very idea that the history of black Americans deserved such treatment. Other whites, however, remained hopeful about the nation's future. They took great comfort and even pride in its ethnic diversity. For many of these Americans, pluralism was a new reason to celebrate the United States and yet more evidence that the country was exceptional.[4]

Above all else, the letters make clear that most white Americans, whether they liked *Roots* or not, as well as some black Americans, now understood the potential for change within the United States to lie within the racial attitudes of individuals. They either praised the television production for improving "understanding" between the races, which would therefore improve race relations, or they criticized it for raising issues best left untouched and thereby damaging race relations. Of the white writers who predicted enriched race relations, most stopped their analysis there. They did not, in other words, suggest much about what this would actually mean for the material circumstances of African Americans, or for the nation in general. "Race relations," as historian Michael Rudolph West has shown, came into its own as a category of social scientific and popular understanding about U.S. society around the mid-twentieth century. It was based on the trope that races should strive for better "understanding" between one another, which was promoted by prominent southern educator Booker T. Washington at the turn of the twentieth century.[5] The remedy to cure the nation's ills, as Washington saw it, would come when black Americans proved to whites that the latter's racism and prejudices were based on false assumptions. The onus was on African Americans, in other words, to prove themselves worthy of white respect.

Letters about *Roots* from sympathetic whites, which rarely called for any substantial change in the United States, bear out West's contention that "race relations" was a rhetorical category that emptied out the radical potential of the civil rights movement. Homilies that dated back to the so-called pragmatism of the late nineteenth and early twentieth centuries triumphed over black power. As letters about *Roots* demonstrate, by 1977 "race relations" had resumed its place as the primary category through which white Americans imagined certain types of social organization nationwide. Once again, the onus for change had come to rest with individuals and their emotional connections to one another, rather than any more thoroughgoing imagining of radical transformation.[6]

African American letter writers appreciated the mammoth effort and financial risk it took to broadcast such a lengthy version of *Roots*, and although many criticized it, a majority who wrote to Wolper, Haley, and newspapers were glad to see the revision of black history. While some black letter writers hoped that new knowledge about the past would prompt a revision of white Americans' behavior, most African Americans, contrary to the majority of white writers, recognized that simply depicting slavery on the television screen would change neither the present nor the future. They described racism, discrimination, and prejudice—words that almost all white letter writers avoided, which in itself says much about the way that most viewers of *Roots* apprehended questions about equality and justice. Even among African Americans, however, there were few calls for government intervention to assist in leveling inequalities in U.S. life. The tide had already shifted since the mid-1960s, and in the minds of these TV viewers, if change was going to come, it would, as almost always had been the case, have to begin with African Americans themselves.

Roots prompted many white Americans to write letters expressing their satisfaction at a job well done. Many of these were only a few lines, with statements such as that from Edward Glockner of Portsmouth, Ohio: "I am a white person but feel you are to be commended for the series—the content and its value to understanding."[7] While that letter arrived with neat penmanship on thick notepaper with a printed personal letterhead, Joyce White in Memphis wrote her missive in pencil on lined paper torn from a notebook. After announcing she was white and that both her family and friends agreed with her assessment of *Roots*, she ended by saying "I wish I had finished school so I could name off a lot of fancy words telling you how much we enjoyed it. But I only have plain words and I hope this is enough. For I want you to know that everyone we know who saw it, agrees with us. From Kunta Kinte to Alex Haley, a family, few people will never forget. Thank-you for a beautiful, moving, heart warming and truthful movie."[8] A well-to-do Virginian housewife, originally from Oregon, was distressed by her neighbors' insistence that *Roots* was "very exaggerated—not totally true," and she confided, "I know better, deep in my heart I know it was so close to the truth it hurts." When she shared morning coffees with three other housewives from out of state, they agreed with her, and so, she urged "ABC, Alex Haley and whoever else is concerned" to screen the series every five years so that all children would come to know their country's history.[9] A group of seven twenty-year-old Tufts University students wrote simply "to thank you for the finest television show we've seen in our lives. Please show *Roots* again and again."[10]

Such letters came from all over the country, and indeed all over the world. (For example, a broadcast of *Roots* in the 1980s inspired school children and adults in Scandinavia, West Germany, and East Germany to write to Haley.)[11] In the United States, people often addressed their mail to the local ABC affiliate that had broadcast *Roots*, and perhaps many of these letters are still in boxes in local archives, but sometimes the stations passed on the notes to network headquarters in New York, Wolper in California, or Haley in Tennessee. For example, a few weeks after the screening, the program/operations manager of KETV in Omaha, Nebraska, forwarded eighteen complimentary letters, including one signed by 114 people.[12] Quite possibly, people who sent letters to their local stations were the kind of people who did not write letters often, or at all, or did not have the resources to find the addresses higher up the line.

Whether inspired, outraged, or something in-between, for many authors this was the first occasion they had written down their opinions of popular culture. Sylvia Kessler of Nebraska opened her letter with "I have never written a fan letter of any kind before, but I simply have to praise *Roots*."[13] "Not that it matters," added Richard Gile from Seattle as a postscript to his short letter to the local television station, "but I am a W.A.S.P. who has never written to a T.V. station."[14] Mrs. M. E. Berry wrote to Wolper care of Warner Brothers, beginning, "I have never written to a TV studio before about anything on TV, whether good or bad. But I just had to take the time out to write to you about the story of *Roots*."[15] Inflammatory newspaper editorials and letters about *Roots* prompted an outpouring of mail, and like the fan letters, some of these were from first-time authors. "This is the first time in my life I have ever written to anyone about something in the paper," wrote one person who agreed *Roots* was terrible; another was so outraged by a negative letter in her local newspaper that she was moved to write although, as she said, "I've never written anyone before about anything."[16] By broadcasting the episodes over consecutive days rather than once a week over eight weeks, the television company produced a sense of an intense and nationwide conversation, which prompted people who might not have usually considered their views and feelings worth sharing beyond a circle of family and friends to convey their thoughts further afield.

Roots was the most successful in a new genre, the historical miniseries, which had commenced in the 1970s with the likes of *Sandburg's Lincoln* (1974), *Rich Man, Poor Man* (1976), and *Eleanor and Franklin* (1976). These television "events" truly aroused people's emotions.[17] White viewers who applauded the series reported that it had made them think harder about history, a process that had a positive effect on them as individuals. Writing a week after the show ended, Patricia Aheimer of Pittsburgh said, "I have done some reflecting about the truth of this story. . . . I feel a deep compassion for the blacks of slavery days—and it carries over to the blacks of 1977. . . . It was indeed an experience to feel and live—for one entire week—and suffer and bleed as Kunta Kinte."[18] A Californian, Joanna Freeland, addressed her letter to *Roots* via ABC headquarters in New York to report she "was deeply affected. . . . I've always considered myself liberal and unprejudiced, but *Roots* has given me a whole new perspective on black people. I think for the first time I'm seeing them as people, individuals with a history and a culture and a spirit, instead of an underprivileged race. Thank you," Freeland concluded, "for opening my eyes."[19] Having watched *Roots* in Houston with her "white upper-middle class family of six," Marian Mulvahill described the "profoundly moving effect on all of us. . . . There was not one evening that we did not weep for the anguish of the blacks or cringe at the hatred and ignorance of the whites or feel some small terrible needed relief when some human decency was exhibited by too, too few whites. Suddenly, I am so proud of our black Americans. *Roots* showed family ideals of Love, Pride, and Good for All of us to live by."[20]

Other white writers, perhaps also influenced by world events to look for ways Americans might now band together more thoroughly, reported that *Roots* made them feel as though black and white citizens were members of a national family. In the words of one white correspondent, Dexter Brown, even though whites were "not responsible for the deeds of their forebears," and nor should black Americans "be ashamed of their heritage . . . nevertheless, the film does motivate one to re-evaluate attitudes, values, and prejudices." Adopting a metaphor that had become a commonplace, and would soon become a number one hit single, "Ebony and Ivory," for Stevie Wonder and Paul

McCartney, Brown concluded, "both keys—black and white—must work harmoniously in the symphony of freedom. America is too small for divisiveness. The world is too dangerous for Americans not to be brothers."[21] Another white writer revealed that "since viewing *Roots* I've had a strong emotional feeling I must express . . . a new realization has come to me. An understanding that black people are people. Not black, not white, but people! People with loves, hates, sufferings, and joys, all the feelings I've known myself. I realize the unjustness and loss of dignity forced upon them through all these years, and their fight to get it back. The words 'created equal' have more meaning. The Good Lord put us all in the same world in the same way and we must learn to understand each other to live in peace as brothers."[22] If not quite brothers, black Americans now seemed to some white letter writers to be, at least, more familiar; as one Californian man put it, "in the very human situations portrayed this past week, I felt I met my neighbors. Each birth, each falling in love and marriage, each death touched me."[23]

For dozens of these authors, the end result of their heightened feelings was, in the words they used most often, a better "understanding between the races." The tone for this assertion was set in William Marmon's long article in *Time*, published on the final day of the miniseries broadcast, and in part atonement for the magazine's earlier prediction that *Roots*, a "*Mandingo* for middlebrows," would flop.[24] Marmon's article became the most often quoted piece about *Roots* in all subsequent literature, and his statistics in particular were repeated: the viewing figures and book sales, the fact that 276 colleges and universities were now setting up courses around the book, and the jump in numbers of African Americans contacting the National Archives. That article also led the way in analyzing the emotional and cognitive effects of the miniseries on viewers, and in predicting outcomes. In Marmon's telling, "most observers thought that in the long term, *Roots* would improve race relations, particularly because of the televised version's profound impact on whites. . . . Many observers also feel that the TV series left whites with a more sympathetic view of blacks by giving them a greater appreciation of black history."[25] Marmon quoted opinions of white people nationwide, including sociologists, a literary critic, journalists, television critics and executives, housewives, teenagers, and a law student. He also cited the views of black men and women, including a sociologist, a biologist, a social worker, politicians, historians, and a secretary. The piece concluded with remarks from two black congressmen and Marmon's supposition that "like black Americans elsewhere, these Congressmen have a sense that because of *Roots*, something good has happened to race relations—even if they cannot quite define what. Perhaps it is simply that the gulf between black and white has been narrowed a bit and the level of mutual understanding has been raised a notch."[26] Most white letter writers who reported on the emotional or psychological impact, like Marmon, did not reflect further on what this might mean, except for a vague sense that "race relations" would therefore improve.

Exceptions to this tendency among white writers were generally limited to self-identified leftists. The newspaper of the October League declared that "*Roots* gave no clue that it is the capitalist system that stands behind Black oppression today, and the effect of the series was to encourage pacifism and assimilationism."[27] The Workers World Party released a similar statement.[28] The Reverend Ivan Backer of Hartford, Connecticut, however, identified more directly a limitation in most white people's responses to the show:

> I have heard many people profess that watching *Roots* was a profound experience. They say that now they have a deeper understanding of the horrors of slavery and the loss of human dignity.
>
> This new understanding poses some old questions with renewed urgency: How can we promote better understanding between all types of people in 1977? How can we eliminate such legacies of the past as discrimination, segregation, and racial hatred? How can we watch people living on totally inadequate public assistance payments without protest?
>
> I ask those who were moved by *Roots*, what will you do with your new understanding? Will you allow you new insight to soothe your conscience, or will it goad you to action? Will you continue to behave as you have in the past, or will you work for freedom and justice for all?[29]

Backer had long been involved in causes for racial justice, both in Connecticut and in his role at the Episcopal Society for Cultural and Racial Unity of the Diocese of Newark. Likewise, Henry Nordin, a fifty-four-year-old white steelworker of Baltimore, responded some weeks after the miniseries broadcast to many white viewers who were either wringing their hands over their guilt or declaring loudly they had nothing for which to feel guilty. "In 1977," Nordin wrote to the *Baltimore Sun*, "if we have anything to answer for, it is not slavery. It is the way we have used the blackness of the blacks to force upon them poor education, poor housing, the worst jobs, the lowest pay, the high percentage of illness because of poor environment and bad diet and, most if not all, of the social wrongs that our society has to offer. The least we can do now is to stop feeling unjustly accused, admit our faults (racial prejudices) and for the good of the entire country make an honest effort to change for the better."[30]

Such voices were the exception, however, with most white viewers content to convey how they felt about the show, without reflecting more deeply about the long-term institutional and structural effects of racism and how they might work to ameliorate them. Most white letter writers, unlike Backer and Nordin, did not use the words *racism* or *discrimination*. Their sentiments were summed up by a Senate Resolution passed in March 1977 to pay tribute to Haley for giving

> a record viewing audience a new sense of awareness of Black Americans' long-obscured rich history by presenting a chronology of Haley's ancestors during the 100 years preceding the Emancipation Proclamation; and
>
> Whereas through the efforts of Alex Haley, individuals of all races have gained new insights into, and a better understanding of, Black Americans' on-going struggle for complete freedom and equality, both historically and at the present time.[31]

Senator John Glenn's statement left unexamined the process by which such "insight" would yield "complete freedom." Most white letter writers likewise left a gap in even describing such a process, let alone indicating a willingness to change their own behavior to bring it about. Instead, they proffered, merely their understanding would "improve" race relations. The fact that so few white letter writers acknowledged the deeper and more difficult structures that shaped, if not determined, chances for African Americans in the United States, reflected the waning of hope that radical change could be effected in the nation.

Other liberal white letter writers found in *Roots* a way to celebrate U.S. ethnic diversity, which many regarded as a new reason to believe the United States was an exceptional nation. From the early 1970s, as historian Matthew Frye Jacobson has put it, the origins of the normative American had moved from Plymouth Rock to Ellis Island.[32] Where earlier in the century, the definition of "whiteness" had expanded to include, for example, those descended from Irish, Italian, Polish, Norwegian, or Jewish ancestors, now descendants of all those immigrants and more were reclaiming their origins and adopting so-called hyphenated identities.[33] Just as black history began to move out of the wings and onto center stage, in other words, other types of difference became ones to celebrate. One of the effects of this was to erase the specificity of the experience of enslavement. One letter writer could therefore say, for example, "We all bear the scars or carry the burden of the history made by our ancestors. Whether our ancestors came to this country on slave ships, sailed from England for religious freedom, followed Cortez, or walked the Trail of Tears, we all carry something of them in us. I feel the only way to lighten that burden is to learn from history."[34] In this manner, *Roots* became a universal story of success, which tapped into a growing interest among Americans in their individual and group "origins," and accelerated the rate at which people began genealogical projects.[35] As the director of the Immigration History Research Center of the University of Minnesota wrote to Haley in 1981, "We at the Center have felt the direct impact of *Roots* in the form of a great number of requests for genealogical information received since its publication. Given our limited staff, we have mixed feelings about all this new business which you have generated for us!"[36]

For many *Roots* viewers, it seemed that if the descendants of dirt-poor immigrants could make it in the great U.S. mosaic, then African Americans' failure to flourish must be their own fault. A woman who announced her own hyphenated identity wrote to a Scranton, Pennsylvania, newspaper to argue that *Roots* showed "Life is what you make it. We can either sit around and complain about our heritage or stand up and make our people proud like Kunta Kenti [*sic*] did. I'm a Polish-American. What am I supposed to do, sit back and cry every time someone calls me a dirty name or tells crude jokes concerning my ancestry. Well, not me. I'm [P]olish and darn proud. So black America, stop bellyaching about your ancestors being slaves and start remembering that they made it possible for you to be free. Every race, creed and color were slaves in one way or another before coming to this country. That is what America is all about. 'All living under God in One Free Nation and helping to do his part in keeping it free.'"[37]

Such attitudes, which reduced slavery to just one difficult experience among many, also found expression at the highest levels of U.S. government and in culture across the country. The committee tasked with shaping the bicentennial celebrations chose not to mark the anniversary with a world's fair or a national tour of a grand exhibition of U.S. history; rather it called for a broad range of modes of commemoration, all to be generated at local and community levels with the participation of a likewise diverse range of individuals and groups. In making this decision, the American Revolution Bicentennial Administration (ARBA) was assisted by a twenty-five-person advisory council that was chaired, not coincidentally, by David Wolper. The council included Alex Haley, too, along with writer and performer Maya Angelou and Betty Shabazz, widow of Malcolm X. Other members were Richard Gambino, whose 1974 *Blood of My Blood* did for Sicilians what *Roots* did for African Americans; senior Catholic and Mormon clerics; businesspeople; academics; community and labor organizers; one "homemaker" from Alaska; and former First Lady Mrs. Lyndon B. Johnson. The ARBA made a virtue of a necessity, as it had only a small budget and Americans were truly disheartened by the federal government by the mid-1970s.[38] But, nonetheless, the character of its plans, and of its reports after the fact, indicates that Americans, too, had taken up the idea that what made the United States unique was its pluralist society and culture. This was, they believed, truly a place where anyone could make it.

Efforts to minimize the uniqueness of black history went all the way to the president; when Jimmy Carter acknowledged the work of Black History Month, he too elided slavery from his remarks and implied that African

Americans were just one group among many. Carter applauded efforts that brought to light "the achievements of Black Americans and their pivotal role in the establishment, development and progress of American life. This celebration highlights the contribution of Black people and gives all of us a keener appreciation of the rich and diverse heritage we share.... May the programs and activities planned for this month encourage many citizens to expand the search for their own ethnic roots. And may they bring about a period of introspection and heightened national consciousness that will lead to greater participation by all in the workings of our democratic society and in our dream for its future."[39] *Roots'* ending no doubt contributed to the idea that the American Dream was indeed color-blind. The miniseries closed when Kunta Kinte's descendant, Chicken George, led his aging wife, two sons, and their families off the plantation on which they had been enslaved to land he had purchased in Tennessee. Enough hard work, the show implied, would lead to success, as some of its critics at the time recognized.[40]

Other groups who believed their heritage to have been unfairly marginalized sought to capture David Wolper's imagination. Letters arrived outlining tales of Jewish, Irish, Native American, and English family histories.[41] Wolper received some ten letters sent as part of what their authors hoped would be "a major letter-writing campaign" to have the producers of *Roots* and ABC adapt Michael Arlen's bestselling and 1976 National Book Award–winning *Passage to Ararat*. A representative letter asserted that Arlen's tale was a "story as large as a whole people yet as personal and focused as the uneasy bond between a father and a son . . . a masterful account of the affirmation and pain of kinship in modern times." They had cannily recognized the characteristics that made *Roots* such a success. *Passage to Ararat* was the perfect choice, they assured Wolper, for "the next dramatization of [a] series to further ethnic awareness and pride in Americans.... the story can be in perfect perimeters considering the multi-cultural, multi-sectarian pluralistic setting of the American society."[42] Wolper appears not to have been moved by such entreaties, going on instead to produce *Roots: The Next Generations* and *The Thorn Birds*, the latter based on Colleen McCullough's novel.

Still others resented that African American history was receiving so much attention. They wondered impolitely why Wolper had chosen to portray a history of black Americans and whether he would redress the imbalance by turning now to other groups. "So-o-o-o, now about the ethnic group.... Let's have some stories of the Polish settlers that came here—or the Hungarians—or the Bohemians??????????? About ROOTS—all we can think of saying is: S*—t," read one note postmarked Albuquerque.[43] Their friends or neighbors asked likewise, using the same typewriter, "Why not some Swedish or Norwegion [*sic*] family? You two sure can rattle on and on. Why not something of the English and the French and yes, someone in the Slavic category? AGAIN ....

about Roots—SO WHAT & WHO CARES?"[44] Such letter writers would certainly have agreed with the sentiments expressed in several editorials and in William Marmon's piece in *Time*, that those who descended from Europeans who migrated to the United States any time after the Civil War had nothing in their family's past for which to apologize.[45]

Expressing their resentment at the gains they perceived black Americans as making, undeservedly, over the past few years, many letter writers used language that anticipated conservative rhetoric regarding color blindness and so-called reverse discrimination, which would become commonplace just a few years later. "The real promise of America was that every man, regardless of his birth, be given the opportunity to succeed by his own efforts. This does not mean that the Constitution guarantees the good life to every citizen regardless of his ability or mentality," wrote one woman to her local, Norfolk, Virginia, paper. "Our country can never prosper if special consideration must be given to any group, be it Irish, Jewish, black, or whatever," she insisted. "In the vernacular of today's youth, let's 'cool it' on *Roots*."[46] In another striking instance, an incensed white letter writer in Michigan wondered if a similar series would be made in years to come in order to chronicle hardships presently endured as a result of "reverse discrimination."[47] Another furious correspondent in Savannah insisted that the Georgia "slave code" was "humane," and that "Kunta did not suffer as much from his severed foot as 'honkies' are now suffering from muggings from young blacks who make a cult of attacking old and feeble whites. . . . One recent victim still has a $9,000 hospital bill to pay."[48] Across the country in Oakland, California, a letter writer fumed the "type of treatment as shown did not happen to all of them and today they get far more assistance and benefits than the whites and if anyone is discriminated against it is us. . . . Now they want to walk in and demand or take by force all the whites have struggled for. I don't intend to sound biased."[49]

Among those white viewers who disparaged *Roots* in writing, however, the far most common response was that it would set back perceived advances in race relations, achieved over the century following the end of the Civil War.[50] "What a crime for the network to stir up so very much hatred of blacks against white," declared E. C. McLachlan of Jacksonville, Florida, "and completely *undo* the good that had taken 100 years to come about. *How can you ever undo the harm that this has caused?*" (original emphasis).[51] Margaret Barry wrote from Long Island to report that the show, "instead of bringing the blacks and whites closer, [has] widened the gap!"[52] David Coleman of Miami Beach, having seen only the first episode, wrote immediately to exclaim, "this showing will prove to be the greatest disservice to ethnic harmony." For evidence he cited a brief exchange he'd had with the African American porter in his building, a formerly pleasant man, Coleman asserted, who now blurted out, "'you whites owe us plenty.'"[53] Mary Mink, of Farmersville, Ohio, typed a seven-hundred-word letter to reprimand Wolper because "the struggle for improvement in black-white relations has been dealt a severe blow by your short-sightedness." She wondered why on earth he didn't consult Margaret Mitchell's *Gone with the Wind*, based, she pointed out, like *Roots*, on twelve years' research "and not once has her book ever been challenged by the most astute historians and not one error has been found."[54] Nobody could know for sure what happened in the past, Mink conceded, but Mitchell's depiction of "the slave community" and of kindly southern whites was much closer, she asserted, to "actual history."

Such writers assumed that African Americans were seething with anger about the past, and that the previous years of struggle amounted to the granting of generous concessions on the part of white Americans, for which black people ought to be more grateful. These white Americans castigated *Roots* as an "all-out attack upon us," about which "we were well aware, and furious at how one-sided it appeared."[55] *Roots*, one writer from Abbeville, Louisiana, claimed, had resulted in "Negroes . . . whipping themselves up into a frenzy of resentment. . . . Hardly what this country needs as we struggle toward understanding and reconciliation."[56] A very long letter in the *Savannah News* opened, "Move over, Harriet Beecher Stowe, and make room in the Hall of Infamy for Alex Haley and ABC television network." This author warned that the series would "go far in spoiling the good relations and mutual regard so carefully nurtured and maintained between the races over the last decade," and concluded that Wolper had performed "a callous disservice to our country which is still struggling to bring about a peaceful and lasting coexistence of the races."[57] Such views found more famous champions. Lillian Carter, the U.S. president's mother, said, "I hate to bring back those awful days. It was so long ago—they're over and gone with. I think we should let it lie."[58] Former first lady of California Nancy Reagan considered *Roots* "inflammatory. Out in Los Angeles we saw on TV people in bars saying they were going out and get the whites, and there were riots in schools." "Nancy's theory," summarized syndicated columnist Betty Beale, was that "we have made tremendous progress in correcting race injustices, so why don't we give some attention to the injustice in the world that's being overlooked?"[59]

In order to charge the makers of *Roots* with meddling in a successful but protracted process of reconciliation, these letter writers accused them of misrepresenting the past, and therefore their letters almost always included some statement about *Roots* being historical fantasy. The primary error, they said over and again, was the underlying claim in *Roots* that "under slavery all blacks were good and all whites were bad . . . a distortion of the truth."[60] They pointed repeatedly to the historical fact that Africans had been involved in the slave trade, which they said was not included in the series (although there is, in fact, a scene in episode 1 in which a caged Kunta Kinte and other slaves are whipped by Africans). More often still, these letters included assertions about there having been good whites in the slaveholding South. Their authors claimed such knowledge through their own reading, or because other, supposedly less biased sources had told them so, or through accounts of their own family's experiences. There were dozens of such letters, and such sentiments found a megaphone in former California governor Ronald Reagan: "Very frankly, I thought the bias of all the good people being one color and all the bad people being another was rather destructive."[61]

Almost all of the letter writers who accused Wolper of historical fabrication on the basis that he portrayed no kind whites ignored the presence in the miniseries of George and Martha Johnson, a young white couple so beloved of Haley's ancestors that they joined them to move to new lands in Tennessee. In overlooking the Johnsons, such letter writers unwittingly demonstrated that they were interested only in Wolper failing to portray kindly slave owners, rather than whites in general. Some were up front about this, claiming Wolper had omitted, for instance, the "compassionate" mistresses who cared for sick slaves and the owners who treated their valuable property well.[62] A woman whose "own roots go deep into Dixie" claimed outright that "high class plantation owners" did not have sex with slave women; "rather the lowtype, illiterate 'sharecropper' type" was to blame, and only then because no white women were available to them.[63] Such myopia was not lost on all who corresponded about *Roots*. As viewer Jesse Casarez wrote to an Austin, Texas, newspaper, "Television columnist Lisa Tuttle criticizes *Roots* for not showing the good side of white folks. She must have failed to watch every episode. The last two dealt fairly well with some good, although poor, whites. The basic issue in the beginning is slavery. If she can find one good thing to say about slavery I recommended she clean her rose-colored glasses."[64] A Savannah, Georgia, woman who did not identify her own race replied even more pointedly on the issue of kindly whites, asserting "You cannot be humane to someone you hold in bondage. The only humane act would be to set the person free. The point is not what you do with the stolen goods, but that the [g]oods were stolen."[65]

Letters from African American viewers of *Roots* likewise poured into newspaper offices and filled Wolper and Haley's in-trays. Many were complimentary, applauding the writers, producers, and cast for their investments of time, cash, and bravery. "I offer my congratulations, thanks and appreciation to the author, producers, movie stars and ABC-TV for presenting to the entire world this true-to-life story with its impact so powerful!," wrote Walter Talbert of La Puente, California.[66] These letters, as with many from white Americans, were saturated with emotion. A Riverside, California, woman wrote a heartfelt letter praising Haley and the screening, which "gave me a sense of pride and dignity. . . . Nothing I have read since the Bible has had such an impact on my life."[67] Janice Smith was relieved and happy "to see the television media present the African-American history in its true light. We so often see ourselves portrayed as comedians, dope pushers, prostitutes, and criminals. . . . It's been such a pleasure to see African-Americans loving each other, struggling together in unity against the racial attitudes in this country.[68] From Houston, one man wrote breathlessly to thank *Roots'* producers for "this monumental display of industry leadership." "Perhaps with shows of this calibre [sic]," he wrote, "depicting 'Black Americans' and their 'heritage,' we will someday make all Americans feels as though we're a united America. For any country to be proud and strong it must have a strong foundation, and part of America's foundation is its 'Black Americans,' of which I'm one and proud."[69]

Many other African Americans, while pleased to see their history on the big screen and the subject of such intense and widespread debate, were not so surprised at *Roots'* content, because such stories had long been a staple of their family and community histories. As Mrs. Bertha King of Benton Harbor, Michigan, put it, the episodes "were no surprise to me because my ancestors and history had already told a similar story," and it had been well rehearsed in the books "which were on the shelves when I GREW UP."[70] Joyann Husband was only one of many letter writers who suggested that those who thought *Roots* was fanciful ought to read a few history books, recommending, for starters, titles by John Hope Franklin and Eugene Genovese.[71] Nathaniel Newsome was likewise moved to reply to letters in a Dayton, Ohio, newspaper, urging readers to consult Julius Lester's *To Be a Slave*.[72] Other writers who commended the series conveyed that nevertheless they had heard firsthand that slavery was "much worse than anything shown in *Roots*."[73] Curt Shelton wrote to a Connecticut newspaper to refute an earlier piece that had accused the television network of a "lopsided" portrayal. By relaying the stories told him by his grandparents, who had themselves been slaves, about violence in general and sexual assault in particular, Shelton implied that, if anything, *Roots* downplayed the harsher elements of enslavement.[74]

Some African Americans were hopeful that the immense reach of *Roots* into people's living rooms would extend to a long-lasting impact on white Americans' attitudes. James Comer, a well-known African American professor of psychiatry at Yale University, asserted that *Roots* "forced all Americans to take a penetrating look at slavery—and thereby helped whites get rid of their burden of guilt."[75] Other specialists in the human sciences agreed. Elaine Pinderhughes, then an assistant professor of casework at Boston College, was the first of twenty-nine signatories to a letter that described in sophisticated language the psychological impact of the program, which others conveyed in more simple ways. *Roots* was a breakthrough, they explained, for black

Americans who had been hamstrung by the pain of the past, "humiliated, nullified, frustrated, angered and trapped that Whites have refused to recognize their reality." Whites, they continued, were "embarrassed, guilty, saddened, outraged and ... trapped" by their unconscious inability to confront black Americans' pain. *Roots* offered an opportunity to "replace mythology with true history." Doing so would enable black *and* white Americans to "understand" that, in repressing the past, they had failed to allow their nation to flourish; "that America may yet be able to face the truth of her past and present, to free both Blacks and Whites from their entrapment, and in so doing, to truly live up to the dreams of her founding fathers."[76]

Whether, in fact, attitudinal change would result in new behavior, was a topic for debate. Maya Angelou, who sat alongside Haley and Wolper on the ARBA advisory council, wrote on the day of the first episode's broadcast that Haley's work did not simply depict black experiences in the past, but, rather, he "has given us the subsequent question: 'Admitting all that has gone before, admitting our duplicity, our complicity and our greed, what do we, all Americans, do next?'"[77] Some responded optimistically, including Francis Kornegay, the executive director of the Detroit Urban League. *Roots*, he said in language so forceful it was as though he hoped he could bring about change just by saying it would happen, "will cause, undoubtedly, the second American revolution. It will be a revolution of the mind, soul and spirit from which action programs will flow to help kill American racism."[78] Others were cautiously hopeful, such as a young black woman, Cynthia Horne, who wrote to her local newspaper to say, "Maybe it's time for some of these scared [white] people to take a good look at themselves and say there's still a lot to be done not only for blacks, but for Mexicans; whites who weren't fortunate enough to be rich or accepted, and for the world of new races with the mixed generations of our society. 'We've come a long way, baby,'" Horne concluded, riffing on a ubiquitous advertisement for a cigarette marketed to women, "but we've got a long way to go."[79]

When it came to predicting or analyzing the outcome of the miniseries' broadcast, many black letter writers were skeptical that attitude changes among white Americans would make much difference to their lives. Clifford Culpepper wrote to the *Los Angeles Sentinel* to condemn television as a distraction from the struggle, which must continue. "Surely you can see if we don't demand our rights, no one, especially your tormentors, is going to hand them over for the asking."[80] Culpepper would have found a friend in Dr. Secil V. House, who addressed head-on the tendency among white supporters of *Roots* to drop analysis when it veered beyond a description of the emotional impact of the series and toward the question of what might be done to change African Americans' material circumstances in the present day. House warned that "to suggest that the major impact of *Roots* was to make many

Americans aware of black history seems to me to be the most extraordinary conclusion possible and the epitome of naivete." Rather, he insisted, viewers needed to understand the continuing impact of slavery, which although no longer manifest in "terrorism and infamy," such as the 1955 lynching of Emmett Till, still "leaves its deadly signature at the close of each day."[81] It was not enough, House pointed out, for viewers to congratulate themselves for the sympathy that the portrayal of black suffering evoked in them. Although a change in attitudes was a good start, action was needed.

Other African American letter writers were quite sure that white behavior was unlikely to change as a result of *Roots*, no matter how many white Americans professed to being profoundly affected by the miniseries. They looked around them and saw violent campaigns to prevent the integration of public schools, and they witnessed continued exclusion of nonwhites from good housing, clubs, and other institutions. Drawing on a long tradition of black self-help, these writers advocated instead that African Americans devote their attention to respectable behavior and education.[82] As Lewis Bohler Jr., rector of Advent Episcopal Church of Los Angeles, put it, "It may be poor strategy to suggest that a group place itself in a defensive posture, but, the truth is, the powers that be (and rule) have already placed us there. My admonition to fellow blacks is: Fight on, pursue on, relentlessly and forever, if necessary. But keep it 'cool, dignified, and orderly!'"[83] Several letter writers likewise drew on a long tradition of self-help among African Americans to propose that *Roots'* impact would be on black youth, who would now know that "segregation and discrimination are not new issues, because they existed during the time of our forefathers. We also know that it stands up and marches this world over like an elite army with total destruction on its mind. It is aimed directly and indirectly toward you! Its purpose is to confuse, harass, intimidate, deceive, evade and deny. But you can defeat it by setting and attaining high goals with quality education."[84]

A final group of African Americans who responded to *Roots* in letters wrote to point out urgently that individual attitudes mattered less than structural change. Ernest Knight was one of several *Los Angeles Sentinel* readers to reply to a provocative editorial by A. S. Doc Young, which had criticized *Roots*. Those perusing the letters' pages could not have missed the derision in Knight's retort to Young's claim that "blacks will be lining up to receive goods and services that whites will dispense because of their aroused guilt feelings that were brought out by viewing *Roots*." As Knight said, "I advise him to get in line early if he plans to get his share, because there certainly won't be many goodies to go around. Reconstruction, 40 acres and a mule, war on poverty, black capitalism and equal justice under the law were a few of the goodies that a so-called guilt-laden white society promised but did not deliver."[85] On the other side of the country, journalist Don Rojas admonished readers of the *New York Amsterdam News* to remember that "capitalists call the shots"; it was now more than one hundred years since Haley's ancestor Chicken George led his family to land in Tennessee following the Civil War, "yet today Blacks are still on the move searching for a peaceful place to rest their load, still waiting to collect on the promise of a mule and 40 acres."[86] As Bertha King of Michigan said in response to an inflammatory newspaper editorial, "regarding privileged access to the federal kitty, it's about time the Federal Government decided to make some efforts, after all they let Jim Crow laws affect their judgment for a number of years."[87]

In raising the question of forty acres and a mule, these critics drew attention to the usually unspoken fear that underlay white Americans' responses to *Roots*: that greater "understanding" on the part of whites about what had happened during slavery would result in an admission that reparations were due. It was the great fear of genuine redress that meant angry white viewers in droves wrote letters to editors, and in lesser numbers to Wolper and Haley, to protest that they did not want to be forced to feel guilty and refused to be ashamed for the actions of their ancestors. In a few cases, they mobilized defenses that had become commonplace—that, as descendants of those who had arrived after the Civil War, they had no personal responsibility for slavery. Occasionally, such white letter writers who descended from slave-era families would even point out that their ancestors had fought for the Union in a bloody war that ended slavery. Their family's debt, they asserted, was therefore already paid.

Liberal white viewers of *Roots* did not express such fears about reparations; however, they did shy away from pledging to alter their own behavior or to become involved in campaigns for broader change. Of course there were, in the 1970s, continuing radical movements for social change, and grassroots activism that continued the project of civil rights and other social movements.[88] Letters about *Roots* show, however, that for a wide cross-section of non-black Americans, the heat of the moment had passed, and for that they were grateful. In the face of apparent national decline in an ongoing Cold War with its threat of nuclear annihilation, and in the aftermath of intense internal and external criticism of the racism of U.S. policies, white Americans tuned in to *Roots* in enormous numbers. As their letters demonstrate, the miniseries' fantasy that if African Americans worked hard enough, they too could make it in the land of milk and honey, was just the salve they needed.

NOTES

1. The literature is too extensive to cite here, but the phrase is from Judith Stein, *Pivotal Decade: How the United States Traded Factories for Finance in the Seventies* (New Haven, Conn.: Yale University Press, 2010).

2. For a summary of this debate see Barbara Keys, Jack Davies, and Elliott Bannan, "The Post-Traumatic Decade: New Histories of the 1970s," *Australasian Journal of American Studies* 33 (2014): 1–17.

3. Ronald P. Formisano, *Boston against Busing: Race, Class, and Ethnicity in the 1960s and 1970s* (Chapel Hill: University of North Carolina Press, 1991); J. Todd Moye, *Let the People Decide: Black Freedom and Black Resistance Movements in Sunflower County, Mississippi, 1945–1986* (Chapel Hill: University of North Carolina Press, 2004); Nancy MacLean, *Freedom Is Not Enough: The Opening of the American Workplace* (Cambridge, Mass.: Harvard University Press, 2006); Stephen Tuck, *We Ain't What We Ought to Be* (Cambridge, Mass.: Harvard University Press, 2009), and "'We Are Taking Up Where the Movement of the 1960s Left Off': The Proliferation and Power of African American Protest during the 1970s," *Journal of Contemporary History* 43 (2008): 637–654; Tracy E. K'Meyer, *Civil Rights in the Gateway to the South: Louisville, Kentucky, 1945–1980* (Lexington: University Press of Kentucky, 2009); Timothy J. Minchin and John A. Salmond, *After the Dream: Black and White Southerners since 1965* (Lexington: University Press of Kentucky, 2011).

4. Matthew Frye Jacobson, *Roots Too: White Ethnic Revival in Post–Civil Rights America* (Cambridge, Mass.: Harvard University Press, 2006).

5. Michael Rudolph West, *The Education of Booker T. Washington: American Democracy and the Idea of Race Relations* (New York: Columbia University Press, 2006), x.

6. On the radical tradition in the civil rights movement, see Nikhil Pal Singh, *Black Is a Country: Race and the Unfinished Struggle for Democracy* (Cambridge, Mass.: Harvard University Press, 2004).

7. Edward L. Glockner (Portsmouth, Ohio) to ABC, MGM, and Mr. Haley, Jan. 31, 1977, David L. Wolper Collection, David L. Wolper Center, Doheny Memorial Library, University of Southern California (hereafter DLW), box 288, folder 1. My thanks to Malgorzata J. Rymsza-Pawlowska for permitting me to read her unpublished work, which alerted me to the existence of this rich trove of letters in Wolper's papers: "Bicentennial Memory: Postmodernity, Media, and Historical Subjectivity, 1966–1976" (PhD diss., Brown University, 2012).

8. Joyce White (Memphis, Tenn.) to ABC Network, Jan. 30, 1977, DLW, box 288, folder 1.

9. Mrs. Michael Hardman (Va.) to ABC, Alex Haley, and whoever else is concerned, Feb. 2, 1977, DLW, box 288, folder 1.

10. Alan Herring, Lynn Berman, Thomas Zesk, Peter S. Ciano, Kem Epstein, Katherine Koucky, and Sarah A. Ticknor to Sirs, Jan. 30, 1977, DLW, box 288, folder 1.

11. These letters are held in the Alex Haley Papers, Special Collections and Archives, African-American Research Library and Cultural Center, Broward County Library, Florida.

12. Gary R. Nielsen (program/operations manager, KETV, Omaha, Neb.) to Mr. and Mrs. John E. Bertenshaw, Feb. 25, 1977, DLW, box 288, folder 1.

13. Sylvia Kessler to KETV (Neb.), Feb. 1, 1977, DLW, box 288, folder 1.

14. Richard E. Gile Jr. to Komo TV et al., postmarked Seattle, Washington, on Feb. 1, 1977, DLW, box 288, folder 1.

15. Mrs. M. E. Berry to David Wolper, Feb. 28, 1979, DLW, box 288, folder 1.

16. Jeffrey Hart, "*Roots* Backlash," *Xenia Daily Gazette* (Xenio, Ohio), March 11, 1977, 4 (syndicated nationwide under various headings); Cynthia Horne (Austin, Tex.), letter to the editor, *American-Statesman* (Austin), Feb. 6, 1977, DLW, box 284, folder 5.

17. Malgorzata J. Rymsza-Pawlowska, "Broadcasting the Past: History Television, 'Nostalgia Culture,' and the Emergence of the Miniseries in the 1970s in the United States," *Journal of Popular Film and Television* 42 (2014): 81–90.

18. Patricia Aheimer (Pittsburgh, Pa.) to ABC-TV, Feb. 7, 1977, DLW, box 288, folder 1.

19. Joanna Freeland (San Jose, Calif.) to *Roots*, c/o ABC-NY, Feb. 3, 1977, DLW, box 288, folder 1.

20. Mrs. Marian Mulvahill (Houston, Tex.) to ABC-NY, Jan. 31, 1977, DLW, box 288, folder 1.

21. Dexter Brown, letter to the editor, *News Leader* (Richmond, Va.), Feb. 11, 1977, DLW, box 284, folder 5.

22. Jerrie Kramer (Indianapolis), letter to the editor, *Indianapolis Star*, March 7, 1977, DLW, box 284, folder 5.

23. Robert Morrison (Fremont, Calif.) to Cast of *Roots*, ABC-TV, Hollywood, Calif., Feb. 25, 1979, DLW, box 288, folder 1.

24. Richard Schickel, "Television: Viewpoint: Middlebrow Mandingo," *Time*, Jan. 24, 1977.

25. William Marmon, "Why *Roots* Hit Home," *Time*, Feb. 14, 1977, 68–75.

26. Ibid.

27. *Guardian* (New York), March 2, 1977, cited in "*Roots*: Reviews and Statements," DLW, box 283, folder 8.

28. "*Roots*: Reviews and Statements."

29. I. A. Backer (Hartford, Conn.), letter to the editor, *Hartford Courant*, March 17, 1977, DLW, box 284, folder 5.

30. Henry Nordin (Baltimore), letter to the editor, *Baltimore Sun*, March 10, 1977, DLW, box 284, folder 5.

31. S. Res. 112, "Resolution to Pay Tribute to Alex Haley for the Impact of His Epic Work *Roots*," March 14, 1977, 95th Cong.

32. Jacobson, *Roots Too*, 7.

33. Theodore W. Allen, *Invention of the White Race*, 2 vols. (London: Verso, 1994, 1997); Noel Ignatiev, *How the Irish Became White* (New York: Routledge, 1995); Matthew Frye Jacobson, *Whiteness of a Different Color: European Immigrants and the Alchemy of Race* (Cambridge, Mass.: Harvard University Press, 1998); David. R. Roediger, *Working toward Whiteness: How America's Immigrants Became White: The Strange Journey from Ellis Island to the Suburbs* (New York: Basic Books, 2005).

34. Vivian Cox (Dayton, Ohio), letter to the editor, *Dayton Daily News*, Feb. 26, 1977, DLW, box 284, folder 5.

35. Jacobson, *Roots Too*; François Weil, *Family Trees: A History of Genealogy in America* (Cambridge, Mass.: Harvard University Press, 2013).

36. Rudolph J. Vecoli to Alex Haley, March 23, 1981, Alex Haley Papers, box STUV, folder 5. My thanks to Myrka Don Fred, Special Collections librarian, who generously emailed me copies of documents from this collection.

37. Mrs. Robert J. Conrad, letter to the editor, *Times* (Scranton, Pa.), March 18, 1977, DLW, box 284, folder 5.

38. Christopher Capozzola, "'It Makes You Want to Believe in the Country': Celebrating the Bicentennial in an Age of Limits," in *America in the Seventies*, ed. Beth Bailey and David Farber (Lawrence: University Press of Kansas, 2004), 29–49; Natasha Zaretsky, *No Direction Home: The American Family and the Fear of National Decline, 1968–1980* (Chapel Hill: University of North Carolina Press, 2007), 142–171.

39. Jimmy Carter quoted in "President Lauds ASALH for Black History Month," *Jet*, Feb. 22, 1979, 18.

40. Russell L. Adams, "An Analysis of the *Roots* Phenomenon in the Context of American Racial Conservatism," *Présence Africaine* 116 (1980): 125–140; Eric Foner, review in *Seven Days*, March 1977, excerpted in David L. Wolper with Quincy Troupe, *The Inside Story of TV's "Roots"* (New York: Warner Books, 1978): 263–264.

41. See *"Roots*: Letters from Public (Solicitations)," DLW, box 288, folder 5.

42. Ara Manougian, M.D., and Sona Hamalian (president and secretary of the Armenian Evangelical College Student Association of America) to David Wolper, March 7, 1977, DLW, box 288, folder 5.

43. Anon. to "Sponsors of Commercials of the ROOTS show, ABC-TV, New York," postmarked Albuquerque, March 30 or 31, 1979, DLW, box 288, folder 3.

44. The Ortiz, Abeyta, and Cunningham families, letter to Messrs Wolper and Margulis, postmarked Albuquerque, April 1, 1979, DLW, box 288, folder 3.

45. Marmon, "Why *Roots* Hit Home"; Jeffrey Hart, "*Roots* Was an Attack," *Piqua Daily Call* (Piqua, Ohio), Feb. 19, 1977, 4 (syndicated nationally).

46. Helen T. Chapman (Portsmouth, Va.), letter to the editor, *Virginian-Pilot* (Norfolk), Feb. 28, 1977, DLW, box 284, folder 5.

47. Lucille Robertson (Warren), letter to the editor, *East Detroit Community News*, March 17, 1977, DLW, box 284, folder 5.

48. Anna H. Nordheimer, letter to the editor, *Savannah News Press*, March 20, 1977, DLW, box 284, folder 5.

49. Anon., signed "The Concerned public," postmarked Oakland, California, to VP, Charge of Programming, ABC TV, New York, Feb. 2, 1977, DLW, box 288, folder 4.

50. David L. Wolper's papers include a folder of negative letters, which contains approximately one-third the amount of complimentary mail. So few of these are profane that I suspect Wolper or a family member or associate threw away some of what he received. Negative letters appeared in newspapers nationwide, too.

51. E. C. McLachlan (Jacksonville, Fla.) to Wolper, Feb. 8, 1977, DLW, box 288, folder 3.

52. Margaret Barry (Huntington, N.Y.) to "Roots," c/o ABC-NY, Feb. 10, 1977, DLW, box 288, folder 3.

53. David Coleman (Miami Beach, Fla.) to ABC, Jan. 25, 1977, DLW, box 288, folder 3.

54. Mrs. Mary E. Mink (Farmersville, Ohio) to Wolper, c/o ABC TV, Feb. 17, 1977, DLW, box 288, folder 3.

55. Two unnamed letter writers to Jeffrey Hart, a syndicated King columnist, cited in Hart, "*Roots* Backlash."

56. Louise Baudreau (Abbeville, La.) to ABC, Feb. 1, 1977, DLW, box 288, folder 3.

57. Marjorie Bruce, letter to the editor, *Savannah Morning News*, March 2, 1977, DLW, box 284, folder 5.

58. Lillian Carter, excerpted in *"Roots*: Reviews and Statements."

59. Betty Beale, "It's a Good Thing New Protocol Chief Enjoys a Party or Two," *Cincinnati Enquirer*, Feb. 20, 1977, H5.

60. Cory Toevs (Baton Rouge), letter to the editor, *Baton Rouge Morning Advocate*, Feb. 8, 1977, DLW, box 284, folder 5.

61. Ronald Reagan quoted in Robert H. Williams, "Postscript," *Washington Post*, Feb. 14, 1977, A3.

62. Baudreau to ABC; Mrs. Carl C. Smith to ABC, Feb. 3, 1977, DLW, box 288, folder 4; Helen Williams (Milwaukee) to ABC-NY, Feb. 2, 1977, DLW, box 288, folder 4.

63. Williams to ABC-NY.

64. Jesse Casarez (Austin, Tex.), letter to the editor, *American-Statesman* (Austin), Feb. 6, 1977, DLW, box 284, folder 5.

65. Geraldine Provence, letter to the editor, *Savannah News Press*, March 6, 1977, DLW, box 284, folder 5.

66. Walter Talbert (La Puente, Calif.), letter to the editor, *Los Angeles Sentinel*, Feb. 10, 1977, A6.

67. Janice Turner (Riverside, Calif.), letter to the editor, *Los Angeles Sentinel*, March 10, 1977, A6.

68. Janice Smith to Wolper, postmarked Feb. 23, 1979, DLW, box 288, folder 1.

69. Charles E. Holiday (Houston, Tex.), to Producers of *Roots*, postmarked Feb. 2, 1977, DLW, box 288, folder 1.

70. Mrs. Bertha King (Benton Harbor, Mich.), letter to the editor, *News-Palladium* (Benton Harbor), March 3, 1977, 31. See also Mr. and Mrs. John H. Saunders Sr. (St. Louis, Mo.) to ABC-NY, Feb. 1, 1977, DLW, box 288, folder 1.

71. Joyann Husband (Lakewood, Calif.), letter to the editor, *Long Beach Independent*, Feb. 17, 1977, DLW, box 284, folder 5.

72. Nathaniel Newsome (Springfield, Ohio), letter to the editor, *Journal-Herald* (Dayton), Feb. 23, 1977, DLW, box 284, folder 5.

73. Jos. J. DeLawrence Jr. (Hartford, Conn.) to ABC, Channel 40, WHYN-TV (Springfield, Mass.), Feb. 12, 1978, DLW, box 288, folder 1.

74. Curt Shelton, letter to the editor, *Bridgeport Post* (Bridgeport, Conn.), April 6, 1977, DLW, box 284, folder 5.

75. *"Roots*: Reviews and Statements."

76. Elaine B. Pinderhughes (assistant professor of casework, Boston College) and 28 other signatories to the Producers of *Roots*, March 7, 1977, DLW, box 288, folder 4.

77. Maya Angelou, "Haley Shows Us the Truth of Our Conjoined Histories," *New York Times*, Jan. 23, 1977, 81.

78. Dr. Francis A. Kornegay (executive director, Detroit Urban League), *Michigan Chronicle* (Detroit), Feb. 12, 1977, excerpted in *"Roots*: Reviews and Statements."

79. Horne letter to the editor.

80. Clifford L. Culpepper, letter to the editor, *Los Angeles Sentinel*, Oct. 6, 1977, A6.

81. Secil V. House (Huntsville, Ala.), letter to the editor, *Huntsville Times* (Ala.), Feb. 19, 1977, DLW, box 284, folder 5.

82. On the tradition see Kevin K. Gaines, *Uplifting the Race: Black Leadership, Politics, and Culture in the Twentieth Century* (Chapel Hill: University of North Carolina Press, 1996).

83. Lewis P. Bohler Jr., letter to the editor, *Los Angeles Sentinel*, March 10, 1977, A6.

84. Talbert letter to the editor.

85. Ernest Knight, letter to editor, *Los Angeles Sentinel*, Feb. 24, 1977, A6.

86. Don Rojas, "*Roots* Captivates Millions of T-Viewers," *New York Amsterdam News*, Feb. 5, 1977, D8.

87. King letter to the editor.

88. Dan Berger, ed., *The Hidden 1970s: Histories of Radicalism* (New Brunswick, N.J.: Rutgers University Press, 2010); Stephen Tuck, "Introduction: Reconsidering the 1970s—The 1960s to a Disco Beat?," *Journal of Contemporary History* 43 (2008): 617–620, subsequent five articles and comment in this special journal section.

CHAPTER TWO

The Politics of Plagiarism
Roots, Margaret Walker, and Alex Haley

TYLER D. PARRY

On April 20, 1977, Mississippi-based black novelist and poet Margaret Walker sued Alex Haley on the suspicion that his *Roots: The Saga of an American Family* substantially plagiarized her 1966 book, *Jubilee*. In *Alexander v. Haley* (Alexander was Walker's married name), she cited multiple passages that bore resemblances to her novel, she claimed that two thirds of *Roots* was collectively based on *Jubilee* and her essay, "How I Wrote *Jubilee*."[1] After nearly eighteen months of deliberations, her legal team was soundly defeated through the ruling of U.S. District Court judge Marvin Frankel, who argued that Walker's accusations fell "into categories of written expression that are not protected by copyright laws."[2] This demoralizing loss was intensified by the earlier victory of Harold Courlander, a white Jewish folklorist who sued Haley on May 22, 1977, for plagiarizing his 1967 novel *The African*. In contrast to Walker's lengthy trial, Courlander's suit ended after only five weeks in an out-of-court settlement of $650,000.[3] While she had befriended Courlander throughout his lawsuit, Walker privately suspected that his speedy conclusion was wrapped within American social politics that favored white men over black women.[4]

By the time the trial began, Walker was over sixty years of age. As a survivor of the Jim Crow South she was, by this point in her life, intimately familiar with U.S. racism. Her ill-fated attempt to sue Haley and his publishing company, Doubleday, verified her philosophy that social control rested within a complex matrix that interweaved capitalism, racism, sexism, and regionalism in the United States. Power was consolidated to benefit a few at the expense of many. The "big business" and "big money" distributed by northeastern media venues and publishing corporations ensured that a black woman from the South could never advance without their approval.[5] But Walker reserved her fiercest denunciations for Alex Haley, whom she accused of willingly submitting to the corporate structure that entrapped black writers: "Poor Mr. Haley has also been used. He knows they used him because he was greedy for white people's money. . . . I wonder what his future will be when those good white folks and New York slicksters get through using him."[6] Haley's greed symbolized his enslavement to corporate America, which Walker hypothesized would lead to his eventual demise. Although she lost the case, Walker believed that, at the very least, she was liberated from the tentacles of northeastern capitalists who preyed on naive African Americans willing to sell their souls.

For Walker, the plagiarism controversy was a foil that exposed not only U.S. corruption but also a world rife with conspiracy. She believed illicit money financed the corporate structures that gradually consumed the global economy, largely at the expense of people of color. Her writings reveal that her concerns went far beyond the immediate issues that encircled the trial. Walker's private musings on the *Roots*' polemic provide a broader critique of the social divisions that defined the racial, political, and legislative dimensions of the United States in the post–civil rights era. She rarely declared these sentiments publicly, at least not with the same intensity. Consequently, her connection to *Roots* and Haley remains largely overlooked. The trial consumed her thoughts for nearly two years, and having examined her private documents I argue that scholars are remiss to overlook her importance when they are examining *Roots*' impact on U.S. culture. Indeed, after Haley's own manuscript collection, Walker's journals contain the most extensive documentation of the hidden controversies that surrounded the trial and her thoughts on the judicial process.[7] These private writings uncover how one black intellectual interpreted *Roots*' position in U.S. cultural history and what it meant for the direction of black America at the end of the twentieth century.

Despite a prestigious literary career, Walker's scholarly legacy remains eclipsed by Haley's. Consequently, her lawsuit is largely absent from U.S. memory. But for us to fully understand the politics of plagiarism that revolve around *Roots* and *Jubilee*, it is necessary to analyze the intricate details of the trial and Walker's reaction, as a black scholar, to *Roots*' literary and factual shortcomings. In five parts, this chapter examines Walker's multifaceted criticisms of *Roots* during and after her lawsuit, analyzing how she used Haley's work as a metaphor to critique the detrimental impact of western capitalism on peoples of African descent. The first section outlines Walker's life and her motivations for writing *Jubilee*. Largely she was forgotten in the history of African American writers, I examine how her public writings were influenced by a philosophy that African people were ensnared by racial oppression, global economics, and neocolonialism. Second, this chapter assesses how this worldview translated into the politics of the trial, showing how Walker utilized Marxist principles to critique *Roots* and denounce Haley as a capitalist tool of white corporations. The third segment explores the repercussions she faced when challenging Haley and his corporate sponsors, which forced her to disconnect, at least for a time, from a black America that once embraced her work. In following this theme, the chapter then investigates how Walker conceptualized such overt discrimination. Viewing her position through a matrix of race, gender, region, and class, she exposed how the sociopolitical environment in the United States bolstered the continual repression of black southern women. The chapter concludes by exploring one critical question: was Walker correct in her assessment? This last section argues that, while Walker's case was not flawless, newly uncovered evidence suggests that her suspicions surrounding judicial inequality held some validity.

Walker consistently kept a journal from her youth to adulthood, allowing scholars to reconstruct a number of intimate details in her life. Growing up, she enjoyed certain privileges allotted to the black middle class in Jim Crow Alabama while she simultaneously faced overt discrimination from the white population. Before her tenth birthday she learned to step off the sidewalk to let white men pass. Neglecting to do this earned her "a sound thrashing by white boys while Negro men looked on helplessly."[8] For Walker, the connections between race, poverty, and social control were not coincidental, for as a young woman of color, she found that "the economic struggle to exist and the racial dilemma occupied all of my thinking." To psychologically overcome such overt discrimination against her, Walker feverishly recorded poems and prose by her "eighth year," hoping to find liberty in a country that allotted freedom based on one's racial identity.[9] Walker left the South to pursue her education, obtaining a degree in literature from Northwestern University in 1935, working with the Works Progress Administration in Chicago in 1936, and earning a master's degree in creative writing from the University of Iowa in the early 1940s. But the South beckoned Walker. By 1949 she had settled in Jackson, Mississippi, a city she once called the "epicenter" of her life.[10]

It is not surprising that Walker returned to the region, as she believed the South was infused by African American culture. For her, "black culture" could not be disconnected from "southern culture," since the two partook "so much of each other." The South was the "deepest manifestation" of Africa's presence in North America.[11] She was not alone in these sentiments, following a long tradition of African Americans who viewed this region as a black space. Even noteworthy abolitionist and former slave Frederick Douglass longed to return to the South, the land of his "fathers."[12] From a practical standpoint, Walker obtained success in Mississippi. Having published volumes of poetry, she was hired as an English professor at Jackson State University (JSU), a historically black college/university (HBCU). Despite obtaining her degrees from predominantly white, state-sponsored institutions, Walker noticed that HBCUs were more progressive regarding gender. She once observed that black women comprised a larger percentage of the faculty at places like JSU than white women did "in coed white universities."[13] By 1965 she obtained her doctorate and a few years later became the founding director of JSU's Institute for the Study of the History, Life, and Culture of Black People, enhancing her reputation as a nationally renowned scholar of the African American experience.

By the 1970s Walker was a premier scholar in the literary arena of African American studies. *Jubilee* had sold well and became an internationally celebrated work that portrayed slavery and the plantation theme from an African American perspective. Walker's research methods were particularly applauded. Film director Phyllis Klotman notes that *Jubilee* was an effective extension of "the slave narrative" tradition, arguing that Walker used her "research into this unique Afro-American literary genre to support the oral tradition of the black family."[14] In essence, it was a historically informed, fictional biography of her ancestors' experiences in the Deep South as both free and enslaved people. The book exemplified painstaking scholarship. Walker imaginatively re-created her slave genealogy by collecting primary sources in archives, published works, and her family's own oral traditions. Although Walker was initially most renowned for her works of poetry, *Jubilee*'s unique premise captured the attention of many black Americans seeking links to a largely undocumented past.

Haley claimed to use similar methods, but one must remember that *Jubilee* was published ten years prior to *Roots*. Walker's fascination with genealogy dated at least to her adolescent years, when she listened to her grandmother's stories of slavery in antebellum Georgia. According to her essay "How I Wrote *Jubilee*," she laid the foundations for her novel by 1934 while still a senior at Northwestern University.[15] By the age of twenty-nine, Walker's journal revealed plans to "write a historical novel about Negro life in America that begins in 1830 in Georgia and ends in 1915 in Alabama. The big character is my great grandmother, whose life-span covers these 85 years."[16] Due to the difficulty of balancing teaching, marriage, and raising children, Walker did not complete the manuscript until the mid-1960s. During the intervening years, however, she actively produced volumes of poetry and taught English at various institutions. These drawbacks may have been serendipitous, as *Jubilee* was published when the civil rights and Black Power movements gained notoriety in the United States. Concurrently, student activists were challenging the Eurocentric curriculums of U.S. universities, and from the late 1960s to the mid-1970s, black studies programs rapidly spread to colleges and universities.[17] Released during this transitional moment, *Jubilee* effectively responded "to white 'nostalgia' fiction about the antebellum and Reconstruction South."[18] While her plans to finish the work were repeatedly derailed, one could counterfactually assume that the book arrived during the historical moment that needed it most.

Jubilee's characters represented the broad spectrum of philosophies that permeated black America, as Walker hoped to reveal that both militant and conservative ideas had always existed among her people. The main character, Vyry, was based on Walker's great-grandmother. As a mulatto slave, Vyry was a product of the plantation setting of the South and represented a more conservative outlook on the transition from slavery to freedom. In contrast, the more militant character, Randall Ware, a free-black artisan based on Walker's great-grandfather, was a more aggressive and assertive force in the fight against racial oppression. Ware's societal viewpoints doubtlessly resonated with the contemporary black political activism of the 1960s. *Jubilee*'s main characters revealed that black Americans were always a multidimensional group of people whose ideas flowed contrary to the domineering systems that attempted to silence them, and they individually subscribed to different methods in combatting racial inequality.[19] In summarizing the symbolic quality of her work, Walker called her novel the "canvas" on which she would paint her "vision" of the world.[20]

Walker's background contextualizes how she became mired in the "*Roots* fiasco," and why defending *Jubilee* was central to her scholarly reputation.[21] As a novelist, Walker hoped to maintain the purity of her work by shielding it from corporations that sought to wrest creative control over her product. By denouncing the corporate system that produced Haley's work, she linked *Roots* to the violent economic and political exploitation that ensured black populations remained subjugated throughout U.S. history. However, such denunciations were not simply reactive. The pretrial journals reveal she was in discussion with film companies and noteworthy black celebrities who hoped to bring *Jubilee* to the cinema. Walker documented her telephone conversations in 1976 with actress Ruby Dee, who expressed interest in the role of Vyry if *Jubilee* ever became a movie.[22] These personal relationships with various black entertainers heightened the possibility for *Jubilee*'s visual depiction on screen. At various points throughout the late 1970s, Walker even fantasized about her ideal cast, including high-profile black actors Ruby Dee, Sidney Poitier, Ossie Davis, and Harry Belafonte.[23] *Jubilee* had already been made into an opera, which Walker interpreted as a reasonably successful venture.[24] At one point, however, she expressed frustration with surrendering creative license to the opera's director, who she believed did not make appropriate musical selections.[25] Even before the *Roots* trial, she also documented her suspicions against Hollywood and similar corporations that stole creative license from black authors and entertainers. Following her conversation with Ruby Dee, she received a letter from a film company requesting "permission for someone to do a treatment" of her work, which she rejected.[26] Walker probably suspected that if she did not assert herself early in the production, it would potentially be stripped from her. Ultimately, this caused her to reject not only this offer but many later offers.

Journal entries reveal that she maintained the same attitude toward subsequent offers from film producers. She practically ignored a letter from an up-and-coming film producer named Jesse Vogel, who wrote to her after hearing of the controversy surrounding *her* trial. Noting that he had never read *Roots* and could therefore not "make comparisons" between the books, Vogel inquired if *Jubilee* had "ever been considered for film or television production," and "if not, perhaps we could reach some agreement regarding this."[27] Walker left no evidence that she gave this offer any serious consideration. But she continued to correspond with Ruby Dee and Ossie Davis throughout the trial, attempting to find financial backing for a cinematic production.[28] Walker often confided to her friends when discussing her case against Haley, and her correspondence enhanced her suspicion that major film companies were suppressing the book.

Ruby Dee held similar misgivings when Walker informed her about Haley's possible plagiarism. Apparently, Dee had previously given a copy of *Jubilee* to an associate at ABC before *Roots* was in production. Although the chronology is unclear, it is possible that *Jubilee* was transmitted to this unnamed production coordinator before *Roots* was even published. Dee also revealed that, despite her own friendship with Haley, she was mysteriously "not included in the ABC screen production." Walker believed this exposed a significant component in the conspiracy.[29] Not only did her work provide inspiration for Haley's subsequent novel, it may have encouraged ABC and Doubleday to finance Haley's novel based on their expectation of a movie to follow. To be sure, it is difficult to validate these private ruminations through any additional sources. However, if this conversation with Ruby Dee was documented accurately, it strongly implies that Walker was not alone in her belief that corporations shut out black authors and entertainers who refused to conform.

Apart from Walker's dealings with the corporate media, the trial also brought new problems for her position among black Americans. She now faced the ire of a black community that had once embraced her, as many of her staunchest critics believed she was driven by envy and a lust for money. The possibility that African Americans might turn against her was not lost on Walker. A 1977 journal entry shows her ruminations on the subject, questioning how one black person "suing another black person" would be received, particularly since she was a woman.[30] While Walker was cordial, or at least diplomatic, in her public reactions to how the black community treated her during and after the trial, her personal writings reveal that she harbored a far more critical view toward her detractors. Walker did not entirely blame them, however, as she believed they were equally the victims of media exploitation that taught them how to think about and react to portrayals of African Americans in popular culture. Building on her beliefs in the historical trajectory of racism, she assumed the white establishment used *Roots* as a "narcotic" for the black populace, serving "to stupefy and control large masses of ... black Americans in the total white western world society."[31] Walker's ideology submitted that black Americans were locked in a common struggle with the African continent against a larger capitalist scheme that extracted natural resources through neocolonialist methods. *Roots* and its attendant media satiated the black American populace, effectively distracting them from global currents that furthered their collective oppression.

As colleagues turned against her, she was convinced that gender was a useful tool for explaining why she was repeatedly "maligned, publicly insulted, and embarrassed" by various detractors.[32] More specifically, she once inferred that her fiercest critics were black men, both academic and laymen. This is not surprising, as she was cognizant that she followed in a tradition of writers who were "seen first as black, then as female," and she dealt with issues not terribly different from previous generations of scholarly black women.[33] Shortly after *Jubilee*'s release, she wrote that black men throughout academia resoundingly criticized it, while the "white press, with few exceptions, was generally kind."[34] Such discriminatory reactions positioned Walker as an outlier in the fraternal black intelligentsia early in her career, and these strained relationships were amplified during the trial. She became particularly suspicious of black scholars such as Lerone Bennett Jr. and Vincent Harding, and she even referenced "an altercation with Derek [sic] Bell" because she refused to "let him get away with rubbing in a lot of snide insinuations and nasty things."[35] However, scholars were not her only critics. She was once verbally attacked during an invited lecture about *Jubilee*, as a man in the audience accused her of harboring jealousy that Haley's book had been made into a movie, while she had not secured the same deal. In contrast to the aforementioned confrontation with Bell, she patiently responded that she was "not mad, [for] whom the gods would destroy they first make mad."[36] In most cases she attempted to avoid the hostility that came alongside the accusations, but she often used her journals to unveil her harshest denunciations.

Walker's criticisms toward her African American detractors were rather vituperative. Whether this was due to stress, anguish, or her disappointment at their willingness to embrace *Roots* is difficult to know with certainty, although it was probably a combination of the three. Throughout the trial the media repeatedly asked black people their thoughts on the lawsuit, and Walker was privately disheartened by the resulting news reports. Many of

Walker's critics believed that bringing the suit was "selfish" and that by doing so she was dismantling black racial solidarity.[37] They worried that if black people were divided among themselves, no other group would protect their interests. Walker probably agreed with this ideology, but she believed the black public ignorantly misconstrued her intentions. For her, their denunciations reflected the "the naivete of black people," as they remained oblivious of the social realities of racial exploitation through law and media.[38] She asserted that the *Roots* miniseries was filtered through "the white point of view, [as] savage, naked black women with long painted finger nails and emasculated black men are what Hollywood tells us our black history and heroes are made [of]."[39] She was increasingly irritated by black people who remained ignorant of how *Roots* fulfilled the goals of white elites. In one of her angriest entries, Walker railed against "the terrible phenomenon of *Roots* and *Haley*, tools of the system, out to sedate the people—a narcotic to keep niggers looking for their roots while the world blows up in their face."[40] In her Marxist worldview, *Roots* was an opiate that satiated black Americans and kept them ignorant of the global struggle against white capitalists and neocolonialists, who continuously bamboozled indifferent black people.

Allegations surrounding Walker's quest for money must have been particularly disturbing to her when one considers that her fiscal ideology aligned with Marxist precepts. For Walker, global capitalism was deliberately developed alongside the forced labor regimes that subjugated African and Afro-diasporic populations. She did not completely reject the value of money, but she worried that if black people did not control their own creative products they opened the door to exploitation. It is likely that the black community's suspicions toward her were connected to Haley's public statements against her. When interviewed by the media, Haley often employed sarcasm to dismiss the trial and claimed that it presented an opportunity for Walker to gain exposure for her book.[41] Such accusations were slanderous, as Walker rejected multiple opportunities to capitalize on *Roots*' success. At one point she even denounced her publisher for attempting to release a new edition of *Jubilee* that advertised it as the primary inspiration for Haley's novel. Any reference to *Roots*, she claimed, was unnecessary, as *Jubilee* stood on its own merits.[42] Walker also refused a bribe from Haley when he promised to exonerate her from court costs if she did not pursue an appeal. In an unsurprising maneuver, she filed an appeal a month later.[43] Thus, even when she had opportunities to advance her socioeconomic status, Walker's Christian Marxism bolstered her belief that a love of money was a poisonous venture.

Such sentiments help explain why Walker condemned Haley's celebrity, for she believed that his tactics were detrimental to future generations of black artists and scholars. In her view, only those willing to surrender creative license gained position in white corporate America. She realized that similar opportunities were not generally available to her, for there was no justice to one that was "relatively poor" or "black[,] . . . female and southern."[44] Each concept resonated throughout the trial, and Walker's journals are strewn with her reflections on these intersecting subjects. In one significant entry, she noted that some of her acquaintances, all of them local black Mississippians, encouraged her to dismantle her legal team and to seek legal assistance elsewhere with hopes that a "rich white Mississippian" would invest in her case.[45] Such beliefs were surely damaging to her psyche, especially when compounded by the facts that black men were overtly criticizing her and the media represented her as "an old crazy jealous woman" (she was only sixty-three at the time) in order to downplay the legitimacy of her case.[46]

But it was Walker's inclusion of regionalism that provides a unique vantage point for contextualizing the themes of gender, race, and class in African American history. Recent scholarship by sociologist Zandria Robinson asserts that black southerners tend to view themselves as distinct from those dwelling outside the region, manifesting a sense that southern culture represents authentic blackness in the United States. Despite the South's overtly racist past, black southerners feel compelled to "rescue the region from the scrutiny of outsiders even as they turn their own cultural gazes on the South's persistent ills and their southern brethren."[47] The very notion of a southern identity among both black and white southerners was birthed through their beliefs that it is culturally distinct from the Northeast and the West and that its social landscape can only be truly appreciated by those rooted in the region.

Regionalism is a prominent factor in Walker's private musings. She was familiar with the popular U.S. conceptions of southern backwardness, and she understood the stereotype to some degree. For despite the national affinity for the "Lost Cause" mythology—the romanticized view that plantation owners and Confederate soldiers, despite being on the wrong side of history, valiantly served their government the same as any northerner—U.S. popular culture maintained that the South intentionally bypassed progress, preferring to remain rural in contrast to the industrialized Northeast.[48] Speaking about Mississippi specifically, she argued the state never obtained a true industrial revolution until the mid-twentieth century, holding no "heavy industry" and only "very little light and diversified industry."[49] This amplified the region's devastating poverty, but Walker still believed African Americans could gain spiritual renewal in the South. After all, black traditions were ingrained in the southern landscape, for black identification with urban spaces in the North and Midwest was still a recent phenomenon in the 1970s.

These regional stereotypes surely increased her anxiety. She assumed her legal problems were compounded by the fact that Haley's corporate team was not only white but also hailed from the capitalist Northeast. Despite his southern roots, Haley typically dwelled outside the South for much of his publishing career and did not return to Tennessee until directly prior to his death in 1992.[50] Given this information, Walker likely did not identify Haley as authentically "southern," especially since he was aligned with financially powerful corporations located in urban spaces outside the South. Walker surely interpreted his move back to Tennessee as a convenient relocation, believing that he returned only after gaining success outside the region. Conversely, Walker pursued her literary career as a southerner. She composed poems about her love-hate relationship with the region that oppressed her, while simultaneously recognizing how it molded her unique American identity.[51]

Walker viewed issues of legislative representation and equity as deeply personal, believing they were inseparable from her precarious position in U.S. society. She was not interested in monetary compensation, as she rejected numerous offers that required her to compromise artistic creativity. Financial assistance surely would have proved useful, but she remained committed to the idea that capitalist ambitions inherently corrupted an individual, even the most pure minded. Beyond the media's portrayal of her supposed jealous rage, Walker's writings reveal she held a far more sophisticated understanding of how the trial symbolized U.S. identity politics in the 1970s and 1980s. She ultimately believed that her multifaceted identity as a black woman in the South forced her to confront overwhelming odds when she challenged publishing companies in the Northeast. Her dignity as a scholar was on the line, and a legal victory could prove that corporate America was not invincible. However, the crushing defeat solidified her suspicions that a league of urban, New York–based corporations controlled a disproportionate amount of the political and financial capital of the United States. Despite her academic prestige, a black woman from the South simply could not compete. It was not so much that Walker was personally wronged, although that surely played a part; it was her suspicions that black creative arts were co-opted by white corporations. She worried that too many black artists in the post–civil rights era were willingly exchanging their artistic autonomy for monetary gain.

But the question remains; to what degree is Walker vindicated in her accusations? Most public records are vague, and scholars—likely due to the fact that she lost the case—have generally overlooked Walker's lawsuit and preferred to explore Courlander's legal victory.[52] After the trial, she was strongly encouraged by friends and family to remain silent about the issue, as they maintained it was unhealthy to dwell on that experience.[53] Many of her public statements on the *Roots'* trial were brief, and at times she even avoided reference to Haley's name when describing her legal battles.[54] Consequently, she is severely underrepresented in the secondary literature. Without further context, it is easy to discredit Walker's complaints as the deranged ranting of a bitter woman, as many of her contemporaries did. From a literary perspective, however, her writings provide readers a pathway to her redemption. The journals were written as if she expected future scholars to rescue her from the bitter obscurity thrust upon her by the *Roots'* controversy.

Today it is impossible to know completely why Marvin Frankel ruled against Walker, but available evidence supports her suspicion that U.S. social politics operated against her. Walker felt victimized by corporate lawyers and suspected that a "conglomerate" within the publishing industry protected Haley's reputation in order to secure their own profits.[55] She suspected this financial cabal reached high legislative offices, including the judge who oversaw her case. Despite her initial optimism concerning Frankel's character, Walker eventually concluded: "I didn't believe Frankel could be bought . . . but he was. He admits similarities, copying et cetera and still ruled against us."[56] While one may not be able to prove that Frankel was "bought," it was strange that he conveniently retired a few days after the trial's conclusion, effectively shutting down any further deliberations. This begs a few questions: What circumstances led to Walker's loss and to Courlander's victory? Was Courlander's case substantially stronger than Walker's? When using her journals in tandem with trial transcripts, select secondary works, and the few public speeches Walker gave related to the lawsuit, I propose that the two lawsuits were not in fact substantially different.

According to Philip Nobile, a freelance journalist credited with publishing the most scathing critique of Haley's plagiarism, the primary difference between the two lawsuits centralized around the usage of the "discovery process," which allows each party to subpoena for evidence that *might* be relevant, rather than *directly* relevant. Nobile argues the discovery process was tremendously helpful in bolstering Courlander's case.[57] This is certainly possible, as the discovery process is designed to lead toward settlement or summary judgment, the exact conclusion to Courlander's trial.[58] For reasons unknown today, Walker's legal team was unable to utilize the same tactic, forcing her to endure over seventeen months of litigation. Such circumstances were unexpected, as Walker claimed a victory in a supplementary opinion provided by New York magistrate Nina Gershon prior to Frankel's ruling. Frankel assigned the trial to Gershon and asked her opinion on the accusations, in which she concluded that "Haley's methods lent themselves to plagiarism" and that Haley had "complete access" to *Jubilee* while writing his own book.[59] But a magistrate could not issue the final ruling. Frankel ignored Gershon's recommendation and ruled in Haley's favor, retiring from the bench shortly after the trial. Such events are surely questionable, but they are not the only inconsistencies.

In its May 12, 1977, issue, *Jet* reported that Haley remembered meeting Walker prior to *Roots'* publication when she invited him to give a presentation at Jackson State University, and a 1971 photo shows the two sharing a table next to their mutual colleague Nick Aaron Ford.[60] But when pressed by Walker's lawyers, he persistently claimed ignorance when asked about *Jubilee*.[61] The closest he ever came to admitting familiarity with the novel was that he possibly read, "here or there," a few reviews of *Jubilee* when it was published, but he refused to substantiate this claim.[62] The assertion becomes especially questionable when compared to the circumstances surrounding the Courlander case. By comparison, *The African* was inferior in its overall sales and was not as widely acclaimed as *Jubilee*. Since Walker's novel was more readily available to him, one should question the notion that he borrowed from Courlander's less prominent work and completely overlooked her critically acclaimed novel. Tellingly, one reason Judge Robert Ward seemed likely to rule against Haley in the Courlander decision was due to his suspicion that Haley lied when declaring he had never "heard" of *The African*, an audacious claim that reportedly left Ward "a little cold."[63] Conversely, Frankel believed Haley's claims about *Jubilee*, *despite* the immense popularity it enjoyed the previous ten years. Such inequitable assessments would certainly cause any plaintiff to question if discrimination was not at play.

In referencing the controversies surrounding both novels, journalist and social activist Herb Boyd put it bluntly: "That Haley failed to read either one of these accessible novels is indeed incredible, especially for a writer of his thoroughness who had spent some 12 years researching and writing the evolution of his family." While this smacks of sarcasm, Boyd intended to revisit the Courlander trial and contextualize the outcome. Scholars have found that Courlander's triumph revolved around three passages in his novel that bore resemblance to those found in *Roots*; the resemblance was sufficient to encourage Haley to settle out of court. However, Boyd submits that the similarities in each passage amount to clear plagiarism, ultimately concluding that the lawsuit was less a "Courlander victory" than it was "a Haley surrender."[64] One of Boyd's selected passages illustrates this summation, and I have italicized the "plagiarized" sentences:

THE AFRICAN (P. 21)

A few days later, Hewsuhunu became aware that the space next to him was empty. *He listened attentively and knew that Grandfather suddenly was not there. He moved his hand until it touched the body.* Then he turned the other way, saying to Dokumi, "Old Grandfather is dead."

ROOTS (P. 225)

Feeling around him, in some strange way, the presence of *his holy-man grandfather, Kunta reached out into the darkness. There was nothing to be felt*, but he began speaking aloud to the Alquaran Kairaba Kunta Kinte, imploring him to make known the purpose of his mission here, if there be any.[65]

The depth of plagiarism here is questionable, as the highlighted passages hold very little in common. The other passages Courlander cited held similar problems, causing one to question how these plagiarism accusations could be supported.[66] Even if Haley was inspired by the concepts found in *The African*, these passages do not necessarily prove that he blatantly plagiarized it. Two authors writing about a character's grandfather in a similar setting are bound to produce selections that resemble each other. Thus, Courlander found no evidence of *exact* passages lifted from *The African*. It is important to note that his charges were not terribly different from Walker's allegations for *Jubilee*.[67] Walker cited similarities in *Jubilee* and *Roots* that revolved around cultural concepts, but Frankel ruled that these "similarities" and "categories of written expression" were not protected under copyright law. From this vantage point, it is difficult to see how Courlander's charge of plagiarism was any different. Such appraisals cause one to suspect that Walker's position, as a black woman from the South, appeared to work against her in this court of law.

This evidence vindicates Walker's qualms or at the very least indicates that she had reason to suspect foul play. Just as Boyd argues that a "guilty" verdict does not necessarily equate with proof of plagiarism, I submit that Walker's courtroom defeat should not exonerate Haley from accusations that he stole her concepts. Far from mere conspiracy theories, one can see that mechanisms were set to ensure that the verdict was placed beyond her control. Whether this definitively led to Walker's defeat in the courtroom is a different issue, but it is troubling that her accusations were dismissed whereas Courlander's were authenticated. Ultimately, the motivations for Walker's defeat might never be proven, but her suspicions surrounding *Roots* must still be taken seriously. If nothing else, the *Roots* trial revealed that Walker viewed her position in a far more global, diasporic context. Walker's writings show that despite the advancements black people made in the post–civil rights era, the pressures of a "sexist, racist, violent, and most materialistic society" continually rendered her existence precarious. But she believed her position as a black woman writer obliged her to remain an "avante-garde [*sic*] for truth and justice, for freedom, peace, and human dignity."[68] Perhaps it is time for researchers to reconsider both plagiarism cases, free from preconceived assumptions of guilt or innocence. Hopefully, future scholarship will examine Walker's important contributions to African American culture, and finally place *Jubilee* alongside *Roots* when discussing how black novelists restructured the U.S. literary canon.

NOTES

1. Margaret Walker, *Jubilee* (Boston: Houghton Mifflin, 1966); Margaret Walker, "How I Wrote *Jubilee*," in *How I Wrote "Jubilee" and Other Essays on Life and Literature*,

edited by Maryemma Graham (1972; reprint New York: Feminist Press at the City University of New York, 1990), 50–65. In the trial transcripts, Margaret Walker was generally referred to by her married name, "Margaret Walker Alexander." For clarity, I am opting to use "Margaret Walker," the name she typically used as a scholar.

2. "The Margaret Walker Case," box 77, folder 2, Margaret Walker, Alex Haley Papers, University of Tennessee–Knoxville.

3. Harold Courlander, *The African* (New York: Henry Holt, 1967). For an extended treatment of the Courlander case, see Philip Nobile, "Uncovering Roots," *Village Voice*, February 23, 1993, 31–38.

4. Journal 102, Aug. 1977–Feb. 1978, 258; Journal 103, May–Dec. 1978, 270 and 72. Both in Margaret Walker Personal Papers—Jackson State University Digital Collections (hereafter MWPP-JSUDC).

5. Journal 102, Aug. 1977–Feb. 1978, 228, MWPP-JSUDC.

6. Journal 106, Dec. 1979–Apr. 1980, 18–19, MWPP-JSUDC.

7. Jackson State University holds 133 of her journals, ranging from the years 1930 to 1998, and six of them reference the controversy surrounding *Roots*.

8. Keith L. Thomas, "Margaret Walker Gives Voice to Literary Legacy of Richard Wright," *Atlanta Journal and the Atlanta Constitution*, December 21, 1988, C1.

9. Margaret Walker, "On Being Female, Black, and Free (1980)," in *On Being Female, Black, and Free: Essays by Margaret Walker, 1932–1992*, edited by Maryemma Graham (Knoxville: University of Tennessee Press, 1997), 5, 4.

10. Jerry W. Ward Jr., "A Writer for Her People (1986)," in *Conversations with Margaret Walker*, edited by Maryemma Graham (Jackson: University Press of Mississippi, 2002), 113.

11. Walker, "Southern Black Culture (1976)," in *On Being Female, Black, and Free*, 79, 80.

12. James C. Cobb, *Away Down South: A History of Southern Identity* (Oxford: Oxford University Press, 2005), 149. For more information on this topic, see Ira Berlin, *The Making of African America: The Four Great Migrations* (New York: Viking, 2010), 41, 155.

13. Walker, "On Being Female," 5.

14. Phyllis Rauch Klotman, "'Oh Freedom'—Women and History in Margaret Walker's Jubilee," *Black American Literature Forum* 11 (1977): 142.

15. Margaret Walker, "How I Wrote *Jubilee*," 51.

16. Journal 22, May–Aug. 1944, 6, MWPP-JSUDC.

17. For a fuller treatment, see Karen K. Miller, "Race, Power and the Emergence of Black Studies in Higher Education," *American Studies* 31, no. 2 (1990): 83–98; Jonathan Fenderson, James Stewart, and Kabria Baumgartner, "Expanding the History of the Black Studies Movement: Some Prefatory Notes," *Journal of African American Studies* 16 (2012): 1–20.

18. Roger Whitlow, *Black American Literature: A Critical History* (Chicago: Nelson Hall, 1973), 136.

19. For Walker's own words, see Phanuel Egejuru and Robert Elliot Fox, "An Interview with Margaret Walker," *Callaloo* 6 (May 1979): 29; Lucy M. Freibert and Margaret Walker, "Southern Song: An Interview with Margaret Walker," *Frontiers: A Journal of Women's Studies* (1987): 50–56.

20. Walker, "How I Wrote *Jubilee*," 65.

21. Ward, "Writer for Her People (1986)," 121.

22. Journal 99, May–Sept. 1976, 30, MWPP-JSUDC.

23. Journal 101, Apr.–Aug. 1977, 52, MWPP-JSUDC.

24. Journal 99, May–Sept. 1976, 31, MWPP-JSUDC.

25. Journal 101, Apr.–Aug. 1977, 53, MWPP-JSUDC.

26. Journal 99, May–Sept. 1976, 56, MWPP-JSUDC.

27. "Jesse Vogel to Mrs. Walker, May 3, 1977," Correspondence, box 4, folder 23, MWPP-JSUDC.

28. Journal 101, Apr.–Aug. 1977, 44 and 52, MWPP-JSUDC.

29. Ibid., 44, MWPP-JSUDC.

30. Ibid., 75.

31. Ibid., 103.

32. Journal 106, Dec. 1979–Aug. 1980, 15, MWPP-JSUDC.

33. Margaret Walker, "Reflections on Black Women Writers," in Maryemma Graham, ed., *On Being Black, Female, and Free: Essays by Margaret Walker, 1932–1992* (Knoxville: University Press of Tennessee, 1997), 44.

34. Walker, "Reflections on Black Women Writers," 52.

35. Journal 103, May–Dec. 1978, 178, MWPP-JSUDC.

36. Journal 106, Dec. 1979–Apr. 1980, 135, MWPP-JSUDC.

37. Journal 101, Apr.–Aug. 1977, 25, MWPP-JSUDC.

38. Ibid., 26.

39. Journal 106, Dec. 1979–Apr. 1980, 13, MWPP-JSUDC.

40. Journal 101, Apr.–Aug. 1977, 131, MWPP-JSUDC.

41. "Notes on People," *New York Times*, April 27, 1977; *Facts on File Yearbook 1977, c. 1978*, box 77, folder 2, Margaret Walker, Alex Haley Papers.

42. Journal 102, Aug. 1977–Feb. 1978, 137, MWPP-JSUDC.

43. This information is from an unpublished autobiography sent to me by Maryemma Graham, who is writing a forthcoming biography of Walker. The original is in her possession.

44. Journal 106, Dec. 1979–Apr. 1980, 25 and 17, MWPP-JSUDC.

45. Journal 103, May–Dec. 1978, 175, MWPP-JSUDC.

46. Nobile, "Uncovering Roots," 37.

47. Zandria F. Robinson, *This Ain't Chicago: Race, Class, and Regional Identity in the Post-Soul South* (Chapel Hill: University of North Carolina Press, 2014), 6.

48. Walker was familiar with this co-option of history; see Walker, "Natchez and Richard Wright in Southern American Literature (1990)," in *On Being Black, Female, and Free*, 118–122.

49. Walker, "Natchez and Richard Wright," 120.

50. Thadious M. Davis, *Southscapes: Geographies of Race, Region, and Literature* (Chapel Hill: University of North Carolina Press, 2011), 43.

51. Margaret Walker, "Jackson, Mississippi," in *This Is My Century: New and Collected Poems* (Athens: University of Georgia Press, 1989), 62–63.

52. Robert J. Norrell's work briefly explores the Walker case, but provides far more extended commentary to Courlander's lawsuit; see Norrell, *Alex Haley and the Books that Changed a Nation* (New York: St. Martin's Press, 2015), 183–198.

53. I am indebted to Walker's biographer Maryemma Graham for this information.

54. Walker, "Epilogue: Race, Gender and the Law (1992)," in *On Being Female, Black and Free*, 234.

55. Journal 102, Aug. 1979–Feb. 1978, 124, MWPP-JSUDC.

56. Journal 103, May–Dec. 1978, 275, MWPP-JSUDC. For her initial beliefs that Frankel "was not for sale" see Journal 101, April–Aug. 1977, 16, MWPP-JSUDC.

57. Nobile, "Uncovering Roots," 37.

58. Thomas R. Van Dervort, *American Law and the Legal System: Equal Justice Under the Law*, 2nd ed. (Albany, N.Y.: Thomson Learning, 2000), 153.

59. Margaret Walker, *Setting the Record Straight*, pamphlet (Detroit, Mich.: Walter O. Evans, 1996), 11; Kay Bonetti, "An Interview with Margaret Walker," *Missouri Review* 15, no. 1 (1992): 126. A copy of *Setting the Record Straight* was generously provided by Maryemma Graham, who still holds the original document.

60. *Jet*, May 12, 1977, 18. The photo appears in Carolyn J. Brown, *Song of My Life: A Biography of Margaret Walker* (Jackson: University Press of Mississippi, 2014), chap. 9 (digital ed.).

61. "Haley Defends *Roots* against 'Snipers' and Gets Honorary Degree," *Jet*, May 12, 1977, 18.

62. Box 48, folder 5, Dec. 15, 1977, Alex Haley Papers.

63. "Alex Haley Settles Suit Out of Court," *Jet*, Jan. 4, 1979, 47.

64. Herb Boyd, "Plagiarism and the *Roots* Suit," *First World* 2, no. 3 (1979): 32, 33.

65. Ibid., 32.

66. See comparisons of all three passages in ibid., 31–33.

67. For Walker's list of plagiarized passages, see box 48, folder 4, Dec. 13, 1977, Alex Haley Papers.

68. Walker, "On Being Female, Black, and Free," 11.

CHAPTER THREE

"My Furthest-Back Person"
Black Genealogy Before and After *Roots*

FRANCESCA MORGAN

At its heart, Alex Haley's *Roots*—both the book and the series—constitute a tale of its author's genealogy research. Haley's plot spans
seven generations, with characters in each generation repeating the same
Mandinkan words to their children that Kunta Kinte had taught his own
daughter before she was sold away from him. As a child, Haley had repeatedly overheard these same words in his grandmother's and great-aunts' conversations.[1] The televised version of *Roots* climaxes with Alex Haley's own appearance onscreen at the end of the final episode, aired on January 30, 1977.
The "things I learned" orally from his kin, and later researched on three continents, "I put in a book called *Roots*," Haley told the camera.[2]

Roots marked a turning point in the ongoing history of black genealogy,
as much as it also broke with that past. I argue for *Roots* as an apotheosis
in relation to earlier histories of African American genealogy because *Roots'*
antecedents help explain the work's subsequent invigoration of genealogy
practice. For a long time previously, including during slavery, African Americans had demonstrated interest in family history.[3] Later, civil rights figures
publicized their own and others' black forebears (especially those who were
U.S. soldiers) as a gesture of protest against the stripping of black citizenship.

Haley's research and publication of *Roots*, however, took place at an especially fertile moment for black genealogy. The decade before Haley published
the book in September 1976, and before *Roots* aired on television in January
1977, featured the flourishing of black historical studies, which in turn accompanied civil rights reforms and Black Power movements.[4] This era also saw
unprecedented commitment to community and do-it-yourself history, the
ascendance of social history ("history from the bottom up") within the academy, and consequent transformations in genealogy practice in which Americans at large embraced ancestors warts-and-all—no matter how foreign,
poor, socially obscure, nonwhite, non-Christian, scandalous, or even enslaved
those forebears had been.[5] *Roots* also shared its historical moment with the

1976 bicentennial, which has been particularly renowned for generating both patriotic hoopla and deep interest in U.S. pasts.[6]

At the same time, however, Haley broke new ground for black genealogists. Most notable were his two sojourns to the Gambia in 1967.[7] Americans' roots travel, as a tradition, is at least as old as Benjamin Franklin, but by far the most-worn paths led to the British Isles and, later, Ireland—also a destination for Haley while researching his white forebears.[8] Only in the wake of twentieth-century decolonizations had Americans begun venturing outside Western Europe in search of family history.[9] Additionally, *Roots* inspired the publication of advice books and the establishment of institutions for the advancement of black genealogy. Only four months after the telecast, in May 1977, Washington-area archivists and other professionals formed the world's first ever African diaspora genealogy society, the Afro-American Historical and Genealogical Society (AAHGS).[10] Such group endeavors succeeded only after *Roots* appeared.

Roots' career as a text after its initial broadcast shows that the story continued to inspire black genealogy endeavors even after scholars and journalists impeached Haley's research. What accounts for the saga's resilience? It has been difficult for U.S. genealogy communities in general to renounce their quests for their respective grails—the documented *Mayflower* ancestor, the royal or otherwise titled ancestor in Britain, the exact location of the small Jewish village in Poland that Nazis had wiped out—and African Americans were no exception. Many who withheld praise from *Roots* after its historical accuracy was challenged have tried their utmost to reconstruct enslaved, free black, and African ancestry.

Early Examples of Black Genealogy

Not surprisingly, my examples of nineteenth-century forms of African Americans genealogy skew toward the upper strata—the lighter-skinned descendants of house servants, the posterity of free black people, and individuals who cannot be placed in either category. Especially before the rise of government archives and large public libraries, genealogy practices were generally restricted to the highly educated and required substantial outlays of time, money, and social connections to other genealogy practitioners. This pattern describes black communities as much as it does other Americans.

Two especially ardent genealogy practitioners born in the nineteenth century, the credentialed historian W. E. B. Du Bois and the novelist Pauline Hopkins, each descended from free black Americans in New England. Among Hopkins's forebears was Nero Caesar Paul, an enslaved man from New Hampshire who had won his freedom in fighting in the French and Indian War.[11]

The Massachusetts-born Du Bois proved his own relatedness to the Revolutionary War soldier and former slave Tom Burghardt, also of Massachusetts.[12]

But histories of working people suggest that the desire to know and perpetuate the knowledge of one's origins flourished even in the absence of any ability to perform research using written documents.[13] Because they researched narrow agendas (particular surnames) very deeply, genealogists in all circumstances were accustomed to turning to "tradition"—lore obtained from oral sources—when paper trails terminated. Writing in 1845, the white historian Frances Mainwaring Caulkins of Connecticut defended her use of "tradition and conversation with aged persons" to supplement her research in written sources: "when tradition contradicts no official record, and when records fail, even history may be permitted to use its aid."[14] However, African Americans had distinctive reasons, starting with laws and working conditions that impeded slave literacy, for their persistent use of what later generations would call oral history.[15]

A case in point is that of the Ohio carpenter James Madison Hemings. Free for decades when slavery was finally outlawed, he could perform the rare feat (among former slaves) of reckoning his ancestry back three generations. Sixty-eight years old in 1873, and in contact with a friendly white newspaperman, Hemings stated that his old master, Thomas Jefferson, had fathered him and his siblings. Madison's maternal ancestors had been house slaves with substantial white ancestry. His mother, Sally Hemings, had been the widely acknowledged half-sister of Thomas Jefferson's long-dead wife, Martha Wales Jefferson.[16] Sally's own grandparents, said Madison, had been an unnamed "fullblooded African" woman and an English sea captain. Their daughter, Elizabeth Hemings, became the "concubine" of her owner, John Wales, a union that produced Sally.[17] Madison Hemings's knowledge of his lineage was almost certainly obtained orally from his mother or other maternal relatives, since it contained information that the otherwise loquacious Jefferson found unspeakable.[18]

The outlawing of slavery in 1865 created many more possibilities for black genealogy. Not only did freed people attempt to locate kin that slave trading had removed from them, but the "people" they sought included ancestors.[19] Lizzie Warrenton Wells, an enslaved cook born in Virginia, was sold away to Mississippi when still a child. Sometime during her transition to freedom, Wells learned to write. She told her own children that her "father was half Indian, his father being a full blood." Before her death in 1878, "[she] often wrote back to somewhere in Virginia, trying to get track of her people, but she was never successful," as her daughter, the journalist Ida B. Wells, remembered.[20]

As the rise of segregation laws and voting restrictions in the 1890s South provoked protests all over black America that would eventually coalesce into civil rights struggles, African Americans performed genealogy and documented ancestors as gestures of protest against racial subjugation. Jim Crow stalked them at the library and at other genealogy repositories. Public libraries in the South, where most African Americans lived at the turn of the twentieth century, either banned black patrons altogether or (in large cities) relegated them to inferior, segregated facilities.[21] The published indexes of periodicals, family genealogies, and other publications, on which genealogists have depended for streamlining their research, often omitted the surnames of nonwhite families.[22]

Despairing over the numerous, race-specific obstacles that separated so many African Americans from knowledge of their forebears' autobiographical facts, some turned their back on the whole enterprise of tracing family origins. In the middle of the twentieth century, Malcolm Little and others in the Nation of Islam substituted "X" for the surnames of their birth, scorning them as slave names, and spurning the painful histories behind them.[23] But some contemporaries did all they could to reconstruct their family histories. Carter G. Woodson, the historian who in 1915 led the formation of the first black-history organization (the American Association for the Study of Negro Life and History), launched the *Negro History Bulletin* in 1937. This periodical sought to connect scholars with teachers and librarians. The *Bulletin* featured genealogical content often as a form of civil rights protest, as when Woodson himself published "Negro Women Eligible to be Daughters of the American Revolution" in response to the Daughters of the American Revolution's notorious exclusion of the black opera singer Marian Anderson from its auditorium stage in Washington, D.C., in 1939.[24]

Another civil rights figure, the jurist and feminist thinker Pauli Murray (1910–1985), became an unheralded pioneer in the area of black genealogy, just as she was an unsung pathbreaker in other areas of twentieth-century reform, including women's struggles against what she called "Jane Crow."[25] She staged sit-ins against racial segregation as early as 1940. Also in her youth, Murray went about transcribing, at length, the family memories of the "race aunts" who had raised her. Murray's parents died when she was a child, whereupon her maternal aunt Pauline Fitzgerald Dame, a schoolteacher, legally adopted her. Murray also grew up surrounded by Pauline's three surviving sisters. When Murray was in her twenties, the white poet Stephen Vincent Benét applauded her plans for a book on her family's history, based on her aunts' reminiscences. He marveled in 1939 that "nobody as far as I know

has really tried to sit down and do a 'Buddenbrooks' or a 'Forsyte Saga'...
from the negro [*sic*] point of view."[26]

Decades later, inflamed by a stinging job rejection from Cornell University
that resulted from the era's red-baiting, Murray began traveling to archives
in Pennsylvania, Delaware, North Carolina, and Virginia to reconfirm her
aunts' information on paper. "I was curious to know how far a Negro family in
America can push into the jungles of its mysterious origins," she ruminated
in 1954.[27] There she found additional material on enslaved and free forebears
going back to the eighteenth century, to solidify her case for the family's, and
her own, patriotic and American roots. She published *Proud Shoes: The Story
of an American Family* in 1956.

Proud Shoes was an important precursor to Alex Haley's *Roots: The Saga of
an American Family* (1976). The two texts share lineages stretching from the
time of slavery to their authors' own lifetimes; stories that originated with
information obtained orally, at first, from older female relatives from the maternal side of their families; and multiracial family trees due to white men's
molestation of female slaves. Murray managed to reconstruct the youth and
ancestry of her maternal grandfather, Robert Fitzgerald, a Union veteran
and educator. She also described her maternal grandmother, Cornelia Smith
Fitzgerald, born a North Carolina house slave. Cornelia's master, an eminent
white attorney named Sidney Smith, had fathered her. Sidney's surviving sister, Mary Ruffin Smith, bequeathed land to Cornelia and her siblings (neither
Sidney nor Mary ever married, or reported other children). But Cornelia's and
her husband's possession of land led to Ku Klux Klan attacks and consequent
loss of their property during Reconstruction.[28]

When published by Harper and Row in 1956, *Proud Shoes* received warm
reviews in white newspapers. Yet it did not give rise to additional endeavors
in African American genealogy, a field widely considered to have emerged
twenty years later, following *Roots*. Murray's book—with her depiction of
Grandmother Cornelia's strong cultural identification with her white forebears—was omitted from black-genealogy canons into the 1980s.[29] Out of
print by the early 1970s, *Proud Shoes* went overlooked to the point that Alex
Haley viewed his own project on forebears as unprecedented. "In America, I
think, there has not been such a book," he told his agent in 1965. "'Rooting' a
Negro family, all the way back, telling the chronicle, through us, of how the
Negro is part and parcel of the American saga."[30] While Murray admitted to
sharing the passionate work habits of genealogists—"my own exhilaration
over successfully tracking down clues to the past sometimes bordered on a
mild sort of lunacy, a common affliction of genealogical buffs"—she preferred
to avoid identifying with genealogy publicly.[31] She pursued other projects until the twin impact of *Roots* and her own simultaneous fame as a pioneering

Episcopal priest in 1977 brought *Proud Shoes* back into print in 1978. In the final years of her life, she rallied her far-flung surviving relatives to help maintain the neglected family gravesites in North Carolina.[32] Murray's presaging of *Roots* made a powerful case for a successful black family's Americanism.

Black Genealogy 1960–1976

Murray's commitment to family history peaked two decades before *Roots*' publication, as her aunts aged and died in the 1950s. Later events shortly before *Roots* reinforce my argument that it was a turning point in an ongoing history of black genealogy, rather than its founding text. The invigoration of black genealogy in the 1960s helps explain why Haley's message resounded: that it was possible for a person to prove, from a combination of oral and textual evidence, his or her descent from multiple generations of enslaved people and across the Middle Passage.

In the 1960s, civil rights confrontations and reforms, including the desegregation of higher education, injected new energy into the field of black history and, by extension, black genealogy. The Reverend Wyatt Tee Walker, vice president in 1965 of a New York publishing firm called the Negro History Library, understood this well.[33] The new ethos of "history from the bottom up" operated not just to transform historians' practices. The ethos also permeated the sensibility of library patrons. They approached catalogs and counters with the new conviction that it was possible to research historical figures similar to themselves. In 1965, Wendell Wray, acting curator of New York's "famed Schomburg Collection of Negro historical materials," described "a very conspicuous increase" in black patrons recently. "So many come in and say . . . something such as, 'I want to find my roots, I want to know who I am.'" That same year, the New York Public Library librarian Timothy Field Beard reported that the previous two years had witnessed a dramatic increase in African Americans' making their way downtown to the library's lion-bedecked edifice on Forty-Second Street.[34]

The academy's new regard for oral evidence was apparent throughout the following decade, the 1970s. Oral historians wielding tape recorders performed research on populations who were otherwise left voiceless by the vagaries and prejudices embedded in documentation.[35] Alex Haley understood the moment well, placing an article on *Roots* in the premier issue of the *Oral History Review* in 1973.[36] The early 1970s also saw outsiders' unprecedented regard for black genealogy projects. In the same years in which Alex Haley traveled the country, delivering lectures that heralded *Roots*, genealogy journals and even the popular press began featuring advice and instructions in black genealogy. In 1974, *U.S. News and World Report* pronounced, "Increasing numbers of blacks, Indians, and children and grandchildren of immigrants—no longer content to submerge themselves in the 'melting pot' of American society—are flocking to libraries to learn more about their own family heritage."[37]

In another sign of the times' invigoration of black genealogy, 1974 also witnessed a pioneering publication—a family genealogy (focusing on just one family or lineage) by an African American. Nora Louis Hicks, a former schoolteacher from New York, produced over seventy pages on eight generations of her family. *Slave Girl Reba and Her Descendants in America* drew on her interviews with relatives to assert that the aforementioned Reba, of mixed "African" and French descent, had been captured in Madagascar and brought enslaved to Charleston in 1828 at age thirteen. Hicks relied so heavily on oral histories, which she left unsourced, that a reviewer complained that one would have to personally meet her to find out where, and from whom, she obtained her information.[38]

The mid-1970s were also dominated by plans for the bicentennial. Patriotic anniversaries in general have long commanded uncanny power to foster interest in the past among Americans—a power that was not lost on the ABC-TV executives who purchased for $250,000 in late 1974 the rights to film *Roots* and began filming before Haley had submitted the final manuscript to his publisher. "No network ever had bought the advance rights to an unpublished book," marveled a reporter in retrospect.[39] Gerald Ford's administration invited Alex Haley onto the American Revolution Bicentennial Administration. Others on the council were the writer-actress Maya Angelou, who played Kunta Kinte's grandmother on the *Roots* show; Malcolm X's widow, Betty Shabazz, long-time friend of Haley's; and the scholar Richard Gambino, author of *Blood of My Blood* (1974), an account of roots travel to his ancestral Sicily. The council chair was *Roots* executive producer David L. Wolper.[40] The members of this advisory council powerfully illustrate the inextricability of the relationship between bicentennial celebrations and the success of *Roots*.

Roots' Innovations in Black Genealogy

Despite all those antecedents for *Roots* in the area of black genealogy, Haley's work must also be understood as a departure from past efforts. Unlike African American genealogists before him, including Pauli Murray—who scorned blacks' transatlantic ambitions, since they seemed impossible to document—Haley crossed the Atlantic repeatedly to research his family history in the Gambia. Although black nationalists had long contemplated African origins and sometimes constructed Zions there, those aspirations had rarely encouraged family history.[41] Conditions after 1945, including the developing world's decolonization, the beginnings of commercial air travel, and travel's increasing affordability, increased the performance of genealogy across continents.[42] Haley was well positioned to take advantage of these developments and was inclined to do so after his conversations with Malcolm X. Malcolm collaborated with Haley to produce *The Autobiography of Malcolm X* (1965), but he perished before he could approve the final manuscript. Haley's newfound interest after 1965 in building new bridges between Africans and African diasporas had been such a commonplace for Malcolm that Betty Shabazz and others have pronounced Haley's indebtedness to Malcolm on that point.[43] Haley ultimately traveled to the Gambia to conduct research twice during the spring of 1967; he also briefly visited Senegal and Mali in 1973.[44]

Any discussion of Haley's journeys to the Gambia needs to explore the forbearance of his publisher. Upon Malcolm's assassination in February 1965, Doubleday, intended publisher of *The Autobiography of Malcolm X*, dropped the project precipitously.[45] By year's end, however, the small, "radical" house Grove Press ushered the book into print, whereupon *The Autobiography* became an unexpected bestseller. It sold six million copies by the 1990s and remains in print a half-century after its first publication.[46] Smarting from its gross financial miscalculation, Doubleday gave Haley wide latitude as he continued the project that would become *Roots* (under contract with Doubleday since 1964) and experienced years of writer's block that delayed his completion of the manuscript for nearly another decade.

Having depleted the advance from Doubleday, Haley garnered financial assistance from a white benefactor, *Reader's Digest* co-owner Lila Bell Wallace, in order to undertake his African travels.[47] Even though most genealogy researchers lacked friendly philanthropists to sponsor their travel—a considerable expense, especially before the 1978 deregulation of air travel—Haley's overseas trips provided others with inspiration decades later. Pilgrimages to West Africa in search of information on family origins became a staple of regional economies. By the 1990s, Ghana alone attracted ten thousand U.S. visitors each year.[48] Knowing that roots travelers predominated among tourists, Ghanaian TV continuously rebroadcast *Roots* some two decades after it first aired.[49]

Another reason to believe that *Roots* broke with its past relates to the subsequent outpouring of advice books on black genealogy, and the new phenomenon of the black genealogy society. Most genealogy works are published privately, as limited markets exist for information on particular family names. Only a few works of instruction had attracted commercial, trade, or university publishers, notably the five editions of Gilbert Doane's *Searching for Your Ancestors: The Why and How of Genealogy* (1937–1980). Following *Roots*, however, commercially and university-published how-tos on African American genealogy joined new counterparts on Jewish and German American genealogy on contemporary bookshelves; Charles L. Blockson's *Black Genealogy* appeared in 1977, and David H. Streets's advice book, *Slave Genealogy*, in 1986.[50]

Before Haley published *Roots*, there had been attempts to form black genealogy societies, such as in Pittsburgh in 1965, but no sustained group existed.[51] However, sixteen years after its own founding in May 1977, the Washington-based Afro-American Historical and Genealogical Society (AAHGS) counted twenty-two chapters in cities and towns around the country.[52] There were also some freestanding organizations, such as the Afro-American Genealogical and Historical Society of Chicago (1979). AAGHSC leaders retrospectively credited the *Roots* broadcast of 1977, which they referred to as a "documentary," for their inspiration.[53]

Roots as a Genealogy Text and Touchstone

Soon beset by scandals, *Roots'* later career as a text shows that Haley's story of his seven generations commanded considerable power to inspire family history projects, even after his story's veracity came under challenge. Some *Roots* book reviewers, including white historians quoted in a controversial *New York Times* article by Israel Shenker, insisted that Haley's story was mythology and therefore fictional.[54] Haley himself admitted to embellishing facts as established by research, asserting the moment had arrived for the concept of "faction" (a blend of fact and fiction). "By far most of the dialogue and most of the incidents are by necessity a novelized amalgam of what I *know* took place together with what my researching led me to plausibly *feel* took place" (original emphasis).[55] But *Roots* was, and still is to this day, labeled as nonfiction by its publisher.

Even more important than its marketing are *Roots'* own aspirations to broader historical and genealogical truths, even while Haley blurred the distinction between fact and fiction. He made the most emphatic claim to broader truths when speaking authoritatively to the camera at the end of the final episode. Many scholars, including scholarly genealogists, initially took Haley at his word. In the nation's most influential genealogy journal, a reviewer of Blockson's *Black Genealogy* and Dan Rottenberg's guide for U.S. Jews, *Finding Our Fathers*, both published in 1977, noted that the authors "establish for their fields what might be called 'the Mayflower equivalent'— the ideal ancestor toward whom the black or Jewish genealogist strives. For blacks, . . . this is the ancestor who was born in Africa and transported to the New World in a slave ship; from the work of Alex Haley we know that this is an attainable goal." The reviewer went on to praise Blockson's pessimism regarding whether others could reach the goal.[56] The sociologist Tamara K. Hareven argued in 1978 that *Roots'* power lay in its factual revelations. Without that "final linkage to Africa, [Haley's story of the search itself] would not have electrified the public."[57]

But some journalists, scholars, professional genealogists, and others found Haley's original research wanting. And multiple nearly simultaneous copyright-infringement suits, with one (involving the author Harold Cour-lander) settled out of court for $650,000, helped to amplify a growing chorus of criticism.[58] Just weeks after the 1977 telecast, the *London Times* revealed the secluded village of Juffure in the Gambia, Kunta Kinte's Edenic birthplace in *Roots*, to have instead been a busy, slave-trading entrepot, with white new-comers, in the 1700s. By 1981, the historian Gary B. Mills and the genealogist Elizabeth Shown Mills located the enslaved Toby Waller, whom Haley alleged had been born Kunta Kinte in Juffure, in North American documents as early as 1763—four years before the arrival of the slave ship *Lord Ligonier* in An-napolis, Maryland, a pivotal event in *Roots*. Also in 1981, the Africa specialist Donald Wright showed that Haley's Gambian informant had not been the "griot" Haley supposed him to be, and that his answers to Haley's questions had been massaged for the book's purposes.[59]

Even though *Roots* underwent a drubbing within the academy and the courts, the tale of Haley's seven generations retained considerable authority with segments of the public. Many African Americans affirmed *Roots* for rea-sons having to do with racial indignities past and present.[60] "I don't care what people say about how he wrote the book," remarked the Chicago entrepre-neur Amy Hilliard-Jones, who reported being one of only twenty-eight black students in her Harvard Business School class (of 746 who graduated in 1978) when *Roots* aired. "Black students watched it instead of studying—we cried and laughed with each other. It was a watershed—We started having family reunions. My father came from a family of 13 brothers and sisters. It was a logistical challenge. . . . [Haley] touched thousands and millions."[61] Starting in 1994, she and her husband Earl Jones organized McDonald's contests that sent hundreds of U.S. winners to Senegal and the Gambia on family-history pilgrimages, called Homeland Tours or Family Reunion Tours.[62]

Another indication of *Roots'* resilience as an inspiration for family histori-ans is the endurance of institutions dedicated to black genealogy, following the scandals and criticisms directed at *Roots*. Impossible questions seemed more possible to answer when people pooled together their findings. The professionals, retirees, and government employees who comprised Chicago's AAHGS chapter (formed in 1989) held monthly meetings through the de-cades, on the city's South Side.[63] Instruction books on black genealogy also continued to find commercial publishers, as in the case of Henry Louis Gates Jr.'s *Finding Oprah's Roots, Finding Your Own*. Genealogy advice for African Americans has also now been televised repeatedly.[64]

Why did *Roots* engender such affection? Haley insisted on portraying his family history as a history of an entire race: "the saga, of us as a people." To him, writing in 1973, black people all shared the same "generic back-ground; . . . every single one of us without exception ancestrally goes back to some one of those villages, belonged to some one of those tribes, . . . was put on some one of those slave ships, across the same ocean into some succession of plantations up to the Civil War, the emancipation, and ever since then a struggle for freedom."[65] Shortly after the book's publication, the educator Nancy L. Arnez returned the favor when she remarked that the book "helped destroy the chilling ignorance of who we are as a people."[66] Such statements ensured that when the story's facticity was challenged, the entire race's reputation came under particular risk. To reject *Roots* publicly might mean airing dirty laundry before the arrayed enemies of African Americans.

But it would be wrong to portray African American opinion as a monolith on the subject of *Roots'* truthfulness. Silences speak as loudly as words. The university professors, archivists, and librarians who wrote for the AAHGS's journal through the decades made no mention of *Roots* at its publication and broadcast anniversaries, or even at the time of Haley's death in 1992. Instead, they upheld the ethos of professionalized genealogy, as when the Howard University librarian Roland C. Barksdale-Hall expressed consternation at *Slave Girl Reba* author Nora Louis Hicks's failure to provide citations for her oral histories in 1974. "It should not be like this," he complained in 1988. "I cannot overly emphasize the point: our research should be repeatable and our publications should contain footnotes and/or a list of sources of materials and documentation."[67] Not until the mid-1990s did scholars in African American studies resume discussing *Roots* within the academy, with the early example of the sociologist Floyd James Davis in 1991.[68]

Conclusion

Today, African American genealogy continues to be hampered by race-specific reasons for the difficulties of performing it. The reasons for the paucity of source material on history's black families include the denial of documentation to slaves' marriages and to white men's fathering of slaves, bans on enslaved people's literacy, and antebellum censuses' failure (with a partial exception in 1850) to list enslaved people as individuals. In coping with the dearth of textual evidence, black researchers have reached for whatever non-textual evidence they can find of their forebears, such as vague revelations of their ethnicity from a DNA sample, or a shared outward, morphological resemblance. In 1999, a Chicago genealogist remarked that he had recently come upon a "tribe in Ghana that had holes over the upper part of their ears. My father had the same trait over both of his ears. My son ... has one hole over his left ear. ... In the near future, I hope to document the authenticity of this finding."[69]

In the 1970s, the story of *Roots* proved captivating because it arrived as interest in African American family history was decidedly building. Therefore *Roots* landed on ears that were keenly poised to listen for its hopeful message: that it was possible, after all, to map one's own lineage through centuries of slavery to a long-ago "African" because Haley had managed to do so. Even though the research connecting Haley to Kunta Kinte has since been questioned, *Roots* carries, to this day, considerable power as a travelogue to inspire endeavors within the arduous field of black genealogy.

NOTES

1. Alex Haley, *Roots: The Saga of an American Family* (New York: Doubleday, 1976), 707–711; Alex Haley, "My Furthest-Back Person—The African," *New York Times Magazine*, July 16, 1972, SM12 (ProQuest ed.); Robert J. Norrell, *Alex Haley and the Books That Changed a Nation* (New York: St. Martin's Press, 2015), 6–8.

2. *Roots: Thirtieth Anniversary Edition* (Warner Brothers DVD collection, 2007), disc 6 (episode dir. Gilbert Moses).

3. François Weil, *Family Trees: A History of Genealogy in America* (Cambridge, Mass.: Harvard University Press, 2013), 29–31, 50.

4. See especially Martha Biondi, *The Black Revolution on Campus* (Berkeley: University of California Press, 2012), including the "Black Revolution Off-Campus" chapter.

5. Peter Novick, *That Noble Dream: The "Objectivity Question" and the American Historical Profession* (Cambridge: Cambridge University Press, 1988), 442 (quotation); Matthew Frye Jacobson, *Roots Too: White Ethnic Revivals in Post–Civil Rights America* (Cambridge, Mass.: Harvard University Press, 2006); and Weil, *Family Trees*, 180–216.

6. Natasha Zaretsky, *No Direction Home: The American Family and Fear of National Decline, 1968–1980* (Chapel Hill: University of North Carolina Press, 2007), 143–182; Tammy S. Gordon, *The Spirit of 1976: Commerce, Community, and the Politics of Commemoration* (Amherst: University of Massachusetts Press, 2013).

7. "Rome Author Alex Haley: Remote Village in Senegambia Was Home of African Ancestors," *Daily Sentinel* (Rome, N.Y.), June 5, 1967, clipping; Peter Calisch, "Author Researches Family Tree," June 4, 1967, *Utica (N.Y.) Observer-Dispatch*, clipping, folder 36, box 29, Alex Haley Papers (MS 1888), Special Collections, University of Tennessee, Knoxville (hereafter Haley Papers 1888). Norrell, *Alex Haley*, 110–112, confirms this chronology.

8. *The Autobiography of Benjamin Franklin, with Related Documents*, ed. with an introduction by Louis P. Masur, 2nd. ed. (Boston: Bedford/St. Martin's, 2003), 27–31; Norrell, *Alex Haley*, 107. The phrase "roots trip" comes from Jacobson, *Roots Too*, 48.

9. When in Ghana shortly after that country's independence in 1957, Pauli Murray encountered "Negro visitors from the United States" who had the "romantic notion of 'coming back to Mother Africa to see my people.'" "What Is Africa to Me?" (December 1960), reprinted in Pauli Murray, *Song in a Weary Throat: An American Pilgrimage* (New York: Harper & Row, 1987), 328.

10. Paul E. Sluby Sr., "History of AAHGS," Afro-American Historical and Genealogical Society, http://www.aahgs.org, accessed May 28, 2014; Weil, *Family Trees*, 198–200.

11. Lois Elizabeth Brown, *Pauline Elizabeth Hopkins: Black Daughter of the Revolution* (Chapel Hill: University of North Carolina Press, 2008), 9–32.

12. David Levering Lewis, *W. E. B. Du Bois: Biography of a Race, 1868–1919* (New York: Henry Holt, 1993), 13, 374–375, 660 n.66.

13. An example is Deborah Samson (later Gannett), a white woman who fought in the American Revolution disguised as a man. Raised near Plymouth, Massachusetts, she claimed descent from two *Mayflower* passengers, but her own generation saw hard times. Samson's father abandoned her mother for another family, whereupon the mother sent five-year-old Deborah out to work as a servant. But Samson named her son for an ancestor and otherwise perpetuated knowledge of her descent. Alfred S. Young, *Masquerade: The Life and Times of Deborah Sampson, Continental Soldier* (New York: Alfred A. Knopf, 2004), 24–25.

14. Caulkins, *History of Norwich, Connecticut* (Norwich, Conn.: Thomas Robinson, 1845), v, quoted in Nancy Steenburg, "Stepping Outside Her Sphere: The Intellectual Adventures of Frances Mainwaring Caulkins," *Connecticut History* 51 (spring 2012): 57.

15. Estimates of slave literacy range from 5 to 10 percent. Antonio T. Bly, "Literacy and Orality," and Tammy K. Byron, "Bible," both in *World of a Slave: Encyclopedia of the Material Life of Slaves in the United States*, edited by Martha B. Katz-Hyman and Kym S. Rice (Santa Barbara, Calif.: Greenwood Press, 2011), 14, 67.

16. Annette Gordon-Reed, *The Hemingses of Monticello: An American Family* (New York: W. W. Norton, 2008), 55–56, 271, discusses the appearance of James Madison Hemings's mother.

17. "Life among the Lowly, no. 1," *Pike County (Ohio) Republican*, March 13, 1873, reprinted in Annette Gordon-Reed, *Thomas Jefferson and Sally Hemings: An American Controversy* (Charlottesville: University Press of Virginia, 1997), 245–248. Wales's name is sometimes spelled Wayles.

18. Madison Hemings himself never identified the source of his information.

19. Heather Andrea Williams, *Help Me to Find My People: The African American Search for Family Lost in Slavery* (Chapel Hill: University of North Carolina Press, 2012), 139–202.

20. Ida B. Wells-Barnett, *Crusade for Justice: The Autobiography of Ida B. Wells*, edited by Alfreda M. Duster (Chicago: University of Chicago Press, 1970), 8.

21. David M. Battles, *The History of Public Library Access for African Americans in the South, or, Leaving Behind the Plow* (Lanham, Md.: Scarecrow Press, 2009), 23–40; Cheryl Knott, *Not Free, Not for All: Public Libraries in the Age of Jim Crow* (Amherst: University of Massachusetts Press, 2015).

22. Johni Cerny, "Black Ancestral Research," in *The Source: A Guidebook of American Genealogy*, edited by Arlene Eakle and Cerny (Salt Lake City: Ancestry Publishing, 1984), 580; James M. Rose and Alice Eichholz, *Black Genesis* (Detroit: Gale Research, 1978), 5.

23. Manning Marable, *Malcolm X: A Life of Reinvention* (New York: Viking, 2011), 85, 96.

24. W. Fitzhugh Brundage, *The Southern Past: A Clash of Race and Memory* (Cambridge, Mass.: Harvard University Press, 2005), 138–183; Carter G. Woodson, "Negro Women Eligible to Be Daughters of the American Revolution," *Negro History Bulletin* 7 (November 1943): 36–37. See also Luther P. Jackson, "The Daniel Family of Virginia," *Negro History Bulletin* 10 (December 1947): 51–57; Eunice Shaed Lewis, "Distinguished

Americans Along the Border: The Cook Family," *Negro History Bulletin* 5 (January 1942): 89–90.

25. Pauli Murray and Mary O. Eastwood, "Jane Crow and the Law: Sex Discrimination and Title VII," *George Washington Law Review* 34, no. 2 (1965): 232–256.

26. Stephen Vincent Benét to Murray, n.d. [after October 23, 1939], folder 1621, box 93, Pauli Murray Papers, Schlesinger Library, Radcliffe Institute, Harvard University (hereafter Murray Papers); Murray, *Song in a Weary Throat*, 132–133.

27. Murray, typed notes, "Fitzgerald Odyssey: Delaware and Pennsylvania," April 29, 1954, 4, folder 1355, box 76, Murray Papers.

28. Murray, *Proud Shoes: The Story of an American Family* (New York: Harper, 1956, reprinted 1978). Scholarly discussions of *Proud Shoes* include Sarah Azaransky, *The Dream Is Freedom: Pauli Murray and American Democratic Faith* (New York: Oxford University Press, 2011), 39–50; Darlene O'Dell, *Sites of Southern Memory: The Autobiographies of Katharine Du Pre Lumpkin, Lillian Smith, and Pauli Murray* (Charlottesville: University Press of Virginia, 2001), 104–143.

29. Exceptions to this pattern are Yaffa Draznin, *The Family Historian's Handbook* (New York: Jove Publications, 1978), 11; Rose and Eichholz, *Black Genesis*, 3. Bibliographies from later times include James Dent Walker, "Family History and Genealogy: Avocation or Necessity?," *Journal of the Afro-American Historical and Genealogical Society* 2 (fall 1981): 103–105 (hereafter *JAAHGS*); Gloria L. Smith, "Some Family Histories," *JAAHGS* 5 (Spring 1984): 44–45. Smith did not claim to be comprehensive, but her list focused on family genealogies, and neither she nor Walker included *Proud Shoes*.

30. Haley to Paul Reynolds, January 30, 1965, folder 10, box 3; bibliography (omitting *Proud Shoes*), n.d., folder 29, box 29; Haley Papers 1888.

31. Murray, *Song in a Weary Throat*, 300.

32. Copy of letter and proposal, Pauli Murray to Regina Brough, March 23, 1978, folder 327, box 12, Murray Papers.

33. Alex Haley, "My Search for Roots," *Tuesday Magazine* (Chicago) 1 (October 1965): 7.

34. Ibid., 5–6. Wray's repository later became the Schomburg Center for Research into Black Culture.

35. The literature on this subject is vast. See especially Tamara K. Hareven, "The Search for Generational Memory: Tribal Rites in Industrial Society," *Daedalus* 107 (fall 1978): 137–149.

36. Alex Haley, "Blacks, Oral History, and Genealogy," *Oral History Review* 1 (1973): 1–25.

37. Thomas H. Roderick, "Negro Genealogy," *American Genealogist* 47 (April 1971): 88–91; Peggy J. Murrell, "Black Genealogy: Despite Many Problems, More Negroes Search for Their Family Pasts," *Wall Street Journal*, March 9, 1972, clipping, folder 23, box 2, Haley Papers 1888; Haley, "My Furthest-Back Person—The African"; "Quest for Identity: Americans Go on a Genealogy Kick," *U.S. News and World Report*, July 29, 1974, 41.

38. Roland C. Barksdale-Hall, review of Nora Louise Hicks, *Slave Girl Reba and Her Descendants: Memoirs* (Jericho, N.Y.: Exposition Press, 1974), in "Book Reviews," *JAAHGS* 9 (winter 1988): 180–181.

39. Norrell, *Alex Haley*, 139 (delivery of final draft in December 1975); Alex Haley, "Carbons of Synopses for Segments," May 15, 1975 (5645), box 47, Haley Papers 1888;

Alex Haley to Waller Wiser, August 29, 1974, folder 1, box 1, Alex Haley Papers 2280, University of Tennessee at Knoxville; Les Brown, "ABC-TV Plans to Stress Serializations of Novels," *New York Times*, December 14, 1974, 59; Marty Bell, "Debts, Stubborn Faith Drive Alex Haley to Write *Roots*," *Chicago Tribune*, February 27, 1977, 12 (ProQuest ed.) (quotation).

40. Zaretsky, *No Direction Home*, 151, 156.

41. Wilson Jeremiah Moses, *Afrotopia: The Roots of African American Popular History* (Cambridge: Cambridge University Press, 1998).

42. Jacobson, *Roots Too*, 130–176.

43. Philip Nobile, "Uncovering *Roots*," *Village Voice* (February 23, 1993), 35; Marshall Frady, "The Children of Malcolm," *New Yorker*, October 12, 1992, 78.

44. G.P., memorandum to J.P. et al., May 31, 1973, Carnegie Corporation of New York, photocopy in folder 4, box 47, Haley Papers 1888.

45. Paul Reynolds to Alex Haley, March 11, 1965 (2790), folder 14, box 44, Haley Papers 1888.

46. Marable, *Malcolm X*, 448, 465–466.

47. Bell, "Debts, Stubborn Faith"; Haley, *Roots*, 715–716.

48. Saidiya Hartman, *Lose Your Mother: A Journey along the Atlantic Slave Route* (New York: Farrar, Straus and Giroux, 2007), 162.

49. Ibid., 57.

50. Dan Rottenberg, *Finding Our Fathers: A Guidebook to Jewish Genealogy* (New York: Random House, 1977); Clifford Neal Smith and Anna Piszczan-Czaja Smith, *Encyclopedia of German-American Genealogical Research* (New York: R. R. Bowker, 1976); Charles L. Blockson, with Roy Fry, *Black Genealogy* (Englewood Cliffs, N.J.: Prentice-Hall, 1977); David H. Streets, *Slave Genealogy: A Research Guide with Case Studies* (Bowie, Md.: Heritage Books, 1986).

51. On Florence Ball-Jones and the evanescent Western Pennsylvania Research and Historical Society, see Jean Stephenson to Alex Haley, August 12, 1965, folder 12, box 3, Haley Papers 1888; Haley, "My Search for Roots," 7.

52. Patricia Liddell Research Associates, *Newsletter* 1 (winter 1993): 28–29, box 5, Patricia Liddell Researchers Archives, Vivian G. Harsh Research Collection, Carter G. Woodson Public Library, Chicago (hereafter PLR).

53. "Patricia Liddell Researchers Archive: Organizational History," http://www .chipublib.org/fa-patricia-liddell-researchers-archive/, accessed January 8, 2016.

54. Israel Shenker, "Some Historians Dismiss Reports of Factual Mistakes in *Roots*," *New York Times*, April 10, 1977, 29 (ProQuest ed.). Other reviewers who considered the book *Roots* to be fictional include John Brooks, "The Epic of the Black Man as Told, at Last, by a Black Man," *Chicago Tribune*, September 26, 1976, F1 (ProQuest ed.; reprinted from the *New Yorker*), and George McCracken, "Recent Books and Reprints," *American Genealogist* 53 (April 1977): 122–123.

55. Haley, *Roots*, 727.

56. Robert C. Anderson in "Review of Books," *New England Historical and Genealogical Register* 132 (October 1978): 315. This journal, the first of its kind in the United States, dates back to 1847. By the mid-twentieth century, its paid circulation (3,403 in 1969) was second only to the Everton family's *Genealogical Helper* (Logan, Utah),

aimed at the do-it-yourselfer (29,414 paid subscribers in 1977). *New England Histori-cal and Genealogical Register* 124 (April 1970): back cover; "Statement of Ownership," *Genealogical Helper* 31 (November–December 1977): 666.

57. Hareven, "Search for Generational Memory," 139. See also Oscar Handlin, as interviewed by Shenker, "Some Historians Dismiss Reports"; Willie Lee Rose, "An American Family: A Review of *Roots*, by Alex Haley," *New York Review of Books* 23 (November 11, 1976): 3–6.

58. Settlement figure in Wolfgang Saxon, "Harold Courlander, 82, Author and Expert on World Folklore," *New York Times*, March 19, 1996, D22; Norrell, *Alex Haley*, 175–177, 183–198.

59. Mark Ottaway, "Tangled Roots: Doubts Raised Over the Story of the Big TV Slave Saga," *Times* (London), April 10, 1977, 1, 17, 21; Gary B. Mills and Elizabeth Shown Mills, "*Roots* and the New 'Faction': A Legitimate Tool for Clio?" *Virginia Magazine of History and Biography* 89 (January 1981): 9; Donald R. Wright, "Uprooting Kunta Kinte: On the Perils of Relying on Encyclopedic Informants," *History in Africa* 8 (1981): 205–217; Nobile, "Uncovering *Roots*"; Weil, *Family Trees*, 196–197; Norrell, *Alex Haley*, 198–201.

60. Helen Taylor, "'The Griot from Tennessee': The Saga of Alex Haley's *Roots*," *Critical Quarterly* 37 (summer 1995): 46–62; David Chioni Moore, "Routes: Alex Haley's *Roots* and the Rhetoric of Genealogy," *Transition*, no. 64 (1994): 10.

61. Anne Romaine, transcript of interview with Amy Hilliard-Jones, n.d. [1993 or 1994], folder 22, box 2, Anne Romaine Collection, Special Collections, University of Tennessee at Knoxville; statistic on class of 1978 from Cullen Schmitt (Harvard Business School), personal communication, June 28, 2016. Amy Hilliard's LinkedIn page lists her 1978 graduation date, https://www.linkedin.com/in/amy-hilliard-b2134, accessed June 28, 2016.

62. Paulla Ebron, "Tourists as Pilgrims: Commercial Fashioning of Transatlantic Politics," *American Ethnologist* 26 (November 1999): 910–932, studied the 1994 tour.

63. Patricia Liddell Research Associates, *Newsletter* (fall 1991): 1, box 5, PLR.

64. Henry Louis Gates Jr., *Finding Oprah's Roots, Finding Your Own* (New York: Crown, 2007). Henry Louis Gates Jr., *African American Lives* (PBS Home Video, 2006).

65. Haley, "Blacks, Oral History, and Genealogy," 20.

66. Nancy L. Arnez, "From His Story to Our Story: A Review of *Roots*," *Journal of Negro Education* 46 (summer 1977): 367–372, quoted in Michael S. Sweeney, "Ancestors, Avotaynu, Roots: An Inquiry into American Genealogy Discourse" (PhD diss., University of Kansas, 2010), 160. Some black reviewers vigorously dissented; see Sandra Rattley, "The Impact of *Roots*," *Africa Report* 22 (May–June 1977): 12–16.

67. "Book Reviews," *JAAHGS* 9 (winter 1988): 181.

68. Floyd James Davis, *Who Is Black?: One Nation's Definition* (University Park: Pennsylvania State University Press, 1991), 124; Moore, "Routes"; Taylor, "'The Griot from Tennessee'"; Linda Williams, *Playing the Race Card: Melodramas of Black and White from Uncle Tom to O.J. Simpson* (Princeton, N.J.: Princeton University Press, 2001), 220–252.

69. "A Word from Our President," PLR *Newsletter* 4 (November 1999): 2, box 5, PLR.

PART II

Rereading *Roots*

CHAPTER FOUR

Roots of Violence
Race, Power, and Manhood in *Roots*

DELIA MELLIS

In the final episode of the *Roots* miniseries, hooded night riders tie Tom Moore (Georg Stanford Brown), the great-grandson of Kunta Kinte, to a tree. They whip him nearly to death in an effort to punish and to make an example of him for going to the police with proof of their attacks on his community. As the young white overseer, Ol' George (Brad Davis), takes up the lash, the terrorists ride away, their leader, Evan Brent (Lloyd Bridges), admonishing him to teach Tom "how to be a nigger." This scene is significant not only because it shows a major character brutalized and humiliated, but because such scenes weave through the series as they wove through life under slavery and in the years after the Civil War. This antiblack, state-sanctioned violence continued to define U.S. life in multiple permutations through the twentieth century—and continues to this day. I argue that *Roots* offers a surprisingly rich exposure and critique of that violence, aimed both at the history the series depicted as well as the period in which it appeared.[1] In a way, *Roots* served as both culmination and death knell for the era of Black Power, exhibiting even as it ultimately undermined the politics of rage, resistance, and self-determination that were so central to the ideology of that movement.

In the mid-1970s when *Roots* premiered, the country was still reeling from the urban rebellions of the 1960s and the shift from the nonviolent phase of the civil rights movement to the forms of activism most often characterized as Black Power. In the two or three decades before the series was broadcast, black anger at persistent inequality had finally begun to seem like a real threat to the stability of the U.S. social order. African American leaders of the Black Power era such as Malcolm X, Stokely Carmichael, Amiri Baraka, Eldridge Cleaver, and Angela Davis called out white violence—physical, economic, social, and political—and condemned not only the whites who abused their power but also the black activists and their followers whom they saw as at worst abetting and at best failing to see this abuse for what it was. Following the activism of the civil rights era, the rage that seemed the dominant note of the Black Power and post-assassination period was perceived as menacing, including to many of the white people who had been sympathetic to and even supportive of calls for black electoral and educational access that were—at least in their eyes—the primary concerns of the civil rights movement. According to Peniel E. Joseph, the Black Power movement "fundamentally transformed struggles for racial justice through an uncompromising quest for social, political, cultural, and economic transformation." In other words, black power called for revolution rather than negotiation.[2] Invoking Frederick Douglass, Black Power advocates asserted that "power concedes nothing without a demand," and pointed to urban riots, beginning with Watts in 1965, as the beginning of real change.[3]

Roots was deeply shaped by this context, with multiple scenes commenting on the ideological significance and political possibilities of the Black Power movement, the central tenets of which were black pride, self-respect, and active, assertive, and if necessary violent resistance to white oppression. While unflinchingly emphasizing the brutalities and humiliations of slavery, the show highlights the dignity, intelligence, and self-awareness of the central characters, who are hurt but never undone by the totalizing racism of their environment. This retention of self-worth in the face of relentless assault, the determination to resist and not just survive, are key to the narrative and the show's complicated political message. The inherent dignity and moral superiority of Kunta Kinte and his family stand in sharp contrast with the moral and psychological rot of the show's villains.

Almost all of the white characters in *Roots* are complicit with slavery. They are always suspect, always dangerous—even the relatively mild among them. Meanwhile, the brutalization of black bodies remains central to *Roots*, as it was to the history the series portrays. From the moment of Kunta Kinte's (LeVar Burton) capture, black men are repeatedly beaten, chained, humiliated; black women are raped and demeaned. The threat—and the fact—of such violence functions to control, contain, and in many ways to define Kunta Kinte and his family. From the repeated beatings and ultimate mutilation of Kunta for running away, to the threatened lynching of his great-grandson Tom for exposing white criminality, black men in the series who express independence face physical violence as an assertion of white male power and control. Their wives and daughters confront that same power in the form of rape. In each instance, white manhood takes shape and finds expression through brutality toward black people who are powerless to defend themselves or each other, or to retaliate.

In showing the brutal consequences for black self-determination, *Roots* depicts the reality of life under slavery as well as under the racial regimes that followed emancipation. Whether deliberately reflecting historiography—and cultural analysis and criticism from W. E. B. Du Bois to Angela Davis—or inadvertently recapitulating reality, *Roots* offers a compelling picture of the psychology and practice of white supremacy. At the same time, however, *Roots* figures as an admonition to those who would overturn the racial status quo through violence or who might take revenge for centuries of oppression. The series sympathizes with their anger and even validates it, repeatedly showing slaveholding whites as duplicitous, vicious, and immoral. But in the end, its message is that black people must corral their impulse to fight back; instead, they are exhorted to respond with patience, tolerance, and even love.

The Slaveholder and Typologies of Whiteness

Like Frederick Law Olmsted, who wrote a travelogue of the slave South for the *New York Times* in the decade before the Civil War, *Roots* offers a catalog of slaveholder types and, in the process, a critique of white supremacy and its reliance on antiblack violence.[4] Echoing Olmsted, *Roots* portrays the physical intimacy of slave and owner—how intermixed their daily lives were—as well as the vast gulf between them. We also see how the institution of slavery shaped slaveholders. Their ideas about their chattel and their social system defined them: white conversations revolve around slaves—how to manage them, their capacities, their innate nature. White characters—the patrician Reynolds brothers, their wives and daughters, their overseers and friends, the vulgar Tom Moore (Chuck Connors)—seldom discuss anything else. The few non-slaveholding whites we encounter also fancy themselves experts on the minds and ways of the enslaved. Whites in *Roots* are obsessed with their chattel and with maintaining power over them.

Each white character represents a particular type of the master class. These characters are played by some of television's most recognizable actors of the day, and there is deep irony in the casting. Lorne Green brings his patriarchal authority from the set of *Bonanza* and dozens of other TV shows and films to his role as the first owner of Kunta Kinte, the aristocratic, dissolute Squire Reynolds. The squire's brother is a doctor, played by another TV paterfamilias, Robert Reed of *The Brady Bunch*. Dr. Reynolds is the responsible intellectual to his brother's profligate authoritarian. And both are deeply compromised. They lack virtue—the squire in his drunkenness and financial recklessness, the doctor through his immoral years-long and barely concealed relationship with his brother's wife, with whom he has a daughter. These flaws are twinned with the characters' saturation in slavery's racial ideologies and practices, as they hold forth sagely on the nature of blacks and the proper way to manage enslaved property.

When Kunta first arrives at the Reynolds plantation he is placed under the protection and guidance of Fiddler (Louis Gossett Jr.), as a kind of double-edged gift from Reynolds to his enslaved factotum. Fiddler is tasked with training the African. The squire warns that Fiddler will face dire consequences if he fails to teach the new arrival to accept his slave status within six months, on the owner's birthday. This is power that Fiddler does not desire—in granting him this responsibility, Reynolds actually undercuts his flimsy authority on the plantation. Fiddler's driving hope is to protect the little privilege he has managed to acquire, and in gaining this new duty he sees his small advantage endangered. The absolute power of the slave master is reinforced here, his whimsy in handing over Kunta entwined with menace.

Inevitably, Fiddler fails to "break" Kunta, who runs away and is captured by Ames the overseer (Vic Morrow). A Scottish immigrant who claims that his years of indentured servitude give him insight into the minds and behaviors of the enslaved, Ames represents another white type. He lives among the enslaved, having, as Dr. Reynolds comments, more contact with black people than white people and basing his authority on that close contact. Ames has in fact been waiting to get his hands on Kunta since he arrived on the place. When Squire Reynolds initially put Kunta under Fiddler's supervision, Ames had warned his boss that it would not work, because "one horse don't break another." Now it is up to Ames to "break" Kunta and he does it with the whip, forcing the captured man finally to acknowledge his slave name, Toby.

In this as in the other instances of physical violence across the series, the actual perpetrator is from the lower classes, brutal but not stupid. Ames brings a level of complication and near ambivalence that makes him impossible to dismiss simply as a villain—though he is indeed that, with his slave concubine and his relentless, deliberate brutality. He contends, in an argument with his boss, that the blacks are not naturally designed to serve, as both Reynoldses believe. "Slaves aren't born, they're made. . . . [F]ear, and the whip to rub it in, that's what makes a slave." From his own experience of servitude and his close surveillance of them, Ames ironically has the strongest sense of the humanity of the enslaved. His moral failure lies in the fact that this recognition makes him no less brutal toward them, no less invested in his power over them. Ames doesn't simply admit that he had been in servitude, a status hardly different from slavery until the contract was up; it's the very fact of his abasement that gives him authority, expertise, and whatever power he has.

In the breaking of Kunta, the symbolic and actual power of the white man is enacted; the squire never dirties his own hands; he does not even watch. Nor does Ames himself administer the whipping; he has a slave wield the lash at his direction. In first restraining and then unleashing his overseer on the African, the patriarch exercises his prerogative, his control over life and death; in turn, Ames demonstrates his own control through the work of another. When Kunta finally gives in and calls himself Toby, Ames is vindicated: he has, with the whip, made the man a slave.

The slaveholder's delegation of the hard and dirty work of control to the lower-class white man—the overseer, the slavecatcher, the posse—reflected the extent to which race had trumped and continued to trump class for white Americans. (Indeed, President Nixon capitalized on this dynamic in the late 1960s, galvanizing the "silent [i.e., white] majority" so effectively that, by the time *Roots* appeared, few could wonder that poor whites reliably chose racial over class solidarity.) In the instances where poor whites dominate blacks, the series enacts a key aspect of the nation's racial conundrum: the deep enmity between poor whites and African Americans, who might—without the divisions created by ideas of racial difference—reasonably have found common ground against a common oppressor. Ames's power over the enslaved despite his own low status is a point of white racial pride, key to what W. E. B. Du Bois would call the "racial wage," and what historian David Roediger calls more specifically "the wages of whiteness." Low as he may be, Ames is never at the bottom. Thus, working-class and poor whites are distracted from their own debasement and consequent resentment of the powerful by their social and political power over African Americans. This racial division supersedes any potential class unity they might find with black people.[5]

Years later, Toby/Kunta (now played by John Amos) has moved, with the squire's other slaves, to Dr. Reynolds's plantation as payment of the squire's debt to his brother. He has married Bell (Madge Sinclair), the doctor's cook and housekeeper, a favorite whom Reynolds calls "as true and loyal a woman as the Almighty ever let draw breath." They have a teenage daughter, Kizzy (Leslie Uggams), a happy and indulged child whose closest friend is Miss Anne (Sandy Duncan), the doctor's "niece"—actually the product of his adulterous relationship with his brother's wife. Dr. Reynolds prides himself on his scientific and humane management of his slaves, declaring that he has "a covenant" with them. But when Kizzy's sweetheart, Noah (Lawrence Hilton-Jacobs), runs away, Dr. Reynolds allows Ordell, the overseer (John Schuck), free reign in tracking him down and punishing him. Having broken the "covenant" that Dr. Reynolds imagines he has with his slaves, Noah is no longer under his protection. Like his brother, Dr. Reynolds takes no direct part in the violence, but he controls it: he later acknowledges that Noah "or what's left of him" has been sold. And he coldly announces to Bell and Toby/Kunta that he has also sold Kizzy because she had forged a pass for Noah to aid his escape. Kizzy is carried away screaming while her mother collapses; Dr. Reynolds impassively observes their separation. Like Noah, Miss Anne, and Kizzy, any claims Bell had on his owner's loyalty or favor are far outbalanced by the patriarch's demand for absolute obedience. Reynolds's investment in his relationship with Bell is meaningless in comparison with any challenge—even by association—to his identity and control as master.

Tom Moore (Chuck Connors), the cock breeder to whom Kizzy is sold, adds a twist to the white class dynamics in *Roots*. From his first appearance, when he stops at the Reynolds plantation to bring news of an attempted slave uprising, Moore is unrepentantly vulgar, a stereotype of the lower-class slaveholder. He deliberately offends the sensibilities of the refined Dr. Reynolds as he slurps his whiskey. Discussing his holdings, he mentions his aspiration to own more slaves: "I got a mind to get me a couple and breed my own ... maybe I only need one, if I find the right one!" He laughs, greedily—and irreverently—pouring himself more of Reynolds's whiskey. He rapes Kizzy on her arrival at his place, and the next morning the woman who dresses her wounds tells Kizzy that Moore makes a practice of "studding" all his young female slaves until they get pregnant, and then he leaves them alone. Kizzy's vow in that moment, that her son would deliver her revenge on Moore, is a rare instance of a black character in *Roots* threatening a white, even in absentia. In this moment of outrage and violation, her rage dominates, and the audience believes she will fulfill her vow. However, it comes to nothing—in fact, she eventually prevents her son from attempting to kill Moore precisely on the grounds that the brute is his father. The ultimate failure of Kizzy's intention, contrasting with the dramatic power of her vow, delivers the message of black women's powerlessness. Just as Bell, the only relatively powerful woman in the miniseries, was ultimately undone and even erased by her daughter's kidnapping (we never see her again after that moment), Kizzy's vow, so intense and certain, comes to nothing in the end.

Moore's vulgarity, in contrast with the refinement of the high-toned Reynolds family, offers yet another angle on the ways of white domination. Moore exercises his power primarily through sexual abuse. He has no overseer, but we never see him whip or hit anyone other than Kizzy. Yet his viciousness goes beyond rape: he is the quintessential duplicitous, immoral cracker. Despite their closeness, he has no compunction about lying to Kizzy's—and his own—son, Chicken George (Ben Vereen), when it suits him, and he coerces him without hesitation, threatening to sell his family away if George refuses to fight his chickens. And he makes no pretense to have or to honor anything like a "covenant" with his slaves, even a slave of his own blood. When hard times hit and he plans to sell away the family of the absent Chicken George, Moore's wife (Carolyn Jones) asks how he'll explain breaking his promise when Chicken George comes back. His response succinctly conveys his attitude toward slaves: "He won't come back white, my dear. He'll still come back a nigger. Really, what's a nigger to do?"

The final model of the slaveholder is the inconsequential Mr. Harvey (Richard McKenzie), to whom Moore has sold Chicken George's family. He is mild and fair, a relative nonentity. He has no overseer, and until he hires the young white war refugee Ol' George (Brad Davis) for the job, his slaves are under the supervision of Chicken George's eldest son, Tom. Harvey provides a contrast to the vicious Brent brothers, a pair of local merchants who go out of their way to humiliate Tom and Chicken George when they come into town. In the final episode, when Harvey must sell the plantation, his parting with his former chattel is revealing. Bewildered and bemused at the changes in his world and his circumstances, he makes an awkward good-bye speech, thanking them for their "kindness" and wishing them well. Tom's mother, Tildy (Olivia Cole), prompts the others to tell him good-bye, offering her hand, her parting words damning him with the faintest of praise: "You was better than some . . . Massa." The stunned Harveys slowly trundle away into their unknown future.

Postwar white power shows up in the pairing of the duplicitous and acquisitive Senator Justin (Burl Ives) and the vile Evan Brent (Lloyd Bridges), who with his brother had earlier humiliated Tom and threatened his father. Determined to overcome Reconstruction's limits on white control, they bind the former slaves to the land with the debt Harvey had promised would be forgiven, as well as with violence. As night riders, Brent and his cohorts had first destroyed Harvey's chance of staying on the land, forcing him to leave by destroying crops and property; after he leaves, they terrorize the former slaves in order to keep them there. Again, white men exert authority through the threat and fact of violence. There is no other way, in *Roots*, for a white man to be effective—to be, in short, a man.

The only white man other than the ineffectual Mr. Harvey who does not lay claim to his manhood through some kind of violation of black bodies is young Ol' George Johnson. He first appears in episode 7, when Tom catches him in a storeroom trying to steal food. Later, as Tom is being bandaged from the beating the Brents gave him when they assumed it was he who had been thieving, Ol' George knocks on the door to beg food for himself and his pregnant wife, Martha (Lane Binkley). They are war refugees from South Carolina, fleeing a part of the state too poor for slaveholding. Tom and his family take them in, and soon Mr. Harvey makes him overseer, because it wouldn't be proper for him to work in the fields alongside the enslaved.

Hapless, childlike, downright comical in his naïveté and goodness of heart, Ol' George follows Tom around like a puppy, asking for and receiving permission, instruction, and protection from the fatherly Tom at every turn. Tom is kind and generous with the young man, teaching him the ways of the world. As he and his brother, Lewis, teach Ol' George how to act like an overseer, Tom forces the newcomer to utter the epithet "Nigger." Ol' George sounds like a small child, the unfamiliar word uncertainly trailing out of his mouth. Although the moment strikes a false note historically, its message for the 1970s is clear enough: not all whites are raised to be hateful toward blacks. Even more, it is the responsibility of black people to be patient and loving toward those whites who do not hate them, to cultivate their innocence and good will.

In episode 8, Lewis, enraged and terrified by the threat of the night riders, turns on Ol' George, rejecting him because he is white. Deeply hurt, George in his turn gives Tom the cold shoulder when he comes to apologize for his brother, and then he accepts the senator's offer to manage the plantation. In one of the show's ironic twists, the young white man has been taught racial distrust by a black man, not other whites. For a time, he and Martha keep themselves apart from Tom and his family. But when Tom is being whipped by Brent and his night riders, Ol' George steps in. Telling them "Nobody whips my niggers but me," he takes up the lash and strikes Tom. He appears to have learned his lesson, to be coming at last into his maturity and authority as a white man.

But as soon as the hooded riders have departed, Ol' George drops his mask and rushes to help his friend and the bond is reestablished. The audience, held in suspense as to Ol' George's intention, learns that he has remained loyal despite Lewis's rejection. The message here is a straightforward slap at Black Power and at black nationalism: in *Roots*, black anger at whites, however justifiable, is dangerous. In this sequence especially, through Lewis, such anger is painted as fear-based, childish, and supremely destructive. Black people must be careful not to lose their white friends, lest they force them to grow up and into their legacy of domination.

Ol' George is the only sympathetic white male in the series, and he is essentially a child, even when he intervenes to save Tom. It is only his refusal— or inability—to grow into a "man" that allows him to escape the villainy that defines the other white men. This is why when he accepts the senator's offer to oversee the farm, we fear that, because Lewis has hurt him, he has finally given in to the culture, to the power of power, like the other poor and working-class whites we have seen. An innocent, unschooled in the ways of white power, he learned what he knew of it from the very slaves he was hired to oversee. He trusted them and did as they taught him, but when they rejected him because of his skin color, the hurt was so deep that we believe it finally awakened Ol' George's own race hate and his lust for power. We believe that he will finally begin to accept the wages of whiteness.[6] And we see—or we fear—that he has finally grown from child to man. The lesson here, again, is aimed primarily at black people, and involves staying true to their white friends, who are thin on the ground and emotionally delicate besides.

In *Roots*, white manhood, in all its violence and moral weakness, is never redeemed. The Reynolds men, ironically depicted by two of the era's most familiar TV fathers, are deeply flawed, morally and otherwise. The other white patriarchs—Tom Moore, Mr. Harvey, Evan Brent, and Senator Justin—are either evil or contemptibly weak. The overseers are horrifying in their pragmatic, savage sadism. Ol' George escapes only because he is a resolute baby. It seems that the only way for a white man to avoid or resist complicity is to remain a child. This is compatible with a simplified view of the youth movement of the 1960s and early 1970s. The hippies, who had turned on and dropped out, had deliberately shirked, abandoned, or sidestepped the roles and responsibilities of adulthood—and in *Roots*, violence against black people is one of those responsibilities for whites. Thus, Ol' George represents both possibility and danger: if he can remain innocent—indeed, if the black people can protect his innocence—he can in turn protect them.

Black Manhood and Power in Slavery and Freedom

The portrayal of black manhood, meanwhile, bizarrely twins Black Power imagery with an evisceration of the politics at the heart of the movement. As the series depicts it, white manhood is entirely based on and enacted through violence and domination, and because the enslaved black characters are so entirely subjugated, black manhood is deeply constrained. This is true even more so because the series was made in a televisual context where conventional, benevolent manhood was constructed as white, and where black men could not, by definition, be portrayed as holding real power, even in the form of anger. The historical and narrative context of slavery simultaneously eased and reinforced this conundrum. Ultimately, in *Roots*, forbearance and survival define black manhood.

Beginning in episode 2, as Kunta Kinte endures the horrors of the Middle Passage, and continuing through the final episode, the series depicts masculine power through violence, and such power always belongs to white men. Meanwhile, in the African scenes, power is signaled rather than depicted, an attribute of age and wisdom, of patriarchal standing and respect. Physical aggression only appears safely within the parameters of "manhood training," when the initiates face the Wrestler (Ji-Tu Cumbuka), in a controlled setting, with no real contest. This contrasts sharply with the brutal violence in subsequent episodes and with their depiction of those holding power as deeply flawed—morally and psychologically.

The battle aboard the slave ship is the only time we ever see Kunta Kinte in a physical fight. Kunta's rage and fear at his capture, his disgust and confusion on the ship are the reason—triggered by the white sailors' attempted rape of one of the African women—he instigates the doomed rebellion. After that defeat, we never see him raise his hand against anyone again. Before his first escape at the Reynolds plantation, we expect that he might be plotting violence when he grabs and hides a broken tool, but he uses it to file away at his leg irons, never to attack the overseer or to fight his way out. To the extent that he expresses his warrior identity it is in his insistence on his Mandinka name, his yearning to go home and refusal to see where he is as a new home, and his repeated attempts to run away. The fact that he is always foiled comes to define him, as defeat defines black efforts at resistance to white imposition and control throughout the series. If, as Black Panther leaders like Fred Hampton and Huey P. Newton pointed out (after Mao Zedong), power grows out of the barrel of a gun—or the wielding of any other weapon—black men in *Roots* got nowhere near power.[7]

Moreover, in an echo of white abolitionist imagery of the bound, kneeling, and shirtless slave exclaiming, "Am I not a man and a brother?," the aestheticized, powerful black male body appears in *Roots* as an inversion, a representation of powerlessness.[8] In episodes 3, 4, and 5, the adult Kunta Kinte is played by the towering John Amos—yet another TV patriarch, the father on the hugely popular *Good Times*. *Roots* repeatedly highlights his physical power, the camera luxuriating in his size, strength, and dignity, his shirtless torso gleaming, his carriage upright, only slumping and dropping his head when whites appear. But Kunta is also the show's primary victim, repeatedly captured, relentlessly defeated. In the end, we learn, Kunta dies alone. After his daughter, Kizzy, is sold, he loses his wife, Bell, too, and although the women who tied him to the place disappear, he himself never escapes.

But the other message of the show is that his identity is his family's deliverance. It is Kunta Kinte's story, his knowledge of and insistence on maintaining who he is and where he came from that defines and sustains his family. This is his real power, and it is a power he is able to pass along to his descendants. Here, *Roots* implies that for African Americans survival, persistence, loyalty, and family are more important than political or economic power, or the ability to resist the abuses of such. A black family that resists the erasure of its history initiated by slavery become a kind of elite—they are different than others, better.

In episode 6, a middle-aged Kizzy takes up with the handsome coachman Sam Bennett (Richard Roundtree), another physically imposing black man.[9] He has physical power and great charm, but in the end he is not strong enough for Kizzy. In a bewildering sequence, she forces him to take her to the Reynolds plantation to see her parents, where she learns that they are dead. Upon their late return to the Moore place, Sam is berated and threatened by his owner (George Hamilton) in front of Kizzy, whom he is supposed to marry and take home with him the next day. Kizzy then refuses Sam, telling her son she couldn't marry him because he wasn't "like us. Nobody ever told him where he come from, so he didn't have a dream of where he oughta be going." The trappings of conventional manhood are not available to enslaved men; physical strength is simply a marker of servitude, because they cannot use it to hurt anyone. Only a sense of identity allows black manhood under slavery, which by its very nature sets out to destroy identity. Here the series celebrates black history and cultural persistence even as it implicitly condemns the majority of African Americans, who have failed to hold on to their stories.

Kizzy's son, Chicken George, is, like his grandfather, a nonviolent resister, choosing to use skill, wiles, and charm as his means of self-definition and escape. He tells his mother, "I'm 'on make a name for myself, and get me some respect, but not by running like your daddy. No, I'm 'on pick them birds until I can buy myself free. And then I'm 'on look straight ahead the rest of my life, not over my shoulder." Although he refers in the final episode to his experience in battle, he is by then an old man, and it is difficult to imagine him at war. He is a sporting man, a trickster, and his adventures take place offscreen. He is moved to violence only once, when he realizes that Moore, his owner, will never set him free, telling him, "You're mine. You are my property.... You're my nigger, George. Can't you get that through your thick skull?" Coming away from this conversation determined to kill the man, George tells his mother why: "He done the worst thing that a man can do to me. He took away all my hopes." Ironically, the only way Kizzy can stop her son from killing Moore is by telling him the very reason she'd once vowed he *would* kill him: Chicken George is the product of her rape by Moore. This moment, when his mother tells him that his enemy is his own flesh and blood, defines one of slavery's central wounds.

Such imagery had profound ideological significance in the post–civil rights era. The sexual terrorism that black women experienced in the Jim Crow South spurred a range of African Americans—from Daisy Bates to Rosa Parks to Robert F. Williams—into activism in the 1950s.[10] And according to Black Power ideology of the late 1960s, the appropriation of black women by white men, through rape or the conferring of favor, served as one of the white supremacist system's greatest offenses. Indeed, in *Soul on Ice*, Eldridge Cleaver claims that his choice to rape white women was a political one, revenge for the centuries of white men's rapine of black resources, women primary among them.[11] In *Roots*, the rape of black women by slaveholders is a fact of life, yet another expression of white dominance and black powerlessness.

And here again, the black characters must rise above. The violence and horror that whites visit upon them provide more than sufficient justification for vengeful hatred, but by the same token *Roots* requires that they forbear. The object lesson in this episode is the Nat Turner rebellion, which created a huge furor among the slaveholders, and provided the first crack in Chicken George's relationship with Moore. We hear more about Turner than we see, although George and Tildy come across the body of one of his followers. Historically, Turner's rebellion helped cause a tightening of restrictions on the enslaved, de jure and de facto. In the show, Turner represents another failure of the black man to escape or overcome the violence of the whites, a mistaken—if only because ineffective—choice.

In the context of Black Power, especially in relation to the Black Panthers, the gun is a central trope for—and means of—rejecting white domination and abuse. In the late 1960s and early 1970s, the Panthers chose to exercise—indeed, to flaunt—their right to bear arms—on the street, in encounters with police officers, and most dramatically on the floor of the California legislature in 1967.[12] In *Roots*, we do not see black characters use or threaten to use guns against whites until the final episode, as the family makes their escape. The gun Tildy and Chicken George see in the dead hand of Nat Turner's follower is dangerously potent—we barely see it, and the couple quickly dispose of it, along with the corpse. In another inverted reference to Black Power imagery, *Roots* keeps guns—a classic symbol of masculine power in American mythology—out of the hands of black people.

Chicken George's son, Tom, is a blacksmith whose physical power is implicit in his trade and, as with John Amos's Kunta, highlighted in multiple shirtless scenes. But Tom, far from being a brute, is remarkable—not to say infuriating—for his ability to humble himself and to insist that his fellows be humble too. He is Christlike in his mildness, in his rejection of anger, his ability to turn the other cheek to white aggression, and his exhortations to others to do the same. And yet, he is the aggressor in the show's only instance of black violence against a white man apart from the uprising on the ship. In a deeply complicated moment, with his bare hands Tom kills the dreadful Jemmy Brent, who has brutalized and humiliated him on multiple prior occasions. Tom comes upon the rebel deserter in a barn, and in a moment that is tortuous for the audience, agrees to help the craven, going to fetch him clothes so he can escape the consequences of his desertion. Jemmy is able to manipulate the idealistic Tom by pretending to recognize that the times have changed, and that they will all have to learn "a new way to get along together," begging Tom to help him as a way of making a start. "Trust has gotta start somewhere, Tom. Let it be here and now." Tom wants to believe and heads off. Brent scowls and mutters a hateful "Nigger" as Tom departs, and is soon leering dangerously at Tom's wife, Irene (Lynne Moody), when she comes to the shop looking for her tardy husband. Tom returns to find his wife struggling in Jemmy's clutches and is lost to mercy. After a fight, he drowns the villain in his cooling bucket, murmuring afterward, "It were him or me. It were him or me."

This incident overturns the classic rape narrative whites used to justify racial lynching in the decades following the end of Reconstruction. Whites—northerners and southerners alike, including those who disapproved of it—threw up their hands at lynching: in their view, red-blooded white men could not be expected to control themselves when white womanhood was assaulted or even threatened. The rape story was consistently effective in silencing criticism of the mob murders of black citizens. Even more, it blotted out the real story of sexual assault in the South. In this scene, though, *Roots* shows what Ida B. Wells and other antilynching activists contended at the time: white men raping black women actually defined the sexual violence and danger of the slave and post-slavery South.[13]

Rape, as we have seen, was central to the culture of white violence, the exercise of manhood through brutality that the show depicts. Angela Davis, icon of the Black Power movement, echoed Wells when she wrote in *Women, Race, and Class* that the appropriation of black female bodies through rape had the double effect of brutalizing their men. The subsequent development of the trope of the black rapist intensified the effects—the psychological, physical, and political violence—a hundredfold.[14]

Tom, like Kunta on the ship, is moved to violence only once: by the threatened rape of a black woman by a white man. He lays claim to a conventional construction of manhood in the eminently justifiable homicide of the hateful and dangerous rapist. But, again like his ancestor, he holds this status only for a moment. Tom repeatedly belies with his words the power his body projects, insisting on obedience to the law, humility in the face of disrespect, submission to the villains. He is an idealist, and his probity contrasts with the emotional recklessness of his brother Lewis and the passivity of everyone outside his family. He insists, after the war ends, that the family must stay put and wait for Chicken George to return. His filial piety defines him, giving him power within his family, and it is one of the ways that the series distinguishes the descendants of Kunta Kinte from other enslaved people.

Conclusion: Rising Above

In the final episode of *Roots*, there is a long moment between Tom's son, Bud (Todd Bridges), and Martha (Lane Binkley), the young wife of Ol' George. These are the boy's only spoken lines, and one of Martha's few bits of dialogue, as well. The two marginal characters carry a great deal of expository weight in this scene. Bud has just seen his father whipped by hooded white men— and then by Ol' George himself—and is in a rage, vowing to kill them all. The camera closes in on his tear-stained, scowling face, which is suddenly iconic, representing the powerless fury of black youths across generations and centuries, including that of the boy's own great-great-grandfather, Kunta Kinte.

But this child is the reverse of Kunta: born a slave, he is suddenly free. And his rage, as the series reads it, is fundamentally different from that of his ancestor, who seeks only freedom. Bud wants revenge; he wants to hurt back. He vows, "I'm gonna kill 'em!"

Proffering the show's central and deeply conservative message, Martha schools Bud about the problem with black rage: if you hate and seek revenge against all white people for what a few bad ones have done to you, "you won't be any better than those men who hurt your daddy." The boy insists that he hates the men who hurt his father. She tells him, "Hate 'em for what they done, not because they's white. Me and mine is white. But we love you, just like our own. If you'll let us love you." Thus, the responsibility falls on the child: we want to love you, but you have to let us, which means abandoning your anger, your fear, your determination to fight back.

With the notable exception of the angelic Tom in his fight with Jemmy Brent, whenever a black character is pushed over the edge by white betrayal and hatefulness to the point of rage and contemplates violence, in retaliation or protectiveness, he is corrected, either by brutal experience, as in the case of the unseen Nat Turner and his followers, or by wiser minds, as in the cases of Chicken George, Lewis, and now Bud. Bud's anger, while legitimate and understandable, must be set aside.

Thus the central message of *Roots*, despite its serious indictment of U.S. slavery and racism, is the message of the white liberal: the descendants of slaves must be patient, must endure, must rise above the hatred and brutality of the unenlightened whites. They must let the "good" whites love them and wait for the day when the rest will change. As the white moderate Martin Luther King Jr. critiques in his "Letter from Birmingham Jail" (and elsewhere), *Roots* puts responsibility for peace on the shoulders of the victims rather than on the perpetrators.[15]

Read this way, the series is a screed against the Black Power movement, against contemporary black doctrines of self-defense or aggression. Although of course such ideas appeared throughout African American history, in the late 1960s and early 1970s they were most visible in the ideas and actions of groups like the Black Panther Party and, by the mid-1970s, the Black Liberation Army. They had also been central to the urban riots of the late 1960s, which were almost always responses to white violence. Some black leaders—most prominently Malcolm X and the Black Panthers—embraced the idea that violence was indeed an expression of manliness, and in fact the only effective way to respond to ongoing white attacks on black individuals and communities.

Roots, then, represents at once a critique of both white violence and black aspirations to fight back. The only resistance that *Roots* legitimates is the effort to escape, and even that effort is always punished. The show consistently refuses sentimentality or the easy resolution; until the very end, no one escapes. This lends veracity as historical account, since relatively few enslaved Americans managed to get away; it also supports the message that the only way through trouble for black people is to suffer and forbear. There is no escape, and any form of resistance is violently punished. Slave rebellion features primarily as a source of hysteria among the whites, the basis for a tightening of restrictions and amplification of dangerous fear. There is no identification among the slaves with such rebels, although Chicken George expresses a furtive, pitying sympathy for the dead man he finds before rolling his body away down a ravine. The message is clear: resistance is fatal.

In the face of brutality and injustice, black people simply have to endure; they must sustain themselves from within, they must simultaneously rise above and cast down their buckets where they are. They should learn and then tell one another their stories, and they must have faith that one day all will be well, that the whites will in the end recognize their humanity and accept them. The series relies on an idea of saintly, even superhuman African American tenacity and faith. "Maybe freedom means we don't have to leave," says Tom in episode 8, in one of the show's most intense moments of cognitive dissonance for a contemporary viewer.

In the end, *Roots* reinforces the inevitability of white male power, although it is deeply critical of that power. In *Roots* as in U.S. society, violence and humiliation are primary expressions of dominance. And in *Roots* as in U.S. society, it is white men who wield power, and who sustain and demonstrate that power through brutality. Forty years later, *Roots* offers a sharp comment on the period and society that produced it, at least as much as the slave society it depicted. Since 2012, the deaths of Oscar Grant, Trayvon Martin, Jordan Davis, Michael Brown, Freddy Gray, Sandra Bland, Alton Sterling, Philando Castile, and too many others have either enraged or confused citizens, depending on their social, racial, or political positions. Contemporary bewilderment at these recurrences arises in part because we fail to fully acknowledge or confront the fact that real power in the United States has always manifested through violence, and that such violence has been primarily the province of white men, policing the boundaries of neighborhoods, of achievement, of expression, and of national identity itself. *Roots* depicts the early American enactment of racial control through brutality. The strands of gender and power run through *Roots*, intertwined through race into a web of domination, violence, and submission. And today, as we painfully and repeatedly watch white men punish African American men—often lethally—for perceived or actual overstepping of gendered racial boundaries, *Roots* is all too resonant.

NOTES

1. *Roots*, directed by Marvin J. Chomsky, John Erman, David Greene, and Gilbert Moses (1977; Burbank, Calif.: Warner Bros. Home Entertainment, 2007), DVD, episode 8.

2. Peniel E. Joseph, "The Black Power Movement: A State of the Field," *Journal of American History* 96, no. 3 (December 2009): 753.

3. Frederick Douglass, "West India Emancipation" (aka "If There Is No Struggle, There Is No Progress"), August 3, 1857, Canandaigua, N.Y., www.blackpast.org/1857 -frederick-douglass-if-there-no-struggle-there-no-progress, accessed March 25, 2015.

4. Frederick Law Olmsted, *The Cotton Kingdom: A Traveller's Observations on Cotton and Slavery in the American Slave States, 1853–1861*, edited by Arthur Schlesinger (New York: Da Capo Press, 1996).

5. See W. E. B. Du Bois, *Black Reconstruction in America, 1860–1880* (New York: Free Press, 1995 reissue of 1935 original), 700–701; David Roediger, *Wages of Whiteness: Race and the Making of the American Working Class* (New York: Verso Books, 1999).

6. Du Bois, *Black Reconstruction in America*; Roediger, *Wages of Whiteness*; George Lipsitz, "The Possessive Investment in Whiteness: Racialized Social Democracy and the 'White' Problem in American Studies," *American Quarterly* 47, no. 3 (September 1995): 369–387.

7. *Selected Works of Mao Zedong*, vol. 2, Marxists Internet Archive (transcription by the Maoist Documentation Project), accessed July 9, 2015; Fred Hampton, "Power Anywhere Where There's People," speech, Olivet Church Chicago, 1969, http://www .historyisaweapon.com/defcon1/fhamptonspeech.html, accessed July 9, 2016.

8. An early and ubiquitous abolitionist symbol depicted a chained and kneeling enslaved man, under the motto "Am I not a man and a brother?" See "Africans in America Resource Bank," http://www.pbs.org/wgbh/aia/part2/2h67.html, accessed July 9, 2016; Library of Congress Prints and Photographs catalog, https://www.loc.gov /pictures/item/2008661312/, accessed July 9, 2016.

9. The fact that Roundtree's defining role was the black private detective John Shaft, the quintessential Blaxploitation hero, is yet more of the show's relentlessly ironic casting.

10. See Daisy Bates, *The Long Shadow of Little Rock: A Memoir* (New York: David McKay Co., 1962); Danielle L. McGuire, *At the Dark End of the Street: Black Women, Rape, and Resistance—A New History of the Civil Rights Movement from Rosa Parks to the Rise of Black Power* (New York: Alfred A. Knopf, 2010); Timothy Tyson, *Radio Free Dixie: Robert F. Williams and the Roots of Black Power* (Chapel Hill: University of North Carolina Press, 1999).

11. Eldridge Cleaver, *Soul on Ice* (New York: McGraw-Hill, 1967), 26.

12. Jane Rhodes, *Framing the Black Panthers: The Spectacular Rise of a Black Power Icon* (New York: New Press, 2007), 68–79.

13. Ida B. Wells-Barnett, *Southern Horrors and Other Writings: the Anti-Lynching Campaign of Ida B. Wells* (Boston: Bedford/St. Martin's, 1996), 60.

14. Angela Davis, "Rape, Racism, and the Myth of the Black Rapist," in *Women, Race, and Class* (New York: Random House, 1981); Darlene Clark Hine, "Rape and the Inner Lives of Black Women in the Middle West," *Signs* 14, no. 4 (summer 1989): 912–920.

15. Martin Luther King Jr., "Letter from Birmingham Jail," August 1963, www .uscrossier.org/pullias/wp-content/uploads/2012/06/king.pdf, accessed October 11, 2014.

CHAPTER FIVE

The Roots of African American Labor Struggles

Reading *Roots* and *Backstairs at the White House* in a 1970s Storytelling Tradition

ELISE CHATELAIN

Today, as was the case when it first aired on television, *Roots'* success is typically attributed to its ability to represent the subjective experience of U.S. slavery and to offer a novel perspective on a troubled era of the nation's history. The story's focus on Kunta Kinte's traumatic entrance into the Euro-American slave trade and on a century of his descendants' struggles, concluding with Emancipation and Reconstruction, highlights the intimate and affective impact of a U.S. past defined by this institution.

These themes both underscore the contours of the text itself and the conversations it generated about a U.S. past defined by hierarchical racial difference. But in the context of its emergence, *Roots* was not alone in offering a new perspective on U.S. history in popular culture. In fact, it was a (particularly well-received) piece within a larger tradition of storytelling and knowledge production common to 1970s television. According to Malgorzata Rymsza-Pawlowska, the tendency toward "nostalgia culture" took shape across television genres but coalesced in a unique way in the miniseries format. In particular, the miniseries offered an image of the past that depicted historical authenticity through reference to the emotional, and especially "emphasized the importance of the historical on the formation of personal identity," offering insight into intrapersonal and familial relationships formed by and within larger historical events.[1]

Situated within its genre, *Roots* reflected not simply a tendency toward the nostalgic but an emerging perspective on historical knowledge production of the time, generally characterized under the umbrella of new social history. This mode of thought worked to uncover the "hidden voices" of the past and illustrate the lived experience of oppressive social institutions from the point of view of subjugated groups. In both academic practice and popular culture, new methodologies and narrative strategies reflected the cultural context following mid-century liberation movements and leftist politics, which informed both the production and reception of a text like *Roots*. And it wasn't simply the desire to uncover the "hidden voices" of the past that motivated this interest, but an impulse to examine the historical oppressions that had shaped these silences in the first place—and how they were such a central part of a national storyline that had been suppressed. Further, in these examinations of "people whose everyday lives have been hidden" family history became central to this new mode of knowledge production, both scholarly and popular.[2]

Keeping that point in mind, I reflect on *Roots* in the context of this storytelling tradition: not just as a popular form of "new social history," but also as a dramatization of the "familial" nature of history's most oppressive social structures. What *Roots* did so powerfully was offer a narrative of these intimate and oppressive power relationships that have come to characterize the telling of African American history, offering a history "from below" through reference to racially structured systems of slavery and servitude. And just two years after *Roots* first aired, another miniseries offered a similar perspective on the African American experience. *Backstairs at the White House* was based on the memoirs of Lilian Rogers Parks, a member of the domestic staff at the White House for nearly thirty years, following in the footsteps of her mother, Maggie Rogers. Spanning a half-century of service to U.S. presidents, from the Taft administration to the end of Eisenhower's presidency, this popular series offered a depiction of twentieth-century economic struggles experienced by working-class black Americans, specifically those laboring under a system of domestic service that contained residuals of slavery itself.

Considered together, *Roots* and *Backstairs* define a collective African American experience through their reference to two centuries of labor exploitation. Both texts drew from a "history-from-below" impulse, bringing to the small screen a popular depiction of how inequalities of race were experienced through powerful economic and political structures. But even more significantly, both offered a sense of a national history through the dramatization of intimate labor relationships in a domestic setting. These popular texts articulated the experience of racial oppression as a distinctly intimate and familial experience, bridging public history with family history in a new way. Importantly, this imagining of the past through reference to domestically oriented power relationships—the master-slave and master-servant dynamic—was not one of an untroubled depiction of family unity. Instead, the familial, private connections between "servant" and "master" that underscored texts like *Roots* and *Backstairs* drew from the historical consciousness of the era in order to unveil the point of view of those "from below" who experienced the oppression of such relationships firsthand. And ultimately, these pivotal moments in television history formed the foundation of new narrative frameworks for African American history, frameworks that persist in twenty-first-century tales of historical labor oppression in popular culture.

Films such as *The Help* (2011) and *The Butler* (2013), as mainstream representations of the past, could arguably be signs of a regressive period in current filmmaking and have been interpreted as such. However, as I suggest below, placing contemporary films within a longer narrative tradition that began with *Roots* highlights the complicated way in which the new social history ethos continues to disrupt dominant histories of race, domestic servitude, and oppressive labor relations.

Roots and the "New Social History"

Roots continues to be recognized as a defining moment in television history and applauded for its role in reshaping U.S. racial consciousness. As evidence to its persistence as a cultural phenomenon, in 2013 it was a central theme in an episode of PBS's *Pioneers of Television* dedicated to the miniseries. The "*Roots* as Untold History" feature offered on the episode's website works to capture the impact of the series on a nation's perception of its racially troubled past. Here, LeVar Burton (the young Kunta Kinte) offers his own position on the role of *Roots* in shifting dominant narratives around slavery: "In every history unit I ever had in school, slavery was always referred to as an 'economic institution.' It was an 'economic engine' upon which this country was built. The human cost was never a part of that module in school. We got schooled through *Roots* about the human side of that equation, the human element, and what that cost was to thousands of souls."[3]

As Burton suggests, the tale of slavery as an "economic engine" was the primary theme that underscored his education in U.S. history. Reflective of the framework that would have persisted during his childhood education (and has not been completely eliminated from historical modes of thought), the "master narrative" presented from a Eurocentric point of view excludes the everyday experiences of many historical actors—particularly those who would have suffered under the oppressive elements of larger social structures like a slave economy. The new social history movement offered a response to these exclusions, and sought to render visible previously untold stories. In a manner to which Burton alludes, it revealed the "human" impact of powerful institutions like slavery by uncovering the subjective experience of those who experienced its oppressions. *Roots*, in a particularly dramatic and novel fashion, revealed the physical and emotional trauma of its violent forces, such as in the gut-wrenching Middle Passage episode (episode 2), which made many viewers reflect for the first time on the actual lived experience of the "economic system" that was the Atlantic slave trade.

Importantly, too, the depiction of subjective experience of oppressions such as these was not in the interest of victimizing historical actors, but in showing how individuals responded to, resisted, and often overcame powerful forces. Kunta Kinte's insistence on sustaining his heritage, represented poignantly in the iconic whipping scene where he refuses to accept the name appointed by his master, illustrates the text's emphasis on maintaining necessary cultural ties. And the celebratory final episode, when patriarch Chicken George helps his family break free from their virtual imprisonment as sharecroppers and the violent antics of racist night riders, displays the family's ability to overcome racial oppression.

In these ways, *Roots* functioned as an empowering source of recognition, dramatizing a heritage that the institution of slavery itself had attempted to erase. As Leslie Uggams (Kizzy) noted: "Alex wrote this story of people with kings and queens, and [who] had a beautiful life, and—strong people—and [they were] taken away, to another country, where they were denied speaking their language, and denied keeping their names, and treated like animals. And that was a story that we—as African Americans—had never seen that part. So . . . it was a lesson for everybody."[4] This theme of recognition was central to the politics of history underscoring both *Roots* and the new social history ethos that defined it. Alongside social movements taking place in the larger culture, this scholarly shift emphasized empowering identity-based politics, bridging developments in ethnic studies, women's history, and labor history. Further, the growing dominance of this "new" form of historical knowledge brought to the forefront of academic practice previously marginalized scholarship, including African American histories offered by writers such as E. Franklin Frazier and W. E. B. Du Bois.[5]

As the political and academic movements driving these epistemological shifts made explicit, knowledge framed through reference to abstract social institutions—politics, the economy, military conflicts—too easily absolved historical actors from the responsibility of their oppressions. A new social history of political, economic, or military structures would expose how they shaped lived social experience—and further, pinpoint the individuals operating through these power structures. However, the task of uncovering these "hidden" voices—and particularly, the everyday lives of those practically erased from the social record—posed unique challenges. Before the new social history movement, the near-absence of "ordinary" people from public documents resulted in their institutionalized invisibility from historical writing. However—and especially in family studies—scholars developed new methodological approaches in the interest of uncovering the lived experience and various features of families' lives.[6] Approaches such as family reconstitution and cultural analysis allowed scholars and cultural producers alike to recapture both the organization of family life and the intimate, emotional quality of the past. As a method, family reconstitution draws from an array of archival sources, particularly birth, death, and marriage records, and other legal documents (e.g., wills), with the "aim of reconstructing the family and household patterns of ordinary people who have passed down little information regarding their way of life."[7] And it involves utilizing interpretive methods in literary and cultural analysis to craft a rich description of everyday history. Haley, in writing the novel on which the television series was based, drew from these methodological shifts, reconstructing a family history that, while fictionalized, presented new perspectives from the past in ways that were based on historical data.

Significantly, though, to examine historical records in relation to the history of slavery requires that one draw from the documents of slave owners. These references to Haley's source material for *Roots* arise in both his novel and the televised production, such as in the pivotal moment after Kizzy's birth, when Master Waller ceremoniously inscribes her name into the family Bible. As *Roots* made explicit, following a family line through the institution of U.S. slavery meant drawing intimate genealogical connections to the white oppressors who operated through this institution—such as in forming white patriarchal familial lines through naming practices or in the often violently formed blood ties made explicit through Chicken George's patrilineal connection to Master Lea.

The intimate, familial relationship of master-servant that underscores *Roots* as an "untold history" reveals an historical process of an intimate power relationship epitomizing larger oppressive structures. While in Haley's novel the perspective of slave masters remains largely at the margins, "black-white" relations form much of the central drama in the television series. In part, this "balanced" presentation was a conscious production decision developed to address network anxieties surrounding the dramatization of a black-centered storyline for an assumed white audience.[8] These anxieties shaped specific choices in the development of the miniseries, such as casting popular white actors in the roles of the most villainous white masters or crafting the character of the conscientious ship captain riddled with guilt for his participation in the Atlantic slave trade.

To be sure, the television adaptation sacrificed some of Haley's intended meaning in order to appeal to a "wider" (i.e., white) audience. However, a consideration of the new social history impulse is also pivotal to understanding these production decisions. In *Roots*, this epistemological and political project was captured largely through the dramatic racial conflicts that defined power relations in a slave-based economy (as well as post-slavery). Further, this relationship offered a distinctly intimate sense of national history, one that drew from the familial-like structure of servitude in order to tell a story about larger systems of oppression. In 1977, when *Roots* premiered, U.S. viewers were primed into the historical ethos of the time through television's focus on familial social history. In *Roots*, these themes came through most poignantly in the representation of power struggles between history's white elite and their subordinated slaves, whose oppressions played out in the most private of spaces of everyday life.

The *Roots* television epic concludes on a theme of freedom and an escape from these oppressive household and property relations that defined much of the black experience since the dawn of U.S. nationhood. The final scenes of Chicken George, Matilda, and family heading west into freedom and opportunity come years after the abolition of slavery. Therefore, what the family is fleeing is the continued ties to white landowners engendered by Reconstruction-era sharecropping, a system that similarly maintained racial stratification through landowners and the workers who lived on and maintained their property. If read as a hopeful narrative of upward mobility, this conclusion can be viewed as "a generic tale of the classic immigrant success story in America."[9] But if viewed (also) as a metaphor of escape from the oppressive labor struggles that defined African American historical experience, the conclusion to television's *Roots* offers a telling tale of a group's escape from labor oppression that was tied to the familial, property-based structure of servitude.

If interpreted on its own terms, *Roots*' conclusion *does* seem to offer a too-neat tale of upward mobility, suggesting a metaphor for the entire black experience that (literally) ends in resounding cries of "freedom!" from racism and economic oppression. Cultural texts, though, only have meaning in relation to the larger interpretive practices in which they exist (and continue to exist). Just two years after *Roots* aired and had such an impact on the national consciousness, another miniseries emerged that offered similar images of U.S. servitude structured around racial difference—this time reflecting patterns of labor and domestic-familial life in the twentieth century and presenting key features of African American labor struggles that were grounded in systems that had preceded this period.

Backstairs at the White House as New Social History

The four-part *Backstairs at the White House* miniseries premiered on NBC in January and February 1979 (it was almost concurrent with the premiere of *Roots: The Next Generations*, which tells the story of Kunta Kinte's descendants). Featuring many of the actors who appeared in *Roots*, including Leslie Uggams (as Lillian Rogers Parks), Olivia Cole (as Maggie Rogers), and Louis Gosset Jr. (as Houseman Mercer), the story followed the lives of an African American mother and daughter and their coworkers, who labored on the White House domestic staff for nearly the entire first half of the twentieth century. Unfolding over four consecutive Mondays, the series enjoyed strong viewership and received overwhelmingly positive critical attention, earning eleven Emmy nominations.

In line with the miniseries format and the new social history device, the series highlights the everyday lives of Parks, her mother, and their fellow staff members as narrated through the "big" historical actors: (white male) U.S. presidents, their wives and children, and significant historical events (wars, scandal, economic crisis, etc.). Importantly, the audience's knowledge of political, economic, and military history is either assumed or presented as marginally important, and the point of view presenting these major events is from the perspective of the people working "backstairs," who narrate the historical register in terms of their own emotional responses to and the intimate impact these events have on their lives as White House workers. For instance, when Calvin Coolidge's son dies, the event itself barely registers on screen but instead unfolds through the reaction and dialogue among the staff members. In fact, after viewing these scenes I had to do a little background research myself on the child's death, for the sequence of events is only presented as it played out in relation to the staff—such as his playing the ill-fated tennis game with a staff member—and the actual cause of death (an infected blister resulting from that game) remains vague in the storyline itself. On the whole, the series appears to consciously represent these families from the "backstairs" point of view. The tone of each presidential reign shifts substantially, from the light and happy feeling of FDR's administration to the somewhat cold and demeaning representation of Eisenhower's reign.

In general, the story told in *Backstairs* is of how servants lived their everyday lives through decades of labor struggles defined by racial hierarchies—including their concerns as political subjects in a racially unequal society. A prominent theme is the racial organization of labor in the White House, including discrepancies in pay among black and white workers and the lack of promotional opportunities available to the "colored help" (often discrimination filtered through the villainous Mrs. Jaffray, who eventually gets what is coming to her when President Coolidge fires her for her bigoted treatment of the black staff members). Further, when First Lady Mrs. Wilson visits Maggie and Lillian in their modest home, they voice their biggest concern: the extent to which the president is going to address the specific needs of the black community.

Other themes relevant to the lived experiences of African American domestic workers—especially women—in the first half of the twentieth century underscore the entire series. For instance, Lillian—spunky, bright, and a talented seamstress—repeats many times that she has no plans to follow in her mother's footsteps into the White House, to the point of critiquing her mother's extreme dedication to her occupation and employers. When the circumstances of the Great Depression force her into an entry-level job as a housemaid, she makes a dramatic entrance into the staff kitchen, smiles, and offers up her metaphor for domestic work to the embarrassment of her mother:

"I've come to take the veil." Her joke references her oft-remarked character-ization of her mother's occupation: she compares the level of dedication re-quired to work as a domestic to entering the convent, a point that is further emphasized by her failed marriage later in life. While a quick blip in the story-line, her husband's exit from her life is presented as a consequence of her time-consuming dedication to her employers and the constant demands of serving on the White House domestic staff.

The series also offers a sense of quotidian domesticity, emphasizing the private home life of Parks and Rogers and further, their family-like connec-tions to long-standing White House staff members. The series opens, in fact, with the conclusion of Lillian Rogers Parks's career, as she and her mother's long-time friend and coworker, Mercer, watch the thirty-fifth presidential in-auguration in their new home. Facing retirement together, they constitute their fictive kinship network in the face of occupations that have diverted their abilities to establish normative family ties—a persistent feature of servi-tude evident in slave narratives (including *Roots*), which continued to charac-terize domestic work as it transformed in particular ways in this period. One such transformation is the transition from live-in to live-out work—a feature that is reflected in the depiction of these central characters' private lives. But even with this structural transition in the occupation, the series illustrates how the work persisted in maintaining too-fluid boundaries between home and workplace—for Maggie, and then Lillian, are constantly getting calls at home to report to their employers.

Scholarship that traces the historical features of domestic work over the course of U.S. history has revealed that, into the first several decades of the twentieth century, this work came to be characterized as an "occupational ghetto" for black workers and especially for women in the U.S. South and along the Eastern Seaboard. In many places, including Washington, D.C., which became a center for black migration and a path out of southern share-cropping, domestic work slowly shifted from a labor category occupied du-ally by African Americans and newly arrived white ethnic immigrants to a primarily "black" occupation.[10] *Backstairs* highlights these racial shifts in the labor market, making explicit how beginning around World War I, many of these white ethnic immigrants were able to access job mobility (or simply aged out of the occupation, in the case of Maggie's coworker). In the series, the White House staff diminished to reflect the changing times, when shift-ing social norms and new technologies shaped the changing nature of service work. But most of those who remained "in service" were the long-standing African American workers—who continued to be segregated by status and pay differentials between the "upper levels" of domestic work. As one ex-ample, the high-status position of head housekeeper, throughout the entire span of time covered by the series, is always a white woman.

In a manner similar to the conclusion of *Roots*, the ending of *Backstairs* portrays Lillian Rogers Parks's exit from her job as a White House maid and seamstress. The final scenes show her slowly walking down the stairs and away from the home that had been both her—and her mother's—workplace, in turn dramatizing the closing of the generational passing down of domestic work that until the mid-twentieth century, disproportionately characterized the contours of black women's lives in a place like Washington. As the historical record has shown, by 1970 black women were no longer laboring as domestic workers in disproportionate numbers: to illustrate, in 1940, almost 60 percent of employed black women were working in domestic service, but by 1970 this number had dropped to 18 percent and has continued to drop since.[11] The general consensus in the scholarship is that these revolutionary shifts were the result of both the decline of the occupation itself (I'll say more on that point below) but also the increasing availability of public service sector jobs that opened up for black women with the passing of the 1964 Civil Rights Act.

Taken together, the trajectory offered by *Roots*, then *Backstairs*, concluding right before pivotal civil rights gains and the mass exodus of black women (and men) from the occupational ghetto of domestic service, can be viewed as a liberatory narrative—especially one that pinpoints labor mobility with the escape from the paternalistic, familial connections that had defined this labor relationship since institutionalized slavery.

Backstairs at the White House and *Roots*: America's Very Own *Upstairs, Downstairs*

In a review of *Backstairs at the White House*, a *New York Times* writer called it the "American equivalent of Britain's 'Upstairs Downstairs,' as it traces the varied lives of servants and masters, and the special ties that bind them together."[12] The reviewer was making reference to what was at the time one of the most iconic televised images of servitude available for popular consumption. *Upstairs, Downstairs*, a British television hit that first aired in the United States in 1974 on public television's *Masterpiece Theatre*, offered a particularly intimate depiction of the occupation of domestic work and historical relations of servitude. One of the most widely viewed television shows ever to be distributed, the series follows the lives of the aristocratic Bellamy family and their "downstairs" staff in their London home for nearly thirty years, from the height of the Edwardian era to the early 1930s.

The series presents an image of Great Britain's "servant past," one that Lucy Delap suggests operated in multiple, complex ways for shaping connections of its contemporaneous viewers to a national heritage. One of the ways in which the text was received by audiences, critics, and scholars alike involved an interpretation of "nostalgia, set against a sense of late-twentieth-century social disintegration." Within this reading, the appeal of such a narrative for specifically U.S. audiences arguably rested in its soothing depiction of what lead actor David Langton referred to as a sense of everyone "knowing their place: it was ordered, disciplined, and people knew where they stood."[13] Particularly for audience members in its original broadcast period—in the context of social and cultural changes of the mid-twentieth century—this nostalgic vision created a "high cultural" space that conflated national identity with a conservative domestic structure and reasserted the strict class hierarchies that defined the master-servant relationship. As Carl Freedman suggests,

> the house at 165 Eaton Place (in which nearly all of the action of *Upstairs Downstairs* takes place) comes to serve as a figure for an England that . . . never quite existed. . . . At the same time, it is an England that well corresponds to what England in the early seventies dearly wished itself to have been and perhaps even to be once again: an all-white society unified by certain generally accepted English values, and one in which class struggle, for the most part, could be charmingly sublimated into domestic foibles and occasional minor tensions between upstairs and downstairs.[14]

In essence, Freedman argues that the Bellamy household and staff—as well as the house itself—can be interpreted as a nostalgic vision for unified national identity, one in which familial labor relationships neatly contained (national) class conflicts.

But as Delap has noted, the success of the series depended on its ability to circulate a range of themes, particularly as it highlighted the lived social experience of the "downstairs" workers that generated an interest in family history and a previously suppressed national heritage.[15] As with *Roots* and *Backstairs*, this kind of new social history ethos relied on representing life "from below." Jean Marsh, cocreator of the series, noted that in depicting the difficult conditions of servitude in early-twentieth-century Britain, "we wanted to show that it was boiling in the kitchen and freezing in the attic."[16] *Upstairs, Downstairs*, similar to *Backstairs at the White House*, was based on a best-selling published memoir chronicling the firsthand experiences of a domestic worker toiling under old structures of servitude. These memoirs—like Haley's emotional "factional" novel on which the *Roots* miniseries was based—offered personal, intimate details of history. Drawing from novels, memoirs, and historical archives, both *Roots* and a *Masterpiece* production like *Upstairs, Downstairs* emphasized emotional and affective connections to the subjugated past in a way that was informed by the new social history movement.[17]

Significantly, the televised version of *Upstairs, Downstairs* did not focus entirely on the lives of domestic workers, but as the title suggests, on the complex relationship between "servants" and their "masters." The upstairs-downstairs device was specifically about dramatizing marginality as it operated through the master-servant power dynamic and the intimacy of historical power relations in the domestic setting. As such, the "domestic foibles" that played out "between upstairs and downstairs" (to which Freedman refers) were central to allegorizing national oppressions. At the center of this narrative was a particular labor dynamic that represented the class relationships structuring the national order—one that placed struggles "from below" directly at the center, while also highlighting the power structures in which these were embedded

As I have suggested, for *Roots*, the "family" as national past was symbolized through the domestic labor relationships that formed a complex and troubled hierarchy of national identity. Similarly, *Backstairs at the White House*, which merged presidential history with the unique features of racialized domestic service that epitomized this history, presented an apt metaphor for these foundational formations of U.S. national identity. If *Upstairs, Downstairs* can be read as a representation of Great Britain's historical class relations through its depiction of the servant past, both *Roots* and *Backstairs* offer a version of U.S. history that depicted how the nation's economic racism played out in everyday domestic life and affected those subjected to these systems over the course of a two-hundred-year economy defined by racialized servitude. As Patricia Williams points out in her use of the "upstairs downstairs" metaphor, "the American phenomenon of black help in white families is overlaid not with the famously cool condescension of the British, but with the radically invasive paternalism in which black servants are often proclaimed to be "just like family."[18] This paternalism is rooted in the historical structures of racialized slavery that formed the basis of twentieth-century domestic work for women like Lillian Rogers Park. Connecting the theme of paternalistic family relations from slavery to the transition into low-paid, exploitative domestic work, both *Roots* and *Backstairs* illustrated a narrative of racial progress in a way that pinpointed the structure of racial oppression in the intimacy of the domestic sphere—and the eventual escape from the "master-servant" dynamic.

In the 1970s, the archaic relations of domestic work, structured around racial hierarchies, seemed to be all but disappearing from the U.S. social and economic landscape. In fact, this was the decade that sociologists, among them Lewis Coser, infamously predicted the disappearance of the occupation altogether, and with it the old structural hierarchies they had come to represent.[19] What texts like *Roots* and *Backstairs at the White House* did in this context (just as *Upstairs, Downstairs* and similar depictions of the "servant past" did in Great Britain) was articulate a shift away from the paternalistic labor oppression that came to characterize the telling of African American history. Narratives of progress and upward mobility were structured around themes of escape from these labor relations, which had also historically been tied to intimate, and oppressive, "family-like" relationships.

As Judith Rollins astutely notes, relations of servitude have reflected "a contradiction between egalitarian values and actual class and caste stratification" that has defined the contours of U.S. history.[20] Shows like *Roots* and *Backstairs* exposed these contradictions in a way that was in line with the political and cultural climate of their era, particularly following the "public relations" disaster of the civil rights movement for the United States. With their new social history ethos, they offered a challenge to—and a narrative of escape from—the paternalistic power dynamic that had defined at least two centuries of U.S. economic racism. To an extent, the ease at which these texts placed racist oppressions in the quickly disappearing system of servitude can be seen as a way to obscure contemporary operations of power, by suggesting a too-easy narrative of racial progress. But by making explicit how the condescending familialism of racialized servitude underscored both public and private social histories, both *Roots* and *Backstairs* offered ways to bring intimate experiences of oppression into the overarching narrative of U.S. historical knowledge.

Conclusion

While highly successful during its initial airing, *Backstairs at the White House* seems to have all but disappeared from public consciousness, particularly when compared with the staying power of *Roots*. Database searches for news stories or academic articles turn up almost nothing following its airing—until the release of Lee Daniels's *The Butler* in 2013, when some reviewers noted explicit connections between the two productions.

In the 2013 film, the narrative bridges centuries of African American labor history with contemporary political subjectivity. While the story begins in the early twentieth century, the expansive shots of black workers farming southern cotton fields load the text with historical meanings of slavery, referencing its agricultural basis (particularly the iconic cotton imagery that has marked historical perceptions of this institution in the South) and the sharecropping system that never quite allowed the culture of the plantation labor structure to fully die after the Civil War. The opening scenes further solidify the film's underlying message about paternalistic servitude: regardless of how much black folks are connected to white folks through shared land, lives, and needs, racism merges in an incredibly volatile way into political and economic oppression—to the point where a child is subject to viewing his father's violent death because he spoke up to the white man who owned the property on which his family toiled.

Throughout *The Butler*, the audience is asked to grasp the centrality of domestic work to twentieth-century paths of upward mobility and historical progression, particularly as a way out of sharecropping, which historically defined both poverty and racial subservience. Cecil, the lead character, establishes a life in Washington, D.C., and secures middle-class stability through his occupation, even as he struggles with a life of racially defined servitude. The film itself is a prototypical civil rights narrative, carefully crafted in relation to the stifling and demanding subjection of life as a domestic worker, and in fact, Cecil's service to the White House plays out as a narrative contrast to his son's participation in multiple mid-century liberation struggles. Eventually, Cecil's retirement is conflated with his transition into political consciousness, for when he leaves his job at the White House, he makes amends with his son and joins a group protest. In this way, the film—in a way that is distinctive from *Backstairs* and *Roots*—connects movement out of servitude specifically with a growing *political* consciousness. The conclusion of *The Butler* centers on the election of Barack Obama in 2008, explicitly tracing a path from a period when black workers could only *serve at* the White House—to a period of the first sitting African American president.

Since the emergence of texts like *Roots* and *Backstairs*, films like *The Butler* have called on their foundational 1970s storytelling traditions. While the "archaic" systems of domestic servitude no longer seem to characterize the majority of African American political and economic struggles (at least not in the popular imagination), these more recent tales often draw from these past events to articulate a narrative of political mobility, often by making reference to the distinctive connections between civil rights–era gains and movements away from domestic work. Civil rights films like *The Long Walk Home* (1990) and *The Help* (2011) are two examples, narrating mid-century liberation movements through personal stories of domestic workers who challenge both legal and economic racism. And, similar to their 1970s predecessors, both *The Help* and *The Butler* offer this representation of political history through an escape from the oppressive master-servant dynamic. Even *The Help* concludes with a scene that parallels the conclusion of *Backstairs at the White House*: this time, Aibileen (Viola Davis) walks slowly, headed north, down a long road away from her employer, who represents the small Mississippi's town's generations-old oppressive system of domestic servitude.

Significantly, in the last few decades of the twentieth century, the exit from identifiable systems of in-house domestic service did not mean an end to racial stratification in the labor market—or an end to domestic service itself. The changing contours of economic racism—including the shift to institutionalized service work and the emergence of a new "servant class" in the form of a globalized, immigrant workforce—continue to underscore structures of oppression in the United States and beyond.[21] Today, as was the case in the 1970s, the placement of these struggles in household labor structures of the past has the potential to obscure contemporary oppressions, drawing on a conservative sense of nostalgia that neatly "domesticates" national tensions and obscures current social dynamics.

As such, twenty-first-century historical films have raised anxieties about the return of representations of potentially idealized master-servant relationships, precisely at the historical moment where these no longer define the reality of many African American lives. This anxiety about the ideological work of historical representations was particularly evident surrounding the release of *The Help*, which stirred an incredible amount of controversy due to what many saw as the unquestioned return of the mammy figure, inaccurate depictions of civil rights history, and particularly, the telling of black women's liberation through a white woman's bildungsroman. In fact, this tension has underscored all of the texts mentioned above: from *Roots* to *The Butler*, critics and viewers ponder whether African American history can be legible only when maintaining whiteness at the center.

But arguably, the nostalgia of these texts operates in complex ways, disrupting the straightforward notion that they are simply recalling racially unequal "master-servant" dynamics. Considering the parallels between contemporary films and their predecessors, films like *The Butler* and *The Help* draw from a new social history perspective to disrupt the notion that race relations can be neatly represented as untroubled family histories. In line with Lucy Delap's analysis, by utilizing an "upstairs, downstairs" trope to retell history "from below," these texts highlight the ways that this particular form of subjugation has been central to the formation of labor consciousness, political consciousness, and ultimately, national history. As such, while it is certainly necessary to continue reflecting critically on how these representations might obscure contemporary power dynamics, we can also reflect on how they represent a relational understanding of African American history—but one that insists on keeping African American perspectives at the center of the narrative. As such, these portrayals of the past, particularly by drawing from the storytelling tradition offered by new social history, offer a space for representing political subjectivity in a changing context of power and oppression.

As Rymsza-Pawlowska argues about the complex role of "nostalgia" in texts like *Roots*, portrayals of the past—especially those that draw from the new social history movement—are also about drawing connections to "social problems that [are] unresolved and ongoing."[22] In the way that *Roots* helped to reshape national conversations about contemporary racial struggles by presenting a new social history of U.S. slavery, texts chronicling twentieth-century oppressions create room for continuously drawing connections to the present day. Contemporary forms of "heritage nostalgia" like *The Help* and *The Butler* offer a vision of emerging political consciousness, one that is not solely tied to older systems of racism and economic oppression, but also allows for consideration of the parallel processes of economic and political racism that persist in our current moment.

NOTES

1. Malgorzata Rymsza-Pawlowska, "Broadcasting the Past: History Television, 'Nostalgia Culture,' and the Emergence of the Miniseries in the 1970s United States," *Journal of Popular Film and Television* 42, no. 2 (June 2014): 81–90, 86.

2. Maxine Baca Zinn, Stanley D. Eitzen, and Barbara Wells, *Diversity in Families*, 10th ed. (Boston: Pearson Education, 2015), 30.

3. "*Roots* as Untold History," *Pioneers of Television*, PBS, February 5, 2013, http://www.pbs.org/wnet/pioneers-of-television/video/roots-as-untold-history/, accessed June 30, 2016.

4. Ibid.

5. Michael Kraus and Davis D. Joyce, *The Writing of American History*, rev. ed. (Norman: University of Oklahoma Press, 1985), 370–379.

6. For in-depth discussion of new methodological approaches developed in the new social history of the family, see especially Sheila McIsaac Cooper, "Historical Analysis of the Family," in *Handbook of Marriage and the Family*, 2nd ed., edited by Marvin B. Sussman, Suzanne K. Steinmetz, and Gary W. Peterson (New York: Plenum Press, 1999), 13–38, and Jay D. Schvaneveldt, Robert S. Pickett, and Margaret H. Young, "Historical Methods in Family Research," in *Sourcebook of Family Theories and Methods: A Contextual Approach*, edited by Pauline G. Boss et al. (New York: Plenum Press, 1993), 99–116.

7. Baca Zinn, Eitzen, and Wells, *Diversity in Families*, 30.

8. See Lauren R. Tucker and Hemant Shah, "Race and the Transformation of Culture," *Critical Studies in Mass Communication* 9, no. 4 (1992): 325–336, for a brilliant analysis of the context of production surrounding the *Roots*.

9. Tucker and Shah, "Race and the Transformation of Culture," 334. Also see Leslie Fishbein, "*Roots*: Docudrama and the Interpretation of History," in *American History, American Television: Interpreting the Video Past*, edited by John O'Connor (New York: Ungar Press, 1983), 279–305.

10. See also Elizabeth Clark-Lewis, *Living In, Living Out: African American Domestics in Washington, D.C., 1910–1940* (Washington, D.C.: Smithsonian Institution Press, 1994), and David M. Katzman, *Seven Days a Week: Women and Domestic Service in Industrializing America* (New York: Oxford University Press, 1978).

11. Judith Rollins, *Between Women: Domestics and Their Employers* (Philadelphia: Temple University Press, 1985), 56. Also see Pierrette Hondagneu-Sotelo, *Domestica: Immigrant Workers Cleaning and Caring in the Shadows of Affluence* (Berkeley: University of California Press, 2007), 16.

12. John J. O'Connor, "TV View: Another Step in Recognizing the Black Experience," *New York Times*, February 4, 1979, D/33.

13. Ibid. Lucy Delap, *Knowing Their Place: Domestic Service in Twentieth-Century Britain* (Oxford: Oxford University Press, 2014), 212.

14. Carl Freedman, "England as Ideology: From *Upstairs, Downstairs* to *A Room with a View*," *Cultural Critique* 17 (winter 1990–1991): 79–106, 82.

15. Delap, *Knowing Their Place*, 209.

16. Cited in ibid., 212; originally in Richard Marson, *Inside Updown: The Story of "Upstairs, Downstairs"* (Bristol, U.K.: Kaleidoscope, 2005).

17. See Rymsza-Pawlowska, "Broadcasting the Past."

18. Patricia J. Williams, review of *Living in, Living Out*, by Elizabeth Clark-Lewis, *Contemporary Sociology* 25, no. 2 (March 1996): 148–151, 149.

19. See Lewis A. Coser, "Servants: The Obsolescence of an Occupational Role," *Social Forces* 52, no. 1 (1973): 31–40.

20. Rollins, *Between Women*, 48.

21. See Evelyn Nakano Glenn, "From Servitude to Service Work: Historical Continuities in the Racial Division of Paid Reproductive Labor," *Signs* 18, no. 1 (autumn 1992): 1–43; Hondagneu-Sotelo, *Domestica*; and Barbara Ehrenreich and Arlie Russell Hochschild, eds., *Global Woman: Nannies, Maids, and Sex Workers in the New Economy* (New York: Metropolitan Books, 2003).

22. Rymsza-Pawlowska, "Broadcasting the Past," 84.

CHAPTER SIX

Letting America Off the Hook

Roots, Django Unchained, and the Divided White Self

C. RICHARD KING AND DAVID J. LEONARD

The airing of *Roots* in 1977 transformed a nation. Disrupting the systemic silence surrounding the history of slavery and enslavement in the United States, *Roots* was more than a miniseries. It was a movement; it was a demand for reconciliation and a national conversation about race and racism. At the same time, it sought to transform the televisual landscape and the persistence of invisibility, antiblack stereotypes, and the all-white-all-the-time television scheduling. As such, its importance rests with its refusal to be silent about the horrors of slavery in the United States and the experiences of African Americans. Its significance rests with its refusal to bury history and its refusal to be silent about the centrality of slavery within African American life and the nation as a whole.

Within this context, this chapter offers a reading of *Roots* as it relates to blackness, Africa, and slavery, arguing that the film both challenges dominant narratives and representations of blackness, providing a counter narrative to the hegemonic tropes "happy slaves" and "uncivilized" "brutes" and "mammies." Its power rests with these counter voices and its challenges to dehumanizing stereotypes. Yet, as we turn to its treatment of whiteness, and more specifically whiteness and racism, we see a film less willing to take on issues of antiblack racism and the systemic realities of white supremacy. Arguing that the film is neither willing nor able to critically interrogate white supremacy as core to U.S. history, we conclude that *Roots* is unable to free itself from the trappings of white pleasure. The film's focus on white bodies and voices, its focus on the redemptive qualities of whiteness, and its inscription of a nation "progressing" toward a unified and authentic self limits its power and transformative possibilities.

This chapter, thus, looks at the ways that slavery and the evils of slavery were offered through a story of white southerners, rendering the American fabric and whiteness as unexamined and unscathed within the national imagination. Its reliance on the tropes of the American Dream and Horatio

Alger necessitated the erasure or dulling of white supremacy as a central component of the American Project. In other words, *Roots*, in its historic accounting of slavery, reinscribes longstanding fictions of a "divided white self" and slavery as fundamentally a southern enterprise rather than as a core U.S. practice. Concluding the piece with an exploration of *Django Unchained* (2012) and its same imaginary as it relates to white supremacy, whiteness, and the southern-northern divide, this chapter reflects on the ways *Roots* lets the nation off the hook even as it shines a spotlight on a history that white America continues to deny and erase from the national consciousness.

"A Novel for Television"

In a twenty-first-century media landscape marked by mass spectacles, niche audiences, on-demand streaming, and digital recording, it is easy to forget the importance of network programming in the late 1970s. It is easier still to underestimate the cultural impact and popular appeal of *Roots* when it aired in 1977.[1]

Not surprisingly, this miniseries had a significant impact throughout the United States. Despite its controversial topic, which some thought had the potential to force white America to reckon with the violent history of one of the nation's "original sins" (along with Native American genocide), Americans as a whole embraced the miniseries. Entire communities and corporations added cultural credence to the film through proclamations and events. Fifty cities declared "*Roots* Weeks" to coincide with the broadcast, 19–21 May 1977 were designated "Alex Haley Days" in his home state of Tennessee, and a department store in New York City hosted a "*Roots* Week" in May 1977, offering consumers genealogy tips and heritage lessons along with their shopping.[2] For a time, it saturated daily life, a seemingly ever-present feature of "conversations, radio call-in shows, classroom discussions, and religious sermons."[3]

Roots was not only popular, it transformed the media landscape. In addition to being among the earliest miniseries and the first to be broadcast on consecutive nights, *Roots* was part of an initial wave to demonstrate the power of docudrama, which "blend[ed] fact and fiction in a soap-opera package."[4] Moreover, it was the first to embrace multicultural themes, shifting a TV landscape that was clearly more receptive to televisual diversity and laying the groundwork for equally important miniseries like *Holocaust* (1978) and *Queen* (1993) and films like *The Color Purple* (1985) and *Django Unchained* (2012). It also facilitated new directions and opportunities for African Americans on television. Other production companies, buoyed by the success of *Roots*, aggressively pursued dramatic specials featuring African American storylines, including *All God's Dangers* (1974) and *Confessions of Nat Turner* (1967), neither of which ever aired on television.[5] Meanwhile, ABC aired *Roots:*

The Next Generation in 1979, and NBC, hoping to capitalize on the Zeitgeist, broadcast *King*, a docudrama about the civil rights leader, which might be deemed a modest success at best.[6] More importantly, *Roots* opened novel pathways for imagining African Americans and their experiences, making viable more complex narratives about African Americans as embodied and fully human characters. That is, the systemic dehumanization that was commonplace in U.S. popular culture, which had rationalized and justified antiblack racist violence from slavery to Jim Crow, was challenged with this groundbreaking miniseries. The depth and humanity brought to the screen was important for both television and the broader cultural landscape.

At the same time, *Roots* relied heavily on the nostalgia that is a powerful reflex to public memory. This is especially the case as it relates to U.S. racial memory, whereupon the past is both sanitized and simplified, rendered as a mere bump in the nation's journey toward racial reconciliation. Now several decades after its release, many have forgotten the controversies surrounding the release of *Roots*. Worse yet is that we have forgotten the struggles to get the film made, which, not surprisingly, often focused on concerns about the white audience—what would they think? will they even watch? will *Roots* alienate this key demographic? These financial and cultural concerns shaped ABC's production and marketing of the series.

For all of *Roots'* success, producers had deep misgivings about developing and broadcasting the miniseries, especially the manner in which white Americans would receive it. In fact, concerns about the content prompted the network's unusual move of scheduling the miniseries on consecutive nights rather than once weekly, as had previously proven successful for the format, such as with *Rich Man, Poor Man* (1976). As we show in this chapter, this was just one of several choices that reveal the efforts of producers to create a program that resonated with the preoccupations and precepts of the white racial frame, and hence ensure its appeal to a largely white audience.

From the start, "its producers primarily were concerned about attracting white viewers." According to Larry Sullivan, an ABC executive at the time, "Our concern was to put a lot of white people into the promos. Otherwise, we felt the program would be a turnoff." Another executive, Brandon Stoddard, echoed these sentiments: "we made certain to use actors white viewers had seen a hundred times before so they would feel comfortable."[7] Although LeVar Burton may be best remembered for his role in the miniseries, *Roots* featured a cavalcade of Hollywood stars—both black and white—including Richard Roundtree, Cicely Tyson, Scatman Crothers, Ben Vareen, Louis Gossett Jr., Ed Asner, Chuck Connors, Lloyd Bridges, and Lorne Greene. In addition to Burton, it also introduced the wider public to the acting talents of Maya Angelou. The familiar actors would be a source of identification. Likewise, black actors were chosen because their age, past roles, or their place in Hollywood contributed to white viewers' sense of safety, necessary to frame *Roots* as just another story, educational entertainment, rather than as a political accounting of the horrors of one of America's worst original sins: slavery.

Creating a comfortable feel for a broad U.S. public also demanded altering Haley's novel, which producers feared had the potential to alienate the white community. At a commercial level, and even with the more pedagogical hopes attached to the miniseries, producers elevated, if not re-centered, whiteness within a narrative about the African American experience within slavery. This is evident in an early scene in episode 1. After viewers are introduced to Africa, which is marked by its villages, women's exposed breasts, its "primitive" existence, and the lack of civilization, the film quickly turns to America, imagined as the embodiment of modernity, "civilization," and the "new world." The clothing, the "classical music," and the sophistication with which they speak of even slavery embodies the modernity of "the new world."

While the evils of whiteness, manifesting within slavery, will soon become visible, the beauty of a civilized (white) America anchors the story. Associating whiteness with modernity and civilization as foundation for this (African) American story are not the only narrative choices that sought to appease potential white audiences. In an effort to draw white viewers into the narrative, to both create characters of identification and fulfill desires to see whiteness as "goodness," the film departed from Haley's novel in other significant ways. It added new characters with whom white audiences would identify. Thus, the slaver captain, Davies (Ed Asner), is transformed from a rather nondescript and loathsome figure in the novel into one who harbors doubts about the morality of slavery, and is rendered as "honorable, innocent, and naive . . . a deeply religious family man . . . who begins his voyage on the Sabbath because it 'seems like the Christian thing to do.'"

When Captain Davies is first informed of the cargo of his new ship being slaves, he is clearly depicted as being at a moral crossroads. His values and Christian ethos put into question the prospect of his participating in the transatlantic slave trade. His ambivalence and concern continue during inventory of the ship's wrist shackles and neck rings. His discomfort at seeing "thumb screws" and the "branding iron" is clearly palpable. While in transit to the Zambia coast, Captain Davies is conspicuously concerned, pacing belowdecks. He is at conflict with himself, divided by slavery from his Christian and benevolent self. His demands to limit the number of enslaved Africans on his ship, his self-medication with rum, his anger over "fornication," the film's juxtaposition between Davies and Slater (Ralph Waite), who clearly finds pleasure in slavery, and his noticeable resentment that he *must* participate in system slavery embodies *Roots'* treatment of whiteness. The narrative juxtaposition of Slater, who is responsible for the dehumanizing conditions belowdecks, and Captain Davies, who expresses regret, brings the divided white self into clear focus. Slavery is figuratively and literally making the latter sick. Davies's anger and anguish resulting from a morally conflicted and divided white self does not cease after his arrival in America. His moral ambivalence is substantiated during a conversation with a slave broker, who, like Slater, seems OK with slavery as a political, economic, cultural, and moral enterprise:

> CAPTAIN DAVIES: Tell me, Mr. Carrington, do you have wonder?
>
> MR. CARRINGTON: On what topic, sir? To what end?
>
> CAPTAIN DAVIES: As to whether or not we are just as imprisoned as those chained in the hold below.
>
> MR. CARRINGTON: I do not follow your meaning, Sir.
>
> CAPTAIN DAVIES: It sometimes feels that we do harm to ourselves by taking part in this endeavor.
>
> MR. CARRINGTON: Harm? What harm can there be in prosperity, sir? What harm is a full purse?
>
> CAPTAIN DAVIES: No—I'd doubt you like to know, Mr. Carrington. I doubt that either of us would truly like to know.

The focus on Captain Davies, and his juxtaposition with those corrupted by greed and slavery, such as Mr. Ames (Vic Morrow), who is presented as the embodiment of evil, alongside the narrative placement of complicit blacks, who capture, brutalize, and otherwise aid slavery, embodies the film's focus on individual choices, morality, and division. Slavery had divided white America and whiteness. In one scene, Mr. Ames, Mr. Reynolds (Lorne Greene), and Dr. William Reynolds (Robert Reed) debate whether Africans are born "slaves" or need to be "made into slaves." This conversation reveals a division on race and on the natural order of things, and a divided white self.

Throughout the miniseries, whiteness is cast in terms of binaries: good and evil, North and South, modern and archaic, and civilized and uncivilized. Slavery had divided whiteness and thus requires reunification. Writing about *Birth of a Nation* (1915), *The Littlest Rebel* (1935), *Gone with the Wind* (1939), *Raintree County* (1957), and *Glory* (1990), Hernán Vera and Andrew Gordon argue that these representations are "defined by the sincere fictions of the white self" but also a sense of disunity resulting from the sins and stains of slavery.

> What we find in these movies is a persistence across time in representations of the ideal white American self, which is constructed as powerful, brave, cordial, kind, firm, and generous: a natural-born leader.
>
> We also find that the Civil War is used as a means to dramatize a split in the white self. These movies are not about white versus black but white versus white, narrativized in *Birth*, *Rebel*, and *Raintree* as North versus South, in *Gone with the Wind* as antebellum South versus post–Civil War South, and in *Glory*

as white liberal Northerner versus white bigoted Northerners. All the movies work toward a final reconciliation or reunification of the split white self, effected through marriage or family reunion in the first four films and through sacrificial death in battle in *Glory*. Blacks in each case are secondary characters coded to enhance certain properties of the white self.[8]

These changes highlight the invisible ways in whiteness impacted the film's narrative, its aesthetics, and its choices; whiteness colored the cultural production and reception of *Roots*. They also underscore a central tension of the post–civil rights United States: white-only and white supremacy no longer have a place in public culture or polite discourse, but white sensibilities and sentiments still dictate the limits of acceptability and intelligibility.

Of Human Bondage

While the focus on whiteness undoubtedly altered the miniseries and shifted the focus to white pleasure at the sight of a reunified white self, they did not drain the series of its capacity to offer counter-narratives or refigure blackness. The civil rights movement, among other movements, had modified the white racial frame, encouraging it to incorporate more positive images of African Americans. In fact, *Roots* exemplifies and advances this project. It centers on sympathetic black characters who are remarkable in television history: they display a range of human emotions, love and laugh, suffer and cry, struggle and strive, build families against the odds, stand up for what is right, and work hard. They are the heroes of this history, which champions the margins and encourages its audience to identify with their plight, if not with the people themselves. And a century after the end of slavery and a decade after the dismantling of legal segregation, it was easy for all Americans, certain they were on the right side of history in a nation beyond race, to want the best for these characters and to curse evil individuals and institutions, even as they enjoyed their legacies in the form of white privilege and accrued wealth. Importantly, *Roots* did not simply have black protagonists; it also opted for an alternative narrative structure. Viewers witness much of the action in *Roots* from the point of view of the African American characters, a technique that not only shifts the focus of most television narratives, decentering whiteness, but also forces the audience to "see through a black man's eyes." Indeed, "*Roots* may have marked the first time many white people had been able to identify with blacks as people."[9] Perspective mattered, redirecting the flow of events, the values attachable to them, and interpretations of the audience.

These shifts made the miniseries especially powerful for African Americans. In speaking of the author and the series following Haley's death, Jesse

Jackson remarked, "He made history talk . . . he lit up the long night of slavery. He gave our grandparents personhood. He gave *Roots* to the rootless."[10] It not only endowed its characters but embodied agents with personhood, situating them in history. For Jackson and many others, *Roots* offered a kind of counter-reading of history and society that opened up new possibilities. As Herman Gray asserts, "For an entire generation of young blacks, *Roots*, also opened—enabled, really—a discursive space in mass media and popular culture within which contemporary discourses of blackness developed and circulated. . . . I would place *Roots* in dialogue with the reactivation and renewed interest in black studies and the development of African-centered rap and black urban style."[11]

The miniseries encouraged or at least contributed to the articulation of a counter-public that validated submerged narratives and efforts to excavate them. What's more, these effects were not limited to the African American community: "*Roots* helped to alter slightly, even momentarily interrupt, the gaze of television's idealized white middle-class viewers and subjects . . . [and] enabled a temporary but no less powerful transitional space within which to refigure and reconstruct black television representations."[12]

Roots tells a decidedly U.S. story, one that insists on reframing the nation, its people, and their place in the world. On the one hand, it foregrounds movement and forced relocation, the dialectics between Africa and the Americas. As such, it highlights the diasporic heritage and condition of African Americans. For example, its efforts to document the "coming of age of Kunta Kinte," in the form of rituals toward manhood, or foreground music or Islamic religious practice disrupt the dehumanizing narratives central to white supremacy. On the other hand, it romanticizes and rehabilitates Africa. It pictures it as a motherland, an origin point, and Eden. While arguably superficial and akin to a "Smithsonian exhibit," its representation challenged prevailing, largely imperial, images of Africa as a backward and savage place, populated by wild beasts and equally exotic and dangerous peoples.[13] While the opening credits roll with multiple shots of animals roaming the prairies of West Africa, only to be followed by the camera's focused gaze on several bare-chested women, the initial images in *Roots* offer a glimpse at the daily lives of those living in the Gambia. From kids playing to family breakfast, the representational field is distinct from the hegemonic signifiers of the late 1970s.

Consequently, *Roots* made it possible for Americans, especially African Americans, to reimagine Africa, encouraging trends already in motion that fostered identification and connection. Or, as Manthia Diawara put it, "Afrocentricity could not have existed without *Roots*."[14] While media portrayals of Africa since 1977 have often recycled familiar clichés about superstitious savages and tribal passions, the significance of the miniseries in its moment and within the African American community cannot be overstated.

While *Roots* offers sympathetic black characters and ostensibly tells the story from the black point of view, the importance of retaining the white audience limited how far or how deeply the miniseries could explore; the white gaze confines the narrative and its representational field in profound ways. Addressing slavery, much less white supremacy, on its face, appears too negative, too extreme for prime time. After all, Americans had not (and still have not) come to terms emotionally, economically, or culturally with the histories and legacies of human bondage in the United States. Even with these structural constraints, *Roots* not only successfully reworks blackness, it also skillfully negotiates the challenges posed by remembering slavery in a (white) nation that would rather not talk about it. As Herman Gray suggests,

> There is little doubt that the success of *Roots* helped to recover and reposition television constructions and representations of African Americans and blackness from their historic labors on behalf of white racism and myths of white superiority. But the miniseries also contributed significantly to the transformation, in [the?] popular imaginary, of the discourse of slavery and American race relations between blacks and whites. That is to say, with *Roots* the popular media discourse about slavery moved from one of almost complete invisibility (never mind structured racial subordination, human degradation, and economic exploitation) to one of ethnicity, immigration, and human triumph . . . this quality is precisely what made the television series a huge success.[15]

When initially aired, the miniseries simultaneously represented slavery and repositioned it. While it arguably romanticizes it and holds under erasure important historical elements, importantly, it dramatizes the violence, exploitation, and dehumanization: slaves beaten and raped, families torn apart, the dismemberment of Kunta Kinte (who loses a foot as punishment), the loss of autonomy, and perpetual servitude.[16] But *Roots* is not a catalog of horrors or an unceasing lament; rather, as Gray asserts, it recasts the slave narrative as a more universal tale of striving for betterment and incorporation, in which the protagonists operate without sovereignty and in the shadow of social death. In a sense, it becomes a reframed immigrant story, albeit rooted in forced migration. It is very much these positive elements of the narrative that gave the miniseries such broad appeal in its day: it spoke a truth about past ills of slavery, showed individuals in a family unit struggling over time for a better life, and held under erasure uneasy questions raised by the lives of its heroes. In a sense, the story of the slave became a U.S. story, joining the master narrative; it became a universal narrative available to all.

Even as *Roots* focused on a single African (American) family ensnared in the brutality and exploitation of slavery, the miniseries opted to tell a more familiar, affirming narrative. Even as it dwells on suffering, loss, and inequity, as a whole, the teleplay offers "a fable of American incorporation."[17] It reworked the classic American myth of individuals who through hard work, initiative, and perseverance make a better life for themselves and their families—they pull themselves up by their bootstraps. Or, as Herman Gray phrased it, the miniseries was a "realization of the American dream."[18] And, according to Louis Kushnick, "*Roots* represents a variant on the Horatio Alger theme of individual striving and individual success which lies at the heart of the American Dream."[19] Framing the African Diaspora in this manner demands accentuating common themes, reworking the stories of those forcibly transported and enslaved to sound like those of other ethnic groups. In other words, even as *Roots* sought to offer a faithful account of diaspora and slavery, it did so through "a generic tale of the classic immigrant success story."[20] While the narrative recasts the African American experience through an immigrant story, with its emphasis on perseverance, bootstrapism, and the promise of a post-emancipation nation, the focus on the American Dream was equally about reimagining a nation where the end of slavery brought about a reunified white self. Slavery threatened U.S. exceptionalism and divided the "modern" and "benevolent" white Americans from their evil brethren. The fulfillment of the American Dream was not evident simply in the film's recasting of slavery and emancipation as a story of immigrants, but through its imagination of an undivided white America.

Importantly, for viewers, likely more so for whites than blacks, the miniseries stops at a happy place. It ends with emancipation, a kind of figurative return to Eden or a release to the Promised Land. Here, history and hence oppression cease, as well—a variant on the "they all lived happily ever after" closing familiar from fairy tales. This, of course, allows the universal immigrant tale to remain in place; the American dream is untarnished, and whiteness remains a marker of modernity, benevolence, civility, and goodness. It also lets (white) viewers and (white) society off the hook.

The historic representation of slavery, and its aftermath, does little to account for the endemic nature of white supremacy; slavery and its legacies in the form of Jim Crow segregation, political terrorism, economic exploitation, lynchings, and bigotry are problems that plagued white America for decades after emancipation. As part of its narrative of racial progress, a divided white self, a nation working to reconcile itself, and the critiques of the racism that flourished after the end of slavery remain stifled. Instead, both *Roots* and its successor, *Roots: The Next Generations*, center whiteness. Thus, the new *Roots* continued to let white people, and the nation's entrenched white supremacy, off the hook *even as it depicted* the political terrorism of Reconstruction, the emergence of the Klan, and the attempts to prevent black men like Kunta Kinte's descendant, Tom, from exercising their new right to vote. Racism was a phase, a manifestation of evildoers, and the legacies of provincial thinking; it was a chapter that had to be reconciled as America became one.

This interpretation of the past fits both miniseries' neoliberal, bootstraps multiculturalism that has become a hallmark of the United States since the late twentieth century. In the end, racial reconciliation and the fulfillment of the American Dream emerge from exceptional heroes. This interpretation is about individuals who rise above, who remain faithful to family against all odds, who remain loyal to self and nation, who know where they come from, and who know their true names. Just as Kunta Kinte struggled to remain true to himself so he could enjoy the spoils of the American Dream, the decision by white people to resist slavery, to be true to their authentic Christian white selves, empowers them to enjoy the essence and exceptionalism of the American Dream.

This is especially true for the character of Ole' George Johnson (Brad Davis), a poor white southerner who, along with his wife, Martha (Lane Binkley), was forced from his land at the start of the Civil War. When a starving George knocks on the door of Mathilda (Olivia Cole), George, Irene (Lynne Moody), and Lewis (Hilly Hicks), they look beyond his whiteness and help the man. They feed him and welcome him into their home; they offer aid and comfort to his wife, as well. And from our initial introduction, it is clear that Ole' George is different: he refers to Mathilda as "Ma'am," averting his eyes. He shows Tom respect, calling him "sir." His behavior and his background make it clear that he is not part of the white planter elite. In fact, when Master Sam Harvey (Richard McKenzie) offers Ole' George a job as an overseer, George doesn't even know what an overseer is and thus has to be taught how to enact racism. As a poor white person, Ole' George has no idea about the logics of slavery and white supremacy.

In an effort to save all of them, Tom and Lewis are forced to teach him to be white. In other words, it is through racism that he is unified with the divided white self. Upon learning the requirements from Tom and Lewis, George refuses to participate in a system of violence and degradation.

> TOM: We're gonna learn Ole' George here about overseeing.
>
> LEWIS: Huh? Why should we? I mean white folks make enough trouble for us as it is.
>
> TOM: Now you bein' an overseer, first thing you need is a whip. Can't be no overseer without whip. Suppose this here is your whip, and suppose you want this here slave to fetch yonder water. How you gonna get him to fetch that bucket? Go on, show him.
>
> OLE' GEORGE: [*Throws whip aside*] Excuse me, Lewis, y'all mind fetchin' me that bucket of water?
>
> TOM: [*Laughing along with Lewis*] That aint exactly how you go about it. Now, you watch, watch me good and I'ma show you how to talk to the slave.
>
> TOM: N*****!

LEWIS: Yas'sir.

TOM: Fetch me this bucket of water.

LEWIS: Ah, master, ask another N*****. I'sa powerful tired.

TOM: Tired, is you, you black trash?

LEWIS: Yas'sir.

TOM: Well, maybe this here [*bending whip*] will perk you up little.

LEWIS: No sir, Massa. Please don't whip me. . . .

TOM: You watchin' and learning?

OLE' GEORGE: No, I couldn't do that. I couldn't whip Louis. . . . You teaching me to be mean, Tom?

TOM: I'm teaching you how to stay alive and how to keep some skin on our backs. Don't ever call me "Sir" again, ya hear?

OLE' GEORGE: Yeah.

TOM: Massa.

OLE' GEORGE: N*****.

In this moment, Tom reminds them that in order for them—Tom, Lewis, and Ole' George—to survive, they must play their respective roles as master and slave. In the end, Ole' George reluctantly uses "the N word."

While emphasizing the theme of a divided white self, George and Martha reveal the potential for unification and redemption on multiple levels. At one level, the embrace of Ole' George by Sam Harvey, Jemmy Brent (Lloyd Bridges), and Senator Arthur Justin (Burl Ives) as long as he maintains the violent racist order of both slavery and sharecropping points to how racism is constructed as a means to reunify whiteness. Despite being offered the spoils of racism in the form of privilege, rights, and opportunities beyond their class position, George and Martha ultimately turn their backs on white racism. Even after Ole' George is hired as overseer rather than continuing as a sharecropper, unlike Tom and the Harvey family, who are forced to work off mysterious "debts," he refuses to play his role and see race. Yet, this all part of the plan, because eventually Tom, Ole' George, Martha, and the entire family free themselves from Brent, finding freedom through interracial resistance. Along the way, Ole' George struggles to find his way as he is offered whiteness. But in the end, he remains true to himself, bringing the nation and the divided white self together. Yet, at another level, Ole' George and Martha's eventual refusal to play their parts, their racial code switching or white double consciousness that leads them to pretend to be agents of white supremacy, all the while resisting and undermining the racial status quo, highlights the ways that color blindness is constructed as a source of freedom and liberation.

This is especially apparent when Ole' George paradoxically helps put out the fires of white supremacy by claiming his rights as an overseer during one pivotal scene. When the Klan arrives to whip Tom, Ole' George must choose sides. While initially staying inside his cabin despite prompting from Martha to stop them, since "like stays with like," he ultimately runs outside, announcing, "nobody whips my N***** but me," and takes up the lash himself in an effort to prevent the Klan from killing Tom. While struggling to fulfill his duties as a white male and yearning to bring his white self together, he can do so only through violence. A series of apologies and pronouncements ensue: While George apologizes for his actions, for becoming white, Irene thanks him for saving Tom's life. Lewis, recognizing his complicity, apologizes to Ole' George. Meanwhile, Martha counsels Bud (Todd Bridges), who wants to avenge the violence inflicted on his father through assaulting some whites. She reminds him that both she and Ole' George are white. He needs to judge people from their actions, not the color of their skin. Evident here and with Tom's defense of Ole' George ("he cannot help being white"), *Roots* sees color blindness as the path to liberation and freedom, as the means to a reunified and authentic United States. Likewise, in focusing on individual prejudice, whether that of Brent or Lewis, *Roots* lets America and its institutions off the hook. In seeing progress as leaving behind the racial baggage of the past, in positioning freedom and equity as coming from Ole' George and Tom simply refusing to "see" color, *Roots* falls short in terms of interrogating white supremacy and its structural location. And in this way, it sets the stage for subsequent representations of slavery and racism in the United States.

From *Roots* to *Django Unchained*

Indeed, the long shadow of *Roots* extended to 2012, when writer and director Quentin Tarantino released *Django Unchained* (hereafter *Django*) with much fanfare and ample public debate.[21] Reflecting both the typical style and narrative aesthetics of Quentin Tarantino, *Django* was a revenge fantasy chronicling a freed slave's efforts to exact revenge on his enslavers while freeing his enslaved wife. While publicizing the film, Tarantino went to great lengths to position *Django* as revolutionary, as a "game changer," and as an exceptional story that others in Hollywood had yet to tell. In doing so, he explicitly positioned his film against *Roots*. Describing *Roots* as "inauthentic" and "corny," Tarantino characterized *Django* as a corrective to the series. "When you look at *Roots*, nothing about it rings true in the storytelling, and none of the performances ring true for me either," he stated. "I couldn't get over how oversimplified they made everything about that time. It didn't move me because it claimed to be something it wasn't."[22]

Not satisfied with elevating his own film through denigrating and denying the transformative impact of *Roots*, Tarantino characterized *Django* in terms that have been used to describe *Roots* for decades. In an interview with the *Los Angeles Times*, Tarantino made this clear: "Even for the movie's biggest black detractors, I think their children will grow up and love this movie. I think it could become a rite of passage for young black males." Since the film purportedly provides black youths with a narrative and understanding of slavery, much of Tarantino's promotion of the film centered around its supposed impact and importance to black America. "I would be surprised if, in five years, that every black person in America hasn't seen my film," Tarantino later told *Ebony*. "I don't know if they are all going to see it on opening weekend, but within five years, everyone will have seen this movie. Why wouldn't you?"[23]

The irony in Tarantino's juxtaposition of *Django* with *Roots*, especially his celebration of his film as a corrective, is each film has whiteness as its center. In many ways, each focuses on white redemption; each falls short in accounting for white supremacy and its persistent roots, which—despite the abolition of slavery, the rise and fall of Jim Crow, and the civil rights movement—continues its grip on the fabric of the nation. Each is bound by a desire to comfort and amuse white viewers, to privilege their feelings and desires and to otherwise center whiteness. We pause here to give two important examples.

First, within the U.S. imagination, racism is imagined through the Klan; the signifiers of white supremacy are the white robe, burning crosses, and "rednecks." *Django* does little to disrupt this narrative, instead embracing and solidifying a comforting narrative that imagines racism as pathological and Southern, as fundamentally "un-American" and therefore exceptional. In one particular scene, *Django* recasts the Klan as bumbling fools: uneducated, uncivilized, and unrecognizable in their whiteness. In this way, Tarantino uses *Django* to remind viewers of the "divided white self." Not only replicating the entrenched Klanification of U.S. racism, the film turns this mainstream terrorist organization into a joke, a source of comic relief

Second, *Django* foregrounds the theme of racial redemption, which was also central to *Roots*. While not limited to narratives focused in or on the South, particularly those films dealing with the post-emancipation and Jim Crow eras, Hollywood has continued to make films that both center and celebrate whiteness as a source of both liberation and transformation. Imagining racial progress through interracial cooperation, white benevolence and brilliance, and the generosity of exceptional white people, the white Hollywood imagination continues to tell stories through white bodies and the presence of a white liberatory impulse. *Django* replicates this proven formula, using Schultz to appeal to its white audiences. Schultz sets Django and Broomhilda free, providing a pathway to not only a new life but also the possibility of both justice and revenge. Without Schultz, whose kindness, guile, and intelligence are invaluable to the revenge fantasy and the redemptive possibilities that anchor the film, freedom remains elusive, a "dream deferred." As Scott

Schomburg notes, "Schultz's one-handed hatred of slavery cannot evade the crisis of whiteness: the totalizing temptation for Schultz to remain the master even in his efforts to help vindicate Django."[24] *Django* takes the classic white savior narrative, with its emphasis on interracial "bromance"—what Donald Bogle describes as a "Huckfinn fixation," and remixes it insomuch as the methods deployed for redemption are those of violence and revenge.[25] *Roots*, while clearly cut from a different cloth than *Django*, similarly relies on the compassion, intelligence, and the redemptive possibilities of whiteness. Ole' George's actions, from his refusal to let the Klan kill Tom to his participation in their emancipation from Brent and the senator, reflect *Roots'* embrace of a narrative of racial redemption. Its positioning of George and Martha as ultimately good, yet tested by the spoils and privileges of whiteness, reveals the centrality of racial redemption. The relationships between Tom and Ole' George and between Martha and Bud further spotlight the ways that color blindness and the interracial buddy narrative operate together.

Whether reflecting on white filmmakers and courageous movie executives, their audiences, the carefully included white bodies within these cinematic fantasies, or the narrative focus on a reunified white self, it should be clear that the thirty-five years between *Roots* and *Django Unchained* saw little deviation in terms of the representation of whiteness within slavery. This sedimented narrative and representation reflects the unwillingness to critically interrogate whiteness and white supremacy, to spotlight the ways that antiblackness is at the core of the U.S. project. By redeeming whiteness as a unified identity and by focusing on the divided yet exceptional whiteness, Hollywood, from *Roots* to *Django*, lets both (white) America and racism off the hook, even for slavery.

Conclusion

One need not have seen *Roots* when it premiered in 1977 to have been touched by or to appreciate the manner in which it changed U.S. society. Unprecedented and unrivaled, the miniseries had a profound impact on television, media images of black people, and popular understanding of the national narrative. At the same time, in speaking to as broad an audience as possible, *Roots* fit itself within a white racial frame. As a consequence, the program did not foster reconciliation, reparation, or racial healing, any more than it prompted effective engagements with persistent inequality and ongoing oppression and their amelioration. Instead, for Euro-Americans, *Roots* affirmed universal messages about family, heritage, and the American dream, at once granting security amid the uncertainties of post–civil rights nation and spawning personal curiosities about their ancestors and their personal histories. Thus, whereas African Americans found in *Roots* an allegory of the diaspora, a larger history, and a collective struggle, Euro-Americans found inspiration to focus on the family and learn their small stories, permission in essence to turn away from the social and fixate on the self. *Roots* provided absolution for those "bad apples," providing redemption resulting in a reunified (white) self and nation. It provided a pathway to allow for focusing on individual choices and histories, to talk about race without racism, to talk about slavery without implicating the nation, to look outward rather than inward, and to otherwise extricate self from the messiness of race by a universal quest for origins. For all of this, in the current moment, it is difficult to imagine that a program like *Roots* could find such a large television audience today. That is its legacy and an important reminder of its cultural, political, and racial importance.

NOTES

This piece builds on C. Richard King's "What's Your Name? *Roots*, Race, and Popular Memory in Post–Civil Rights America," in *African Americans in Television: Race-ing for Ratings*, edited by David J. Leonard and Lisa A. Guerrero (Santa Barbara, Calif.: Praeger, 2013), 69–81.

1. David A. Gerber, "Haley's *Roots* and Our Own: An Inquiry into the Nature of a Popular Phenomenon," *Journal of Ethnic Studies* 5.3 (fall 1977): 87–111.

2. Helen Taylor, "'The Griot from Tennessee': The Saga of Alex Haley's Roots," *Critical Quarterly* 37, no. 2 (summer 1995): 46–62, 48; Gerber, "Haley's Roots and Our Own," 88.

3. Alison Landsberg, *Prosthetic Memory: The Transformation of American Remembrance in the Age of Mass Culture* (New York: Columbia University Press, 2004), 103.

4. Museum of Broadcast Communications, *Roots*, http://www.museum.tv/eotv /roots, accessed December 9, 2016.

5. Gerber, "Haley's Roots and Our Own," 88.

6. John De Vito and Frank Tropea, *Epic Television Miniseries: A Critical History* (Jefferson, N.C.: McFarland, 2010), 10.

7. Lauren R. Tucker and Hemant Shah, "Race the Transformation of Culture: The Making of the Television Miniseries *Roots*," *Critical Studies in Mass Communication* 9 (1992): 325–336, 328.

8. Hernán Vera and Andrew M. Gordon, *Screen Saviors: Hollywood Fictions of Whiteness.* (Lanham, Md.: Rowman & Littlefield, 2003), 17.

9. Landsberg, *Prosthetic Memory*, 103, 104.

10. Jesse Jackson quoted in Taylor, "'The Griot from Tennessee,'" 50.

11. Herman Gray, "The Politics of Representation in Network Television," in *Channeling Blackness: Studies on Television and Race in America*, edited by Darnell M. Hunt (New York: Oxford University Press, 2005), 155–174, 61.

12. Ibid.

13. Tucker and Shah, "Race the Transformation of Culture," 332.

14. Landsberg, *Prosthetic Memory*, 102.

15. Gray, "Politics of Representation in Network Television," 160–161.

16. "Responses to *Roots*," *Race and Class* 19, no. 1 (1977): 77–105.

17. Matthew Frye Jacobson, *Roots Too: White Ethnic Revival in Post–Civil Rights America* (Cambridge, Mass.: Harvard University Press, 2006), 43.

18. Gray, "Politics of Representation in Network Television," 161.

19. Louis Kushnick quoted in "Responses to *Roots*," 81.

20. Tucker and Shah, "Race the Transformation of Culture," 334.

21. This section builds on David J. Leonard's "Django Blues," *Crisis* (April 2013): 26–29, http://www.academia.edu/3249551/Django_Blues; this was further developed in David J. Leonard, "Django Blues: Whiteness and Hollywood's Continued Failures," in *Quentin Tarantino's "Django Unchained": The Continuation of Metacinema*, edited by Oliver C. Speck (New York: Bloomsbury, 2014). For additional discussion of *Django*, see William Jelani Cobb, "Tarantino Unchained," *New Yorker*, January 2, 2013, http://www.newyorker.com/online/blogs/culture/2013/01/how-accurate-is-quentin-tarantinos-portrayal-of-slavery-in-django-unchained.html, accessed January 2, 2013; Salamishah Tillet, "Quentin Tarantino Creates an Exceptional Slave," *Time*, December 25, 2012, http://inamerica.blogs.cnn.com/2012/12/25/opinion-quentin-tarantino-creates-an-exceptional-slave/, accessed November 10, 2013.

22. Kirsten West Savali, "Quentin Tarantino: *Roots* Was Inauthentic," December 27, 2012, http://newsone.com/2114168/quentin-tarantino-roots-inauthentic/, accessed January 5, 2015.

23. Erin Aubry Kaplan, "*Django* an Unsettling Experience for Many Blacks," *Los Angeles Times*, December 28, 2012, http://articles.latimes.com/2012/dec/28/entertainment/la-et-django-reax-2-20121228/2, accessed June 22, 2016; Amy Elisa Keith, interview, "Quentin Tarantino, Untamed," *Ebony*, December 12, 2012, http://www.ebony.com/entertainment-culture/interview-quentin-tarantino-untamed-999#axzz2kIfBa2ZA, accessed November 10, 2013.

24. Scott Schomburg, "The Enduring World of Dr. Schultz: James Baldwin, *Django Unchained*, and the Crisis of Whiteness," September 6, 2013, http://theotherjournal.com/2013/09/12/the-enduring-world-of-dr-schultz-james-baldwin-django-unchained-and-the-crisis-of-whiteness/#disqus_thread, accessed November 10, 2013.

25. According to Donald Bogle, in a Huckfinn fixation, "the white hero grows in stature from his association with the dusty black." See Donald Bogle, *Toms, Coons, Mulattoes, Mammies, and Bucks: An Interpretive History of Blacks in American Films* (New York: Continuum, 2001), 140.

CHAPTER SEVEN

The Black Military Image in *Roots: The Next Generations*

ROBERT K. CHESTER

Although less seen and discussed than the original televised version of *Roots*, the sequel, *Roots: The Next Generations* (*RTNG*), was nonetheless an important cultural event in its own right. Airing in seven two-hour episodes on ABC in February 1979, *RTNG* benefited from a production budget three times higher than that of its predecessor, costing around $16.5 million and employing over a thousand extras. A talented collection of black actors, including James Earl Jones, Irene Cara, and Ruby Dee, made up the ensemble cast alongside white stars such as Henry Fonda, Olivia de Havilland, and Marlon Brando.[1] Despite strong scheduling competition from the other networks (CBS and NBC ran high-profile movie premieres against it), the show fared well, earning a Nielsen rating of 27.8 percent for its debut on February 18.[2] Critical reception was generally positive, and all or part of the series was seen by around 22.5 million U.S. households (a hefty number, although significantly lower than the 32 million households that tuned in for the first *Roots*).[3]

The title sequence claims that the series is based in part on "Search," a book by Alex Haley, but no such work has ever been published. Instead, the narrative draws from the brief coverage of the late nineteenth and twentieth centuries in the final chapters of Haley's original *Roots*, and from hours of oral records, transcripts of which Haley gave to the liberal Jewish screenwriter Ernest Kinoy as the basis for Kinoy's teleplays (Kinoy wrote the first three episodes and supervised the writing of the remaining four).[4] White directors John Erman and Charles S. Dubin took charge of five episodes between them, while African Americans Lloyd Richards and Georg Stanford Brown (who also reprised his role as Tom Carver) directed one each. *RTNG* opens in 1882, approximately twelve years after the end of *Roots*, and follows the descendants of Kunta Kinte from post-Reconstruction Tennessee to Alex Haley's 1967 trip to the Gambia, where he located the village from whence slavers abducted his forebear two centuries earlier. As well as continuing to explore black Americans' African heritage, *RTNG* covers the racial and economic degradations of the Jim Crow South and the Great Depression, the service of African Americans in two world wars, and the radicalization of black political dissent in the 1960s.

As the subject of academic study, *RTNG* remains overshadowed by its older sibling. Scholars have examined audience reception of the sequel series, but little scrutiny has been paid to its representational politics.[5] The original *Roots* has received more attention and is accused (by Herman Gray and others) of soft-pedaling its attack on racism, ignoring black struggles in favor of an uplifting emphasis on the ascent from slavery to relative prosperity and security.[6] This critique might be leveled equally against *RTNG*, which foregrounds middle-class values in pursuit of the American dream as the family climbs from enslavement to business ownership, success in academics, and Alex Haley's eventual status as a celebrity author.

This chapter, however, suggests the presence of more subversive elements in the sequel. Exploring *RTNG*'s treatment of twentieth-century issues of assimilation, exclusion, and disaffection through the theme of black Americans serving in the U.S. military, I contend that the show creates a landmark departure from prevailing (and succeeding) narrative conventions of U.S. films and television series, in which black service was either overlooked or written into a simplistic, celebratory narrative of progress toward equality. Rather than emphasizing seamless multiracial unity or presenting war as a cure for prejudice and division (what we might call racial triumphalism), *RTNG* taps into African Americans' post–civil rights, post–Vietnam War reconsideration of assimilationism and military service as viable responses to exclusion. The experiences of Simon Haley (Alex's father) in World War I and Alex Haley in World War II situate black service and the challenges confronting black veterans not in a teleology of uplift and equalization, but as part of ongoing and shifting patterns of bigotry and betrayal. This constitutes a significant expression of a dissenting vision of war and its repercussions for U.S. racial formations, all the more so for its appearance on a major network reaching millions of the nation's homes.

Black Soldiers and Veterans in U.S. Popular Culture

At the time of *RTNG*'s release, there existed in U.S. culture a long-established practice among African American cultural producers and sympathetic whites of referencing black military service to challenge racial injustice. Such arguments were gradualist in tone, requesting integrationist reform as just reward for patriotic risk of life and limb. Recalling African American servicemen from the Revolutionary War hero Crispus Attucks to the black troops who fought overseas in the twentieth century, African Americans and their allies used remembrance of their military sacrifices as a way to chip away at the edifice of inequality.[7]

World War II lent such appeals special impetus. In U.S. popular culture, war against Nazi ideals of white supremacy gave rise to a new image of the U.S. military as a multiethnic, multiracial entity. Hollywood war films threw together on screen soldiers of diverse backgrounds, depicting the nation as far more democratic and united than it actually was.[8] After the Second World War, African Americans pressed harder the notion that the history of black service merited full and equal citizenship. Liberal white filmmakers addressed racism through military scenarios, creating narratives that called on Americans to shape in reality the democratic society envisioned in those wartime films.

Yet such stories were rare breaches of a rule of silence. It was more often the case that soldiers of color were altogether neglected. When the author Niven Busch's 1944 novel, *They Dream of Home*, was adapted for the screen (as *Till the End of Time*) in 1946, the character Perry Kinchloe, a black Pacific combat veteran, triple amputee, and labor rights activist in the book, was altered to a white character who was pointedly apolitical.[9] In postwar culture, Cold War conservatives' effort to undermine antiracism by associating it with communistic rabble-rousing also inhibited appeals to racial justice. The purge of the Hollywood left in the late 1940s and early 1950s saw the FBI and the House Un-American Activities Committee (HUAC) target progressives who had produced antiracist World War II films or positive images of veterans of color.[10] Postwar Hollywood began promulgating a form of racial triumphalism suggesting that antifascist warfare had cured the malady of prejudice (or that race was never an issue in the first place), so that no "race problem" remained to be solved—1952's *Red Ball Express* is an illustrative example.[11]

Alongside the many combat stories, the travails of white veterans were well represented in postwar popular culture, while black GIs' often difficult homecomings received little attention. Where he did feature, the black veteran, rather than acting as an agent in his own future, was reduced to a passive vessel by which a bigoted white's reformation is enacted. For example, Universal Studios' *Bright Victory* (1951) centers on a friendship between white and black southerners, each recuperating in a hospital for blinded WWII veterans. Once the white GI realizes that his companion is black, the relationship is shattered. The two quickly reconcile, though, as the black soldier is instantly open to forgiving the white after the latter makes his apologies.

Away from the screen, more leeway existed for black artists to express dissent. In William Blackwell Branch's 1951 play, *A Medal for Willie*, the mother of a southern black Korean War hero rejects the medal her son has been posthumously awarded, hurling it at the general who has come to present it. "Willie should'a had that machine gun over here," she says. "So you can take this medal back on up to Washington and tell 'em I don't want it! Take it back! Pin it on your own shirt! Give it to the ones who keeps this big lie goin' and send boys like my Willie all over the world to die for some kind'a freedom and democracy they always gets the leavin's of!"[12] *A Medal for Willie* articulates a challenge to racial triumphalism that gained momentum through the 1950s, as national war-weariness and Cold War anxieties were exacerbated by the unpopular stalemate of the Korean War (1950–1953). By the early 1960s, left-ist filmmakers, free of the blacklist, began to represent the U.S. military as an institution corrupted by prejudice. In Carl Foreman's 1963 World War II film, *The Victors*, for example, a group of white GIs enters an Italian bar and se-verely beats a pair of African American soldiers. Only the blacks are arrested by the military police.

Changing Images in the 1960s and 1970s

From the mid-1960s into the 1970s, the cultural climate facilitated further cri-tiques of racism in U.S. military history. Gradualist approaches to inequality and exclusion lost credence in black communities. Having fought hard and long for legislative change, African Americans grew increasingly frustrated with the slow pace of reform and the bitter way in which whites contested it. "Every advance revealed a new wall," wrote Lerone Bennett Jr. in a 1963 article for *Ebony*. "Every step forward revealed unbearably the precise nature of the American racial system: naked and violent power organized in the de-fense of special privilege."[13] These circumstances induced rising militancy, with the Black Panthers and the Nation of Islam endorsing armed resistance against and cultural separation from an oppressive white society. Spokes-men such as Stokely Carmichael and Malcolm X derided black participation in the U.S. military as misguided subservience to white power, mocking the once-venerated sacrifices of men such as Crispus Attucks. Malcolm X's 1965 autobiography (written on X's behalf by Alex Haley) recounts how he avoided conscription in 1943 by informing an army psychiatrist that he hoped to "get sent down South" in order to "Organize them nigger soldiers, you dig? Steal us some guns, and kill crackers!"[14] War in Vietnam further strained black Americans' relationship with the military, piquing black leaders who consid-ered it the expansion of white supremacist policies overseas. In the late 1960s, as conservatives inveighed against the antiwar movement and the cause of racial equality, the Black Panther leader Eldridge Cleaver accused them of "fighting the same war" on "different terrain." "Black Americans are consid-ered to be the world's biggest fools to go to another country to fight for some-thing they don't have for themselves," he claimed.[15]

The Vietnam-era military was far removed from the seamless cohesion imagined in so many World War II films. Displays of black power allegiance were commonplace among African American servicemen, while the unequal treatment of black troops provoked violent interracial clashes on army bases across Vietnam and on navy ships at sea.[16] As the United States extracted itself from Indochina in the early 1970s, the end of the draft in 1973 ushered in the phase of the all-volunteer force (AVF). No longer able to compel young men into uniform, the services launched an image makeover focusing on recruiting black Americans, who often viewed this with skepticism. After the Vietnam War, the historian James Westheider writes, "It now appeared that African Americans no longer viewed military service as an honorable obligation owed to one's country or as a route to social and economic advancement."[17]

The late 1960s and 1970s remained bleak in terms of opportunities in mainstream media for black actors and directors to express such sentiments. In 1979, a U.S. Civil Rights Commission study of television found black performers occupying a "disproportionately high number of immature, demeaning, and comical roles."[18] A rare sight in film, black soldiers and veterans were scarcer still on TV. ABC's World War II drama series *Combat!* (1962–1967) featured no African American characters during a five-season run encompassing more than 150 episodes. The black actor Ivan Dixon did have a prominent role as Kinch, a U.S. prisoner of war, in the CBS comedy series *Hogan's Heroes* (1965–1971). In the six seasons it ran, it avoided tackling racism even from a comedic perspective (in one episode, Kinch impersonates a visiting African official, but that's about it). At the time of *RTNG*'s release in 1979, no major TV show or film had explored the black veteran's return to U.S. society.

Television did offer some critical images of U.S. military history, however. In 1970, Aaron Spelling produced the made-for-TV film *Carter's Army*, set in Europe during World War II. In the film, an all-black sanitation company is relieved of its duties digging and emptying latrines in order to be sent on a dangerous mission to save a vital bridge. The soldiers' anachronistic Afro hairstyles, manners of speech, and Black Panther–style berets mean that these maltreated World War II troops (among them Richard Pryor and Billy Dee Williams) make easy surrogates for those serving in Vietnam. The GIs are defiant in the face of racism, threatening white aggressors—even superior officers—with violent retaliation. Although some whites (including their commander, a racist Georgian) learn enlightening lessons about black capabilities, the war is not presented as any kind of spur to equalization. Instead, it becomes, as James Baldwin wrote in 1962, a moment at which "a certain hope died, a certain respect for white Americans faded."[19] This is conveyed as the soldiers, having defeated a German outfit and saved the bridge so that the Allies might advance, are passed by a U.S. jeep flying a Confederate flag. A white GI throws a shovel at the surviving combat heroes, yelling, "Hey, boy, you better get some latrines dug."

Although *Carter's Army* was produced by whites, it nevertheless resonates with themes emergent in black visual culture at the time. After a relatively barren period, a more overt tone of dissent was apparent in independent black-produced cinema beginning in the late 1960s. An important figure in this was Melvin Van Peebles, whose films made him "something of a folk hero for the black community."[20] In 1967, Van Peebles, an air force veteran, released *Story of a Three-Day Pass*, which he had shot in Europe using a French government grant.[21] The film expresses the splintering of black U.S. subjectivity through service in a white-dominated institution. A black corporal, known only as Turner (played by the Guyanese actor Harry Baird), is serving as an orderly in postwar France. In an early scene, Turner confronts himself in the bathroom mirror, wondering aloud whether his white captain will promote him. At this, the screen divides into two images of Turner, with the mirror-image speaking as part of his conflicted mind. Should he seek success within the system, or does such ambition involve too much subjugation of the self? Someone must be promoted, Turner reasons, so "why not me?" The mirror image offers a contending perspective, arguing that if Turner advances it will be due to his subservience to white authority. "Because you are the captain's new good colored boy," the image accuses. "You are the captain's Uncle Tom, baby."

In Van Peebles's film, World War II lurks as historical memory contained in the postwar French landscape (a poster of James Brown on a barroom wall places the narrative in the 1960s). Turner travels with Miriam, a white Frenchwoman with whom he is involved, to Normandy, its beaches enshrined in U.S. memory as "a synecdoche for the Allied victory, for the triumph of democracy over totalitarianism."[22] Yet, more than twenty years after D-Day, Turner remains subject to undemocratic prohibitions, and Van Peebles uses the iconic beaches as the stage for an oppressive encounter during which Turner is accosted by three white GIs. Spotting Turner with Miriam, the whites bully and intimidate him, towering over the camera. They report their meeting to the captain, and Turner's promotion is lost. Black subjectivity, Van Peebles implies, cannot cohere within the racist structures of the armed services.

Military narratives in the post-Vietnam era also voiced severe doubts over the nation's capacity for progressive change. In the 1976 film *Brotherhood of Death*, three black Alabamians join the military to escape the attentions of the local Ku Klux Klan. After fighting in Vietnam with an all-black guerilla outfit, they return to find their hometown openly dominated by Klansmen. The veterans at first seek democratic solutions, organizing a mass voter registration movement in the black community. Ultimately, this effort proves fruitless and, after local politicians (who are also Klansmen) go unpunished for burning a black church, raping a young black woman, and murdering a college-bound black athlete, the veterans are compelled to use their expertise in jungle warfare to exact bloody revenge.

Black Soldiers and Veterans in *RTNG*

Intended for a network television audience, *RTNG* does not go as far as *Brotherhood* in its elevation of armed resistance above reform enacted within existing political structures. Nonetheless, the series echoes certain of the radical elements of this film and others, drawing attention to historical ironies and betrayals and placing African American soldiers in a trajectory of increasing radicalization. Spanning Booker T. Washington's accommodationism, W. E. B. Du Bois's summons to fight in World War I, and the separatism advocated by Malcolm X in the post–World War II era, *RTNG* grapples with the dilemma of fighting for a nation that denies blacks full citizenship. To do so, the series' writers allude to what Du Bois, in his 1903 work *The Souls of Black Folk*, describes as "double-consciousness." As Du Bois explains, double-consciousness is the "sense of always looking at one's self through the eyes of others, of measuring one's soul by the tape of a world that looks on in amused contempt and pity. One ever feels his two-ness—an American, a Negro; two souls, two thoughts, two unreconciled strivings; two warring ideals in one dark body, whose dogged strength alone keeps it from being torn asunder."[23] Like *Three-Day Pass* and *Brotherhood*, *RTNG* implies that reconciliation of these "two souls" is yet to occur.

In episode 3, as the First World War rages in Europe, Simon Haley (to become Alex's father and husband to Bertha, Kunta Kinte's great-great-great granddaughter) is in agricultural college. Reading *Souls* unsettles his allegiance to Booker T. Washington, whom Simon previously idolized but now considers too obsequious. After the United States enters the war in 1917, Du Bois's July 1918 article in the National Association for the Advancement of Colored People (NAACP) journal, the *Crisis*, motivates Simon (Dorian Harewood) to volunteer. In "Close Ranks," Du Bois calls on black Americans to "forget our special grievances and close our ranks shoulder to shoulder with our white fellow citizens and the allied nations that are fighting for democracy."[24] Through military service, Du Bois hoped (and Simon hopes), black Americans might "make it possible for a man to be both a Negro and an American without being cursed and spit upon by his fellows, without having the doors of Opportunity closed roughly in his face."[25]

RTNG quickly shows how those hopes are undermined. Simon sets off optimistically, quoting Du Bois and telling Bertha that he will be helping to create a fairer world. However, even before Simon and the other black troops depart the train station, a white captain and sergeant complain about the "damn coons" they must command. In the background, posters bearing slogans such as "Americans All!" underline the gap between patriotic rhetoric and lived experience. More dangerous still, even as the "war for democracy" is being decided overseas, Klan activity is on the increase in Henning, Tennessee. White-robed Klansmen parade holding banners reading "White Is Right" and "The South Will Rise Again," and they later burn the store of a Jewish tailor. Perturbed at the prospect of "niggers with guns" returning from war with a new sense of empowerment, the local Klan leader, Earl Crowther (Paul Koslo), who is intimately connected to the town's political machine, organizes further efforts to intimidate Henning's black population. Jim Crow reaffirms its grip on the American South; military service offers no escape route.

Episode 4, directed by Charles S. Dubin (the director of many *M*A*S*H* episodes), moves back in time a little, beginning with a somber sequence depicting the December 1917 execution at Camp Travis, San Antonio, of thirteen black troops from the 24th Infantry Division. The opening shot captures the Stars and Stripes fluttering above a vast gallows from which multiple nooses descend. The hanging of black men, the director suggests, is a most American practice. After ascending to the platform in chains, the condemned soldiers sing "Go Down, Moses"—with its famous refrain of "let my people go"—in a last defiant gesture. The scene recalls the deaths of black soldiers who took up arms against whites in what is known as the Camp Logan Riot or the Houston Uprising. In August 1917, responding to what one historian calls "the abuses heaped on them by white Houstonians," black soldiers seized weapons and ammunition and traveled into Houston, where they killed seventeen whites.[26] Their subsequent treatment by the military was secretive and deathly swift. *RTNG* thus creates a powerful marker of the military's history of racial injustice, reminding audiences once more of the abundant hypocrisies present within the "war for democracy." In Henning, the African Methodist preacher denounces the affair. "The army called it mutiny and murder," he says, "but those boys of the 24th Infantry had no chance to testify to the provocation, the indignation, and the humiliation they suffered at the hands of the police of Houston, Texas." This was not "military justice" but a "lynching" like so many others in U.S. history.

Despite the presence of some enlightened whites in the army, Simon and his comrades soon become disillusioned. In their barracks, they debate the reasons for the war, with the conscripts questioning why Simon volunteered. "President Wilson says the world must be made safe for democracy," Simon explains. "That's alright for them white boys," replies Doxey (Charles Weldon), "but what's in it for us?" Simon returns to Du Bois's high aspirations, quoting from "Close Ranks": "we make no ordinary sacrifice, but we make it gladly and willingly, with our eyes lifted to the hills." Bubba Haywood (Bernie Casey) and the others just laugh. "I'll make a deal with you, Haley," Haywood replies. "Now you and your Dr. Du Bois keep your eyes lifted to the hills, and I'll keep your behind out of trouble down here in the mud where we all gonna be."

Du Bois's and Haley's democratic ambitions seem very distant during training at Camp Grant, Illinois, especially after Haywood returns to base having been attacked and beaten by local police. The army refuses to intervene on Haywood's behalf, and the men in Simon's company are furious. "Where's they respect for this damn uniform?" asks Doxey, and the troops, including Simon, begin arming for a retaliatory action not dissimilar to that for which the men of the Houston Uprising died. Haywood talks them out of it, telling them they will be hanged or imprisoned. "You wanna shoot somebody? Wait 'til you get to France and you can shoot yourself some Germans." "What I got against them Germans?" Doxey asks. "Seem to me we fighting the wrong white men."

Deployment brings further cause for grievance. Sent on a perilous mission to disable two German machine guns, the troops do not receive the essential artillery support promised by their white commanders. Haywood reasons that they were neglected because there was "nothing out here but a bunch of niggers." Compounding the injustice, the men are blamed for the failure by their captain, who dubs them "dumb darkies" and berates them for "rolling their big bug eyes" instead of fighting. When the November 1918 armistice brings an end to the miseries of trench warfare, the men fraternize with French women and sing "Mademoiselle from Armentieres." Doxey is so taken by the color blindness of French citizens that he hopes to "turn frog" rather than return to the "miserable, low-down, nigger-hating country" from which he came. Haywood is going home regardless. "It's *my* miserable, low-down, nigger-hating country," he says.

Importantly, *RTNG* also takes up the veterans' homecoming in 1919. Simon forecasts that things will have improved, and stock footage confirms the celebrations that greeted black veterans as they sailed into New York Harbor. Yet Simon, Doxey, and Haywood are met upon their return to Tennessee not with fanfare but with violence. A white mob, anticipating the return of black troops with "wild ideas about all kinds of things," travels to Knoxville to destroy black homes and businesses. Doxey and Haywood begin to shoot in defense, but the mob sets fire to the house from which they are fighting. As the men, still in uniform, spill into the street, Haywood is shot dead by the Klan leader, Crowther. Doxey takes timely revenge, accosting Crowther and slitting his throat with a razor blade. As is the case in *Brotherhood of Death*, violence in response to violence is represented as legitimate and necessary, the only feasible defense of the black veteran's right to live in peace.

His prewar optimism diminishing, Simon reads bitterly from Du Bois's May 1919 *Crisis* article, "Returning Soldiers," which lists grievances against the

United States, among them lynching, disenfranchising, and stealing from its black citizens. "This country of ours," Du Bois writes, "despite all its better souls have done and dreamed, is yet a shameful land." The article tells First World War veterans, "we are cowards and jackasses if now that that war is over we do not marshal every ounce of our brain and brawn to fight a sterner, longer, more unbending battle against the forces of hell in our own land."[27] This call to arms Simon hopes to answer, but the war has done little to improve his life or that of his family. Pessimism sets in, especially after his share-cropper mother is evicted from her Georgia home following his father's death. Simon struggles to find work and begins to feel that he remains, unchangingly, inferior in the eyes of white Americans. Bertha (Irene Cara) reminds him of their ancestors' strength and the need to keep fighting as Du Bois instructs.

World War I is not a conflict that is generally esteemed in U.S. cultural memory. World War II is far more often associated with the advance of democratization, so it is notable that the narrative of disillusionment and betrayal told through World War I is essentially repeated after the later war.[28] During episode 6, despite his disappointments during the First World War, Simon pushes Alex toward the military. In 1939, Alex enlists in the coast guard, but his treatment there is little better than that dealt to his father by the army twenty years prior. At first, the young Alex (Damon Evans) is impressed by the uniforms and weaponry, but he soon relinquishes any dreams of a gallant military life. Alex is assigned to the cramped and claustrophobic kitchen, where southern racial codes persevere. A fellow recruit tells him, "All that hero stuff is for the white boys. You and me are gonna be messmen, stewards, or maybe ship's cooks. That's all there is for colored, coast guard or navy." The coast guard motto, "Always Ready," he continues, means that "as long as you're in that uniform, you better always be ready to be house nigger for these white officers."

Alex's duties involve polishing shoes, cleaning, and waiting tables under the authority of Steward First Class Percival "Scotty" Scott (John Hancock). In December 1941, when news breaks of the Pearl Harbor attack and the declaration of war against Japan, Scotty reminds the stewards of their place in the pecking order. "Well, men, we got ourselves a war," he says. "Now, you know what that means to you. You gotta do your duty, so get yourselves down to the galley and polish them pots." Haley spends the war performing boring and menial tasks in the South Pacific. He does, however, take the opportunity to develop his writing, charging less-literate crewmates for letters home. In truth, *RTNG* rather rushes by the World War II years, and this in itself is a significant narrative choice, refusing to attach to black service therein any form of racial triumphalism.

After Alex returns home, Simon's optimism is restored. "These are exciting times," he tells his son. "We won the war overseas and now we have to win the one here at home. And we are moving!" Yet the postwar nation appears unmoved by the battle against Nazi philosophies of white supremacy. Alex remains in the coast guard, where he is assigned to New York City as a writer. With Alex still in uniform, the family heads north, encountering multiple indignities as they seek lodgings. Initially, a white woman turns the Haley family away from her motel, claiming to be full despite the "Vacancy" sign outside. At the next motel, the same thing happens: "*Boy*," the owner says, "I am telling you that there's no vacancy here, *for you*." Increasingly desperate, Alex turns to the Veterans of Foreign Wars (VFW). "Need a place to stay?," asks the sign outside. "We can help you!" But, even at an institution founded to benefit veterans, the Haleys are denied aid. "Ordinarily we would try to arrange something," lies the manager, "but it's a very crowded time of year" (it is November). At this last instance of thinly veiled racism, Alex becomes visibly angry, slamming his fist on the countertop before leaving.

Directing this sixth episode was the seasoned African American stage director Lloyd Richards, whose understanding of the importance of the visual is reflected in this scene's politicized cues.[29] On his way into the VFW post, Haley pauses to straighten his tie in a mirror hanging in the lobby. Smart in his dress uniform, Haley is captured here alongside the U.S. flag, entering the building as a proud serviceman. After his humiliating rejection, Richards repeats the shot as Haley exits and assesses himself once more in the glass. This time, the camera zooms in to cut the flag from the frame and leave Haley alone in medium close-up, seeing his image in a wholly different light.

Here, the dilemma of service and rejection consumes Haley's self-image just as it did Turner's in Van Peebles's *Story of a Three-Day Pass*. As he returns to the car, passing the "Need a Place to Stay? We can help you!" sign again, Haley tells his wife, Nan, "I heard about it, but it never happened to me. So I took a long look at myself. My medals were right here, the United States eagle was right here, and you know what I saw? Not a war hero, no sir. Not a veteran, not a serviceman. I saw what they [the VFW] saw: a nigger in a fancy monkey suit." White America appears unreformed by the war, while for black veterans such as Haley "double-consciousness" remains intact.

Rather than focusing on progress toward integration, *RTNG*'s postwar sections emphasize the unresolved legacies of inequality, as Haley's career in journalism (covered in episode 7) brings him into contact with figureheads of differing racial separatisms. First, *Playboy* magazine accepts Alex's proposal to interview Malcolm X (Al Freeman Jr.). Malcolm regards Haley as a "tool of the white man," but the writer (now played by James Earl Jones) wins his trust. Haley attends a speech in which Malcolm denounces the "white devils" and "Uncle Toms" who advocate integration. "Integrate with the devil?" X asks his audience. "They gotta be outta their minds." Considering the repeated acts of violence against African Americans (in uniform and otherwise) that the series has dramatized, his assertion that "we will defend our-selves against anyone who attacks us, and we know who our enemy is" does not seem unreasonable.

Later, *Playboy* asks Haley to profile George Lincoln Rockwell, a World War II veteran and commander of the American Nazi Party. Rockwell is played by political leftist Marlon Brando, who contacted the producers of *RTNG* in hope of securing his first television role (for which he won an Emmy). Brando portrays Rockwell as a childish man who delights in his fervent bigotries. Haley visits the swastika-bedecked U.S. Nazi HQ in Arlington, Virginia, where Rockwell, attempting to incite Haley's anger, claims blacks have done "noth-ing" in America that "horses or trained monkeys" could not have achieved. The Nazi leader recites the lyrics of songs about black inferiority, one of which takes the tune of "Mademoiselle from Armentieres," which the black troops had sung in celebration after the First World War.

Rockwell claims that he and Malcolm preach the same message: "race mixing isn't going to work." Haley sees an important difference, describing X as "some sort of a distorted reaction to a very real problem" while calling Rockwell "a stupid fascist." Malcolm X also shows a capacity for change that Rockwell entirely lacks. *RTNG* covers Malcolm's reform after his trip to Mecca, where he witnessed people of many races worshipping together and came to believe that "not all whites are racists." Of course, the fact that he is soon as-sassinated for his change of heart reiterates the series' implication that race and racism remain unsolved sources of violence and fracture in American culture.

While it did not reproduce the impact of the original, *RTNG* rated well among audiences. For some, the series' immediate connection to recent history was pivotal to its power. "If the first series was about the struggle for freedom," producer Stan Margulies said, "this *Roots* is about the struggle for equality." As many noted at the time, *RTNG* brought the issues of history, genealogy, and inequality raised by the original book and series into a period of living memory, removing the safety net of temporal distance and reminding view-ers of their close proximity to a historical and contemporary landscape of racism. "None of us lived 200 years ago," Margulies noted, "you could watch the first *Roots* and say 'I wouldn't act like that.' In the new group of shows, you have to look at yourself in the mirror."[30]

In light of this, some hoped that *RTNG* would produce a national round of mirror-gazing, offering viewers "a clearer understanding of legalized segre-gation as it permeated every aspect of Southern life from the 1870s through [the] mid-twentieth century."[31] Yet public responses to the first *Roots*, whereby a serious engagement with slavery and racism was deflected into an outbreak of personal genealogical research, meant that such a reaction was far from guaranteed.[32] Surveys conducted around the time of *RTNG*'s initial broadcast suggest that the show was often preaching to the converted. Those predisposed to "egalitarianism" in matters of race were more likely to watch more often, while audience responses revealed no appreciable increase in egalitarian sentiments after viewing the series.[33]

Elsewhere, reactions to *RTNG* exposed the still-heated atmosphere surrounding race in the United States. Members of the KKK in Haley's home state of Tennessee burned crosses outside the Nashville offices of the NAACP and at the local ABC affiliate that was carrying the show. Television stations were picketed by Klansmen in Huntsville, Alabama, while the American Nazi Party rallied against the series in Philadelphia.[34] Some black critics found different reasons for dissatisfaction. In the *Baltimore Afro-American*, Ida Peters assailed the show's tendency to "gloss over" injustice and emphasize passive black victimhood rather than active resistance.[35] She objected to the treatment of the hanging of troops from the 24th Infantry in particular, charging that insufficient context was provided. On the whole, Peters chided, *RTNG* was "a light, fluffy piece of entertainment" created by whites in an effort to "psychologically con you and me into further complacency and calmness."[36]

If Peters was dissatisfied with the ideological content of *RTNG*, what followed in terms of the black military image in visual culture would have done little to assuage her concerns. In the late 1970s and after, World War II in particular was used to re-hoist an integrationist framework through which the possibility and desirability of assimilation was defended. Even as, in the wake of the Vietnam War, *RTNG* and a few other productions questioned the value of military service as a source of social advancement, African Americans were elsewhere being recouped into a newly recharged paradigm of racial triumphalism. The 1978 film *Force Ten from Navarone*, for example, written for the screen by Carl Foreman, lacks the critical tone of *The Victors*, preferring to emphasize the power of combat service to mollify black dissent and create multiracial unity.

The narrative of racial triumphalism has been predominant in U.S. visual culture in the era of the AVF. This is, again, most often true of representations of World War II, which remains the most revered of U.S. twentieth-century conflicts. In the past twenty or thirty years, made-for-television films such as the Hallmark Channel's *Decoration Day* (1990), as well as feature films including *U-571* (2000), have either elided historical racism or depicted it as overcome in the crucible of war (often by attributing to black heroism the reform of previously prejudiced whites). In *Decoration Day*, an elderly veteran who believes he was racially abused and shot at by white Americans while serving in World War II discovers he was actually attacked by Germans in disguise. Thus, his forty years of anger and resentment at white America have been misplaced. Images of war and remembrance thus continue to help contain what Gary Gerstle calls the "cultural revolt" of antiassimilationism.[37] In light of this, *RTNG* still stands out as a unique and dissonant engagement with race and military history.

NOTES

1. Frank Rich, "A Super Sequel to Haley's Comet," *Time*, February 19, 1979, 84–88.

2. Les Brown, "*Roots II* Draws Well, But Not Like the Original," *New York Times*, February 21, 1979.

3. Sandra J. Ball-Rokeach, Joel W. Grube, and Milton Rokeach, "*Roots: The Next Generations*—Who Watched and with What Effect?," *Public Opinion Quarterly* 45, no. 1 (spring 1981): 58–68, 58.

4. Alex Haley, *Roots: The Saga of an American Family*, 30th anniv. ed. (New York: Vanguard, 2007 [1976]), 845–888; John J. O'Connor, "Strong *Roots* Continues Black Odyssey," *New York Times*, February 16, 1979; and "*Roots II* Boon to Hungry Actors," *Baltimore Afro-American*, January 13, 1979.

5. See Ruth A. Protinsky and Terry M. Wildman, "*Roots*: Reflections from the Classroom," *Journal of Negro Education* 48, no. 2 (spring 1979): 171–181; and Ball-Rokeach, Grube, and Rokeach, "*Roots: The Next Generations*."

6. Herman Gray, "The Politics of Representation in Network Television," in *Channeling Blackness: Studies on Television and Race in America*, edited by Darnell M. Hunt (New York: Oxford University Press, 2005), 155–174.

7. See Jennifer C. James, *A Freedom Bought with Blood: African American War Literature from the Civil War to World War II* (Chapel Hill: University of North Carolina Press, 2007); and Cecilia O'Leary, *To Die For: The Paradox of American Patriotism* (Princeton, N.J.: Princeton University Press, 1999). See also William Cooper Nell, *The Colored Patriots of the American Revolution* (New York: Arno Press, 1968 [1855]).

8. Richard Slotkin, "Unit Pride: Ethnic Platoons and the Myths of American Nationality," *American Literary History* 13, no. 3 (2001): 469–498.

9. Niven Busch, *They Dream of Home* (New York: D. Appleton-Century, 1944).

10. See Gordon Kahn, *Hollywood on Trial* (New York: Boni and Gaer, 1948), 99, 106–109.

11. Robert K. Chester, "'We Feel the Wound Is Closed': *Red Ball Express* (1952), the Department of Defense Pictorial Division, and the Reluctant Embrace of Postwar Integration," *Powerlines: An Interdisciplinary Online Journal* 1, no. 1 (April 2013), http://amst.umd.edu/powerlines/robert-k-chester-red-ball-express, accessed June 21, 2016.

12. William Blackwell Branch, *A Medal for Willie* (Alexandria, Va.: Alexander Street Press, 2013 [1951]), 55–56.

13. Lerone Bennett Jr., "The Mood of the Negro," *Ebony*, July 1963, 27–30, 32, 34, 38; quotes on 27, 30.

14. Quoted in George Lipsitz, "Frantic to Join . . . the Japanese Army," in *Perilous Memories: The Asia-Pacific Wars*, edited by T. Fujitani, Geoffrey M. White, and Lisa Yoneyama (Durham, N.C.: Duke University Press, 2001), 347.

15. Eldridge Cleaver, "Rallying Round the Flag," in *Soul on Ice* (New York: McGraw-

Hill, 1968), 112–120, 116; Eldridge Cleaver, "The Black Man's Stake in Vietnam," in *Soul on Ice*, 121–127, 127.

16. James E. Westheider, *Fighting on Two Fronts: African Americans and the Vietnam War* (New York: New York University Press, 1997), 18–36, 169–173; Kimberley L. Phillips, *War! What Is It Good For? Black Freedom Struggles and the U.S. Military from World War II to Iraq* (Chapel Hill: University of North Carolina Press, 2012), 188–272; and John Darrell Sherwood, *Black Sailor, White Navy: Racial Unrest in the Fleet during the Vietnam War Era* (New York: New York University Press, 2007), 55–102.

17. Westheider, *Fighting on Two Fronts*, 169.

18. Roscoe C. Brown Jr., "Let's Uproot TV's Image of Blacks," *New York Times*, February 18, 1979.

19. James Baldwin, *The Fire Next Time* (New York: Vintage, 1993 [1962]), 54.

20. Donald Bogle, *Toms, Coons, Mulattoes, Mammies, and Bucks: An Interpretive History of Blacks in American Film*, 3rd ed. (New York: Continuum, 1994), 236.

21. "The Story of a Three-Day Pass," *Ebony*, September 1968, 54–60, 54.

22. Marianna Torgovnik, *The War Complex: World War II in Our Time* (Chicago: University of Chicago Press, 2005), 22.

23. W. E. B. Du Bois, *The Souls of Black Folk* (New York: Dover Publications, 1994 [1903]), 2.

24. W. E. B. Du Bois, "Close Ranks," *Crisis*, July 1918.

25. Du Bois, *Souls of Black Folk*, 3.

26. Adriane Lentz-Smith, *Freedom Struggles: African Americans and World War I* (Cambridge, Mass.: Harvard University Press, 2009), 44.

27. W. E. B. Du Bois, "Returning Soldiers," *Crisis*, May 1919.

28. See, for instance, John Bodnar, *The "Good War" in American Memory* (Baltimore, Md.: Johns Hopkins University Press, 2010).

29. Sandra G. Shannon, "From Lorraine Hansberry to August Wilson: An Interview with Lloyd Richards," *Callaloo* 14, no. 1 (winter 1991): 124–135.

30. Stan Margulies quoted in Rich, "A Super Sequel to Haley's Comet," 85. See also Lee A. Daniels, "*Roots II* Strikes Personal Chords," *New York Times*, March 8, 1979.

31. Protinsky and Wildman, "*Roots*," 178.

32. Matthew Frye Jacobson, *Roots Too: White Ethnic Revival in Post–Civil Rights America* (Cambridge, Mass.: Harvard University Press, 2006), 42–44.

33. Ball-Rokeach, Grube, and Rokeach, "*Roots: The Next Generations*."

34. Samuel Yette, "We Ought to Learn from the Past—Not Live It," *Baltimore Afro-American*, March 3, 1979.

35. Ida Peters, "Showtime," *Baltimore Afro-American*, March 3, 1979.

36. Peters, "Showtime"; also Yette, "We Ought to Learn from the Past."

37. Gary Gerstle, *American Crucible: Race and Nation in the Twentieth Century* (Princeton, N.J.: Princeton University Press, 2001), 327–341.

PART III

Rerouting *Roots*

CHAPTER EIGHT

The Same, but a Step Removed
Aspects of the British Reception of *Roots*

MARTIN STOLLERY

This chapter explores aspects of the British reception of the television version of *Roots*. The miniseries has been discussed and viewed in Britain in ways that, although not radically dissimilar, are different from U.S. debates and perceptions. The British reception of *Roots* initially polarized between mainstream media commentary and less publicly visible "black British" engagements with the *Roots* phenomenon.[1] In this chapter I explore the terms of that polarization, focusing in particular on a range of black British responses to *Roots*, an issue that television scholars have not previously investigated. As I demonstrate, *Roots'* multidimensional resonance among black British audiences has had, over time, as much, if not more, staying power than the predominant, limiting framework utilized in most newspaper and magazine discussions of the miniseries when it was first broadcast in Britain.

Mainstream British media commentary, when *Roots* was first broadcast, was generally couched in the guise of a relatively distanced, objective evaluation of or relationship to the miniseries. This commentary tended to conform to dominant British discourses about the history of slavery. On the other hand, some personal engagements with *Roots*, especially black British ones, involved more intense and intimate responses, sometimes persisting long beyond its initial broadcast. Tracking these engagements leads into the domain of what Janet Staiger describes as "memory studies," which "do not inform us about the initial impact or significance of the movie or TV program on the individual at the time but rather how the memory of that event becomes woven into our personal narratives."[2] My discussion therefore begins with a consideration of responses to *Roots* published soon after it was first broadcast in Britain, and concludes with discussion of the focused interviews I conducted in 2014.

Temporal and Geographical Distancing

Four days after *Roots* premiered on British television in April 1977, the *Times* quoted Alex Haley as saying "the story of black people in England is the same [as in the United States,] but it's a step removed. They went to the Caribbean in slave ships instead of going to America. And now their descendants have come here to England" (although Haley neglected to consider black Britons of African rather than Caribbean descent, I do so briefly later in this chapter).[3] Haley emphasized African Americans' and black Britons' common historic legacies: African heritage and the Middle Passage. At the same time, he acknowledged some variation due to the different routes traveled, forced and elective. (Some commentators, such as Judie Newman, posit a clear distinction between *Roots'* Afrocentrism and Paul Gilroy's black Atlanticism.[4] Haley's statement in the *Times*, invoking shared African origins and an acknowledgment of diasporic differentiation, complicates this division.) Haley was afforded this platform in the *Times* because *Roots* was by then recognized in Britain as a major publishing and television event, following its initial U.S. television broadcast in January 1977. Media commentary extended beyond book reviews and television columns; Haley, for example, appeared on the leading British television chat show, *Parkinson*, the day before BBC1 began broadcasting *Roots*. Yet a significant proportion of surrounding media commentary avoided the implications of Haley's statement, "the same but . . . a step removed." Instead, *Roots* was repeatedly framed as primarily, even exclusively, a U.S. narrative.

At one level this is self-evident; the majority of *Roots'* narrative does indeed unfold in the United States. However, the frequency with which the "Americanness" of *Roots* was emphasized supports historian Ross Wilson's contention that there is "an ingrained perception of 'distance' in the popular memory of the slave trade in Britain."[5] In their discussion of the "abolition discourse" framing the bicentenary celebration of the British Parliament's 1807 Abolition Act, Emma Waterton and Wilson argue that one of its features is "temporal distancing—which emphasises that these events are 'all in the past.'"[6] As far as *Roots* is concerned, one feature of the initial British media commentary surrounding the miniseries was geographical as well as temporal distancing. This distancing emphasized that slavery occurred somewhere else, unconnected with Britain, and that revisiting its history was primarily a U.S. concern.

To take some examples, W. Stephen Gilbert suggests, in his April 3, 1977, *Observer* newspaper column on forthcoming television highlights, "ABC's blockbuster is unlikely to grab British audiences in quite the way it took America by the short hairs . . . it's not difficult to see how a saga tracing the story of American blacks with some veracity would touch raw and ready nerves in the

Carter era."[7] Iain Johnstone, in the BBC listings magazine, the *Radio Times*, collates a feature article, "Americans on *Roots*: Some Personal Views."[8] This again focuses on *Roots'* relationship to the culture in which it originated, rather than on its potential impact in Britain. In one discussion piece published after the miniseries had been aired, George Hutchinson reflects in the *Times* on how *Roots* had prompted him to think about the "traffic in persons" that persisted in parts of Africa, Asia, and Latin America. He commended the ongoing work of the Anti-Slavery Society, one of "England's historic, romantic causes," in which some of abolitionist William Wilberforce's descendants were still active.[9] Pride in Britain's abolitionist credentials coexists here with a disavowal of its historic complicity in the slave trade.

Of course, newspaper and magazine commentary gives at best a partial, limited picture of media reception. Billy Smart, one of a growing number of television scholars exploring the reports produced by the BBC's Audience Research Unit (ARU), recommends moving "away from contemporaneous television and literary criticism to examining a different range of sources that prioritise the responses of non-professional critics."[10] The ARU produced a number of such reports on *Roots*. These were initially routine ones, compiled shortly after the miniseries was broadcast. They were followed, in February 1978, by a longer special report, partly modeled on the U.S. survey carried out by Cleveland State University. ARU reports do indeed broaden the picture of how *Roots* was received in Britain, albeit with one major caveat.

The special report on *Roots* estimates British viewing figures for *Roots* as averaging approximately one-third of the population—significant but "not in the record-breaking class."[11] The report subdivides its data according to social class, but gives no indication, in statistical terms, of whether *Roots* broke records for black British viewers. To date there has been no specific research on how the ARU operated in this larger context, for example in relation to how viewers were selected to take part in surveys and whether the sampling included black British respondents. However, as a public service broadcaster, the BBC has a long history, as Darrell Newton puts it, of "attempt[ing] to assist White Britons in understanding the impact of African-Caribbeans" in the post-*Windrush* period.[12] Newton demonstrates how the ARU played an important mediating role in the BBC's ongoing internal assessment of whether specific television programs contributed to harmonious race relations. Yet the unit's analyses of responses to programs dealing with race relations aimed at a general, and therefore ethnically diverse, British television audience focus predominantly on the attitudes of white viewers. The headline findings of ARU reports on television programs such as *Race and Colour: A Scientific Introduction to the Problem of Racial Relations* (aired November 9, 1952) or *Fable* (January 20, 1965), a *Wednesday Play* episode that imagined an apartheid Britain where blacks oppress whites, are predicated on an ingrained assumption of what Sarita Malik calls "the racial (White) homogeneity of the British television nation."[13]

ARU reports on *Roots* partly circumvented the geographical and temporal distancing of the "abolition discourse" by focusing on the miniseries' relevance to British race relations at the time of its initial broadcast. The pervasiveness of "abolition discourse," however, is suggested by one of the special report's conclusions: "British viewers . . . did not feel themselves to have any affinity with the white slave-owners, and hence did not need to protect themselves from the discomfiture of being made to feel guilty by avoiding the series." In addition to effacing British involvement in the slave trade, this sentence conflates "British viewers" with white British viewers. Some survey questions cited in the special report make this even more starkly evident. They include "would you be willing to have a black person as part of your family" and a question about whether "the logic and philosophy of the blacks [in *Roots*] is far in advance of what I would have expected."[14] The wording and structure of the survey frames the British television nation as homogeneously white, regardless of whether any black British viewers were among the respondents. This framing is also present in the few examples of mainstream media commentary that similarly considered *Roots'* potential impact upon contemporary British race relations. James Murray wrote in the *Daily Express*, after discussing the miniseries' impact in the United States: "There are lessons in *Roots* for us too. There are few people who watch it who will not be looking with new eyes at the coloured bus conductor or station ticket collector tomorrow."[15] The implied white addressee of this sentence is invisible, not "coloured." No consideration is given to the possibility of the bus conductor or ticket collector under observation having his or her own distinctive, perhaps strongly felt, response to *Roots*.

Race and Class and the Late 1970s Moment

Race and Class: A Journal for Black and Third World Liberation, published by the Institute of Race Relations (IRR), was an important British publication that generated extensive feedback on *Roots'* significance, from a black perspective, with black defined as "the colour of our politics."[16] The IRR was taken over by a new collective in 1972. One of its key figures, Ambalavaner Sivanandan, describes the transition:

> The Institute had been set up as an independent think-tank . . . but its work was becoming increasingly partisan—carrying out policy-oriented research which supported the racist acts of successive governments, particularly over immigration . . . this kind of research was defining "the problem" as one of racialism not racism, i.e. personal prejudice not structured injustice. Policy-oriented re-

search inevitably pandered to the concerns of government, not its subjects. It was not relations between races that needed looking at but power relations on the ground. And that meant research which would speak to the needs of the subjected to overcome oppression and injustice.[17]

Race and Class, the IRR's newly radicalized journal, included in July 1977 a lengthy dossier relating to the miniseries, "Responses to *Roots*." This dossier encompassed a different, wider range of engagements with *Roots* than mainstream media commentary or BBC audience reports. These run from personal reflections on *Roots*' affective impact to passionately engaged ideological critiques.

The dossier concludes with a summative contribution from Sivanandan, editor of *Race and Class*. Sivanandan contrasts *Roots* with U.S. socialist historian George Rawick's *From Sundown to Sunup: The Making of the Black Community* (1972). Sivanandan accepts *Roots* as in some respects a collective history for African Americans, and he acknowledges that it represents acts of resistance and rebellion, but he draws on Rawick to argue "survival, resistance and rebellion are part of the same continuum—and their (dialectical) progression, unlike in the televised *Roots*, must be seen not in individual acts but in the 'continual creation of a community whose primary function was to struggle against their oppressors.'" For Sivanandan, excessive focus in Haley's book on individuals, rather than on the ongoing social and political development of the African American community, marginalizes civil rights activism, Black Power, and the Black Panthers, despite the narrative continuing into the present. Sivanandan extends his ideological critique by concluding that *Roots*' individualism blocks any opening onto the "revolution inherent in the black condition." Instead, *Roots* finally "ceases to be the whole story of a people and becomes the tale of one man—the tale of a man who awakens from the American nightmare into the American dream—a man whose roots are in Africa but whose traditions are wholly American."[18] In other words, as a mainstream product of the American culture industry, *Roots* ultimately endorses U.S. capitalist ideology by celebrating Haley's individual success, both within its narrative and in the publicity surrounding the book and the television miniseries.

Colin Prescod, another writer closely associated with *Race and Class*, is more caustic in his contribution to the dossier. He begins by quoting the lyrics of Billie Holiday's classic song "Strange Fruit," attributing them to the U.S. Communist writer Abel Meeropol (pseudonym Lewis Allan), who was provoked into writing them by Lawrence Beitler's horrific photograph of the 1930 lynching of Thomas Shipp and Abram Smith. The lyrics elaborate a tree metaphor, with "blood at the roots" graphically dramatizing how violent oppression of African Americans has become almost second nature in American culture, persisting long after abolition. Prescod then draws on the U.S. Marxist economist Harry Braverman to make a related point about the ongoing economic exploitation of the majority of African Americans. Prescod finally arrives at a conclusion similar to Sivanandan's. He confesses to "nagging doubts about the meaning of [Haley's] *Roots* for America today . . . Mr Haley . . . I am pointing to an irony which I'm sure you know about but haven't told us about on the TV. Ultimately the truth of *Roots* for Haley is a lie for blacks in the U.S.A."[19]

Sivanandan's and Prescod's critiques are significant responses to *Roots*, developed within a specific historical, political, and institutional context. And they are, at one level, convincing. *Roots* is not C. L. R. James's book *The Black Jacobins* (1938), nor is it the film *The Last Supper* (Tomás Gutiérrez Alea, 1976), both of which can much more readily be characterized as offering revolutionary perspectives on slavery. Tellingly, *The Black Jacobins* has never been adapted for film or television, and *The Last Supper* has received only limited distribution outside Cuba. However, Robin Nelson's comment about criticism of contemporary television drama is equally applicable to these late-1970s British assessments of *Roots*: "the contingency of critical readings . . . should be located in the force-field of influences upon them."[20] Sivanandan's and Prescod's focus on structured injustice, rather than on individuals, inevitably entails blind spots as well as insights.

Other black British responses to *Roots* during this period emerged from differently constituted, albeit not completely dissimilar, "force-fields of influences." These can be considered within the framework Helen Taylor uses to account for *Roots'* phenomenal success: "A wide variety of consumers of most ages, races, genders and nationalities . . . have actively used *Roots* as a cultural resource to generate a variety of (often contradictory) meanings and pleasures. This is, surely, what John Fiske calls a 'producerly' text—an accessible book and TV series which may be understood within the dominant ideology but which, containing limitations, gaps and contradictory voices, is open and amenable to popular production."[21] There is not an absolute opposition between Taylor's approach and that of the *Race and Class* editors in 1977, led by Sivanandan. The latter implicitly acknowledge the value of *Roots* as a generative cultural resource by encompassing such a wide range of contributions in their dossier. One of the most thought-provoking in this respect is Olive Morris's. Morris, who died of cancer at the age of twenty-seven, has been described by Ana Laura Lopez de la Torre as "someone who was [not] famous in the sense of leaders" but "really a grass-roots activist."[22] Morris's contribution to the *Roots* dossier is written in the plural, yet this plurality encompasses the detail of individual responses. Morris therefore aspires to what Raymond Williams describes as the "reciprocal discovery of the truly social in the individual, and the truly individual in the social."[23] Morris begins, "we are a group

FIGURE 1. The cover of the 1979 handbook published by the Advisory Service for Squatters featured this 1973 photo of Olive Morris. Olive Morris Collection, Lambeth Archives image collection.

of Black women based in Moss Side [Manchester]." She anticipates Taylor's argument when she writes, again in the plural, "We have taken from *Roots* what is relevant to us, and we have learnt from it as we have always been able to learn from the various contributions made to the Black struggle by our sisters and brothers all over the world."[24]

Morris concurs with Sivanandan and Prescod when she highlights some of what she sees as *Roots*' shortcomings, for example its failure to represent the true harshness of the working conditions and domestic lives of African American slaves, and the degree of oppression that incubated some revolutionary struggles. However, Morris is confident these shortcomings can be overcome by black viewers, for whom it is nevertheless an important resource: "we are basically with Alex Haley and his efforts. Black people will fill in the rest of the story for those who are not clear." Filling in the rest of the story is, presumably, one of the responsibilities of organic intellectuals such as Morris. It is also a process described by one of my interviewees. She recollected, after *Roots* was first broadcast on BBC1, "the Black Power Movement in the UK [in its widest sense] became stronger and like-minded friends would meet in community halls to read further literature on black history and the slave trade" (Doreen, fifties). Collective attempts to create more informed and assertive communities are often preceded by individual perceptions and actions that eventually accumulate to the critical mass that constitutes cultural change.

The value of Morris's contribution to the *Roots* dossier is that she profiles ordinary people's responses. She does so in ways that go beyond portraying them as passive recipients of ideologically compromised media messages. Morris recounts incidents where black Britons in 1977 creatively deployed *Roots* in their everyday lives. This is further contextualized by her friend, Liz Obi, who emphasizes the importance of paying close attention to what Paul Gilroy has described as "small acts," "the opportunities for democratic, oppositional agency that can exist even in the most restricted circumstances."[25] Obi situates Morris as "part of a black youth movement that had developed in Britain in the 1970s, a generation that had fought against the racism of the state and society but whose contribution seemed to have been lost between the *Windrush* arrivals and the 1981 riots."[26] Red Chidgey argues that focusing on lesser-known figures such as Morris contributes to a more nuanced understanding of cultural history, one preferable to "propping up the status quo with selected examples of the past," for example by solely valorizing the "race men" Hazel Carby discusses in her book of that title.[27] For Chidgey, paying attention to people such as Morris, and the "small acts" she chronicles in the *Roots* dossier, counters the view "that change only happens periodically, in ways that can be marked and contained by state-sanctioned memorials or anniversaries."[28]

Among the specific examples Morris cites are the following:

> We have been told of Black people in factories, on the buses and elsewhere being addressed with titles from *Roots* as an insult. One woman was called Kizzy.... But instead of throwing a fit, as [her white antagonist] expected, she responded by bowing and saying, "Yes, massa." He nearly had a heart attack. Another woman, when picked on by someone at work, said, "You can't break me; I must survive, I am from the Mandinga tribe."
>
> There have been many other positive reactions. One mother who likes to plait her hair and wear various types of African head scarves reported that her children (all boys) began to show a lot of appreciation for how she wore her hair and to tell her that they like this or that African tie or cane row.[29]

These small, seemingly inconsequential anecdotes cannot be immediately related to commonly acknowledged, major turning points in black British history. Yet they represent women and children, not normally seen as historical agents, engaging with *Roots* in ways that are quite different to the geographical and temporal distancing that was a characteristic feature of mainstream British media commentary. All of them find it easy to take the step Alex Haley describes, which bridges the story of black people in England and the United States. The woman picked on at work also provides a different perspective on Prescod's, and indeed Morris's, criticisms of *Roots'* failure to represent the grinding labor exploitation to which enslaved African Americans were subject, perpetuated after emancipation in the modified form of lower wages and poorer working conditions than white counterparts. Despite this absence, the woman mentioned by Morris translates something *Roots* does represent, the dignity and strength of the Mandinka, to help her in a workplace struggle.

Women are conventionally associated with less critically distanced, emotional responses to film and television. Morris's anecdotes could at first glance seem to confirm that stereotype. On closer inspection, however, they hint at more complex transactions between *Roots* and black British viewers. As feminist research, such as Purnima Mankekar's work on Indian women viewers of television serials, has shown, intense emotional engagement does not preclude a simultaneously reflexive response.[30] When the woman addressed as Kizzy rebuts her white antagonist, she is arguably both embracing a comparison with an admired female character in *Roots*, and consciously performing the role in a manner designed to provoke maximum discomfort, by sardonically insisting on the link between casual, unthinking, everyday white British racism and the institution of slavery. Similarly, the woman targeted at work creatively performs an African ancestry, using *Roots*, an (African) American popular cultural product, as an empowering cultural resource. These "small acts" can be considered in relation to a tendency Leila Kamalli has tentatively suggested is evident in black British writing:

The exuberance inspired by the gaze towards black America is initially accompanied by doubt over its significance for black identity in a British context. Yet that doubtful stance often quickly gives way to a realisation that what is most inspiring about an African American position is the freedom and confidence to *perform*. Encouraged by this show of confidence, black British writers seize the opportunity to perform identity anew, embracing the influence of American blackness and any dramatisation of Africanness that might seem appropriate to enable the individual to enunciate an identity often composed of a multiplicity of cultural inheritances.[31]

The anecdote about sons acquiring new admiration for their mother's hairstyle suggests the impact of Binta (Cicely Tyson), Kunta Kinte's mother, the only major character with cane rows in *Roots*. At one level, this is a straightforward example of *Roots* binding a black British family more closely together around what they perceive as an authentically African style and around shared African origins. However, in his classic essay, "Black Hair/Style Politics," Kobena Mercer favors suspending judgements about the superiority, or greater authenticity, of one black hairstyle over another. Mercer sees Afros, cane rows, curly perms, conks, and numerous other hairstyle options as legitimate parts of "a popular art form articulating a variety of aesthetic 'solutions'" to a range of "problems created," at different historical and cultural moments, "by ideologies of race and racism."[32] Styles change as new circumstances arise. The sons' increased appreciation, when *Roots* was first screened in Britain, for their mother's hairstyle may also have marked the moment when they realized black hair is not a trivial matter, nor solely a woman's concern.

LKJ, *Roots*, and Reggae

Linton Kwesi Johnson, also known as LKJ has long been a name to reckon with in British cultural history, unlike Morris. LKJ's literary eminence was confirmed when he became one of only two living poets to be published in the Penguin Classics series. Yet, as Robert McGill argues, LKJ's "If I Woz a Tap-Natch Poet" (1996), included in his Penguin Classic, *Mi Revalueshanary Fren: Selected Poems* (2002), can be interpreted as a determined effort to maintain "a commitment and debt to black politics even as it acknowledges its own increasing trajectory towards the world of printed, canonized poetry." One marker of allegiance to collectivist politics in LKJ's writing is the use of "'we' as often as 'I.'"[33] Using different methods, LKJ aspires, like Morris, to speak in the plural, "us" as well as "me." In his contribution to the *Race and Class* dossier, he asserts, "For black people in Britain, *Roots* has given us a new sense of identity and belonging, a new feeling of racial pride."[34]

For some black Britons, like some African-Americans, *Roots* catalyzed an emphatic assertion of African heritage. British playwright and actor Kwame Kwei-Armah, for example, adopted a Ghanaian name as a direct result of watching the miniseries. LKJ's stance is not opposed to this kind of metaphorical "return to the source," but he gives the "new feeling of racial pride" a contemporary, rather than backward-looking, inflection when he writes that *Roots* helps to answer the question, "how can I as a black person place myself in the modern world, in the twentieth century?" This is more in tune with Sivanandan's argument, in the previous issue of *Race and Class*, that the liberation of the black intellectual should involve "discovering where he came from . . . not in a frenetic search for lost roots," but in order to more fully realize "where he is at, and where, in fact, he is going to."[35] It also resonates with LKJ's skepticism regarding some of the mysticism and "return to Africa" strands in the Rastafarianism that otherwise influenced him as a youth. As he puts it in "Reality Poem" (1978),

> dis is di age af reality
> but some a wi deal wid mitalagy
> dis is di age af science an teknalagy
> but some a wi check fi antiquity.[36]

The British, specifically London, dimension of LKJ's response to *Roots* is most evident when he hears a soundtrack different from that provided by the show's composers, Gerald Fried and Quincy Jones. LKJ concludes his contribution: "On another level, [*Roots*] provides us, in very concrete terms, with a meaning to one of the most frequently used terms of popular black parlance, namely 'roots.' So that when the black youth hear reggae singers like Johnnie Clarke singing: 'roots, natty, roots natty congo,' or Peter Tosh singing: 'so don't care where you come from / as long as you're a black man / you're a African'—if they once had difficulty in comprehending the meaning of those songs, after seeing *Roots*, they have no such difficulty."[37]

LKJ's linkage of *Roots* and reggae music, at the precise moment of the late 1970s, can be seen in the context of one of the great fixtures of West London's calendar, the Notting Hill Carnival. Sound systems playing reggae had become an increasingly prominent element in the carnival by 1977, articulating a younger, more rebellious structure of feeling than that associated with calypso. Reggae tracks such as the Revolutionaries' "Kunta Kinte" (1976), or selections from Ranking Dread's *Kunta Kinte Roots* (1979), would have been heard in this context. The Notting Hill Carnival became, for a time, more overtly politicized after major clashes between black youths and the police in the mid-1970s, which can themselves be related to the moral panic around "mugging," analyzed by Stuart Hall and his colleagues in their classic study, *Policing the Crisis* (1978).[38] The "Forces of Victory" the Carnival's organizers adopted as a theme in 1978 was also the title of LKJ's second album of dub poetry, released the same year. Carnival sounds became more widely accessible to listeners who did not attend through Alex Pascall's live broadcasts on his Radio London show, *Black Londoners* (1974–1988), from 1975 onward. For a different audience, disc jockey John Peel also led the way during the 1970s in playing reggae on the BBC's national service, Radio 1. In related developments, British reggae bands, such as Steel Pulse and Aswad, and LKJ himself, lent their support to concerts organized as part of the Rock Against Racism (RAR) campaign in the United Kingdom.

LKJ's alignment of *Roots* and reggae was therefore part of a distinctively British cultural constellation during the late 1970s. He certainly emphasized the importance of second-generation black British youths expanding their cultural and historical horizons, and engaging with their African diasporic roots, both through the eponymous miniseries and reggae music. Yet at the same time, this generation, born in Britain during the 1950s and 1960s, faced racist taunts telling them to "go back where they came from," as well as more violent forms of racism, often encouraged by the fascist politics of the National Front party. Methods used to counter these threats included cultural transactions and tactical alliances with other minority ethnic groups, under the banner of black politics, and with antiracist white youths, in the type of "contact zone" exemplified by the RAR campaign. As a number of scholars, such as Ashley Dawson, argue, "Britain's Black Power movement . . . seemingly riding the coattails of developments in the United States, had a far more cross-cultural character at the grass roots than did its American counterpart."[39] This situation arose from a number of factors, including the specific character of British immigration and race relations legislation, as well as the relatively small size, geographic concentrations, and social and political histories, of British diaspora populations. This cross-cultural character is reflected in LKJ's output from this era, for example in his dub poem "It Dread Inna Inglan," which includes these lines:

> Maggi Thatcher on di go with a racist show
> But a she haffe go
> Kaw
> Right now
> African, Asian, West Indian, and Black British
> Stand Firm inna Inglan.[40]

The lines probably refer to Margaret Thatcher's notorious appearance on the current affairs television program *World in Action*, which aired on ITV on January 27, 1978; discussing immigration, she suggested that white British people feared they might be "rather swamped by people of a different culture."

From a different standpoint, Jayaben Desai, a leading figure in the bitterly protracted Grunwick labor dispute in Dollis Hill, London (1976–1978), insisted the strike was not only about pay but also, fundamentally, "about human dignity." To underline her point, Desai claimed, "the treatment we got was worse than the slaves in *Roots*."[41] Considered in the abstract, this is an utterly incommensurate statement. However, that Desai could make such a comparison, despite her personal history as a Gujarati who left Tanzania in the wake of its Africanization policies, says something about the late 1970s cultural constellation that framed some of the most interesting British receptions of *Roots*. Shortly afterward, Dennis Bovell, LKJ's regular musical collaborator, released an instrumental dub reggae track, "The Grunwick Affair" (1978), affirming solidarity with the strikers, although the dispute primarily involved South Asian women. *Roots*, reggae, and Grunwick became common reference points in newly forged cultural and political connections during this period of black British culture.

Continuity and Change

Exclusive emphasis on the initial moment of a film or a television series' reception can obscure its longer-term impact and changes in how it is perceived over time. *Roots'* presence in British culture extends from the late 1970s to the present, partly due to reruns and new distribution formats. It was repeated on BBC1 in September and October 1978, accompanied by a documentary, *Haley's Comet: The "Roots" Phenomenon*, produced by Tony Laryea, one of the few black British BBC television producers during that period. *Roots* was broadcast again on BBC1, in May and June 1981, falling between the Brixton and Handsworth riots. Video cassette recorders became more widely available from the 1980s onward, part of the shift toward what John Ellis calls the televisual "age of plenty," where today one can consume the miniseries through satellite or cable television, DVD purchase, or internet access.[42] Now available across diverse platforms, *Roots* will never again be the "event television" it was in April 1977, but it has become closely woven into some accounts of black British personal and family histories.

To explore this further, and to open up questions about elements of continuity and change in *Roots'* reception, I briefly consider here the four email and face-to-face interviews I conducted in 2014.[43] Given the small size of the sample, and my limited focus on continuity and change over time, I have only differentiated between interviewees on the basis of age. My minimal aim was to pay homage to Olive Morris's approach, by addressing ordinary people's memories and perceptions, to supplement the occasional journalistic canvassing, for example during *Roots'* thirtieth anniversary in 2007, of black British celebrities and public figures for their recollections.[44] Howard Becker argues that even "one interview is sometimes quite sufficient to establish that something is possible."[45] My interviews demonstrate that it remains possible, nearly forty years after *Roots*' first screening, to bridge the distancing effects of "abolition discourse."

There was one clear element of continuity in my interviewees' responses. Everyone endorsed Haley's view that "the story of black people in England is the same [as in the United States], but it's a step removed." Doreen, for example, wrote "the anger, frustration and of course the humiliation that was portrayed in *Roots* bore similarities with slaves that were brought to the Caribbean; therefore my forefathers had the same treatment." Kisi (thirties), named after the character in *Roots*, said "we all came from slavery... so wherever it was, everyone was able to identify with it." Another woman described *Roots* as impressing on her the "human face" of slavery more vividly than was the case during her schooling in Ghana, where the main focus was on its more abstract economic, social, and political dimensions (Amma, fifties).[46] Amma's perspective, as a Ghanaian who moved to London in the 1970s, differed from those respondents who "came from slavery," but she was just as emphatic about *Roots*' relevance and emotional resonance for black British viewers. She recalled how *Roots* further accentuated "two extreme reactions" she had experienced, prior to her viewing of the miniseries in the early 1980s, in social relationships between black African Britons and black Britons with links to the Caribbean: "some are very hostile ... those who resented being sold into slavery ... others love you because they see you as representing the source, a part of their heritage they would like to know about."

Strong emotional engagements with *Roots* did not preclude the posing of questions about its relationship to more complex or challenging aspects of black history. Doreen, for example, wrote, "over time I have felt that certain aspects of the story must have been 'airbrushed.' In particular, I would have liked to have seen more of the lives of the African people prior to the enslavement. Why were they enslaved, how did that come about?" All of my interviewees expressed views about *Roots* in relation to African involvement in the slave trade, despite me not soliciting comments on this point. In episode 1 of *Roots*, both black and white characters mention African chiefs' and traders' involvement in the supply of slaves, and the four men who physically capture Kunta Kinte are black men (supervised by whites). It is open to debate whether this constitutes airbrushing or sufficient acknowledgment of this issue within a narrative primarily focused on experiences of slavery after capture. The salient point is that this issue had a higher profile for my interviewees than it did for the *Race and Class* contributors.

This issue may have been foregrounded in the interviews partly because I was a white male interlocutor. As Howard Schuman and Jean Converse have pointed out, politeness and a desire not to offend may be factors in this situation.[47] In this case, black interviewees' references to African involvement in the slave trade could be their attempts to mitigate what they perceived as my white guilt. Although this possibility cannot be ruled out, the fact that all four of my interviewees independently broached this issue suggests a broader trend. Doreen's comment, for example, can be linked to the "further literature on black history and the slave trade" that *Roots* prompted her to read. The "textual environment" surrounding *Roots* has changed since 1977 with the production of more books and television programs by or involving black British and African American writers and intellectuals that address, in various ways, the question of African involvement in the slave trade.[48] Examples include Caryl Phillips's novel *Higher Ground* (1989); Ekow Eshun's *Black Gold of the Sun* (2005); the documentary series presented by Henry Louis Gates Jr., *Wonders of the African World* (aired in Britain as *Into Africa*, BBC2, July–August 1999); and *Motherland: A Genetic Journey* (aired BBC2, February 14, 2003), described by participant Rick Kittles as "*Roots II, Roots* revisited."[49]

This changing "textual environment" is embedded in what Alison Donnell describes as the further consolidation and diversification of black British culture, since the 1980s, to a point where it "could now afford to entertain internal disputes and controversies without being under threat."[50] Likewise, most contemporary historians acknowledge "the export of slaves emerged through a complex process in which Africans most certainly were not without agency," while firmly rejecting any insinuation of equivalency, or that "Africans were to 'blame' for the slave trade."[51] This changing textual and cultural environment has contributed to different individual perspectives on *Roots*, without necessarily diminishing emotional engagement. As Doreen put it, "my feelings [about the miniseries] have not changed," despite the questions her further reading encouraged her to pose.

My analysis does not purport to offer a complete picture of *Roots'* reception in the historical moments I have considered. There were many other black British responses to *Roots* in the late 1970s, beyond the circle of *Race and Class* contributors and sympathizers, although Morris's, and to a certain extent LKJ's, contributions provide some insight into this wider field. Future research into the historic and contemporary British reception of *Roots* could also consider white Britons' ongoing relationship, or lack of same, with the miniseries. *Roots'* resonance for other British minority ethnic populations, "mixed-race" viewers, or black British audiences from various class, regional, and gendered backgrounds, could also be explored. Nevertheless, one thing is clear. Over and above the tendencies in different historical moments, or the standpoints of particular individuals, the evidence considered here suggests there are many stories to tell about *Roots'* British reception that go beyond the myopia of "abolition discourse."

1. I use the term *black British* to refer to Britons who identify as being of African or Caribbean descent, although not everyone who could be designated as such would wish to be described in this way. I therefore follow Lola Young, *Fear of the Dark: "Race," Gender, and Sexuality in the Cinema* (London: Routledge, 1996): "The issue of language constructed with a discourse of 'race' is difficult: it is hard to discuss events, issues, material and attitudes without using terms which are problematic. One way of indicating unease with particular terms is to place them in quotation marks. . . . Generally speaking, I problematize terms when they are first used and trust that the reader will remember not to take them at face value" (198).

2. Martin Barker and Janet Staiger, "Traces of Interpretations: Janet Staiger and Martin Barker in Conversation," *Framework: The Journal of Cinema and Media* 42 (2000), accessed June 30, 2016, http://media.wix.com/ugd/32cb69_2b962808928e4649a5f3c436a3e64ab1.pdf.

3. Alex Haley quoted in "Sticking Pins into a Best Seller," *Times* (London), April 12, 1977, 12.

4. Judie Newman, *Fictions of America: Narratives of Global Empire* (London: Routledge, 2007), 75–76.

5. Ross Wilson, "Remembering to Forget?—The BBC Abolition Season and Media Memory of Britain's Transatlantic Slave Trade," *Historical Journal of Film, Radio and Television* 28, no. 3 (2008): 391–403, 395.

6. Emma Waterton and Ross Wilson, "Talking the Talk: Responses to the Bicentenary of the Abolition of the Slave Trade in Government Documents, Media Responses and Public Forums," *Discourse and Society* 20, no. 2 (2009): 382.

7. W. Stephen Gilbert, "The Week in View," *Observer*, April 3, 1977, 30.

8. Iain Johnstone, "Americans on *Roots*: Some Personal Views," *Radio Times*, April 9–15, 1977, 15, 17.

9. George Hutchinson, "The Signals from the Voters Are Unmistakable," *Times* (London), April 30, 1977, 12.

10. Billy Smart, "The BBC Television Audience Research Reports, 1957–79: Recorded Opinions and Invisible Expectations," *Historical Journal of Film, Radio and Television* 34, no. 3 (2014): 458.

11. BBC Audience Research Unit, "A Study of British Viewers' Reactions to the *Roots* Series," February 1978, BBC Written Archives Centre (WAC), VR/78/29, 3.

12. Darrell Mottley Newton, *Paving the Empire Road: BBC Television and Black Britons* (Manchester, U.K.: Manchester University Press, 2011), 4.

13. Sarita Malik, *Representing Black Britain: Black and Asian Images on Television* (London: Sage, 2002), 179.

14. BBC Audience Research Unit, "A Study of British Viewers' Reactions to the *Roots* Series," 4, appendix A, 3.

15. James Murray, "A New Lesson—Black Is Noble," *Daily Express*, April 12, 1977, 17.

16. Avery F. Gordon, "On 'Lived Theory': An Interview with A. Sivanandan," *Race and Class* 55, no. 1 (2014): 3.

17. Ibid., 2.

18. Ambalavaner Sivanandan in "Responses to *Roots*," *Race and Class* 19, no. 1 (1977): 391–403, 104, 105.

19. Colin Prescod in "Responses to *Roots*," 83.

20. Robin Nelson, *State of Play: Contemporary "High-End" TV Drama* (Manchester, U.K.: Manchester University Press, 2007), 163.

21. Helen Taylor, "'The Griot from Tennessee': The Saga of Alex Haley's *Roots*," *Critical Quarterly* 37, no. 2 (1995): 55.

22. Ana Laura Lopez de la Torre quoted in Red Chidgey, "Do You Remember Olive Morris?," *Red Pepper* 173 (2010): 34. But compare Tracy Fisher, *What's Left of Blackness: Feminisms, Transracial Solidarities, and the Politics of Belonging in Britain* (Basingstoke, U.K.: Palgrave Macmillan, 2012), 74–77; Tanisha C. Ford, *Liberated Threads: Black Women, Style and the Global Politics of Soul* (Chapel Hill: University of North Carolina Press, 2015), 142–150.

23. Raymond Williams, *Marxism and Literature* (Oxford: Oxford University Press, 1977), 197.

24. Olive Morris in "Responses to *Roots*," 94.

25. Paul Gilroy, *Small Acts: Thoughts on the Politics of Black Cultures* (London: Serpent's Tail, 1993), 10.

26. Liz Obi quoted in Chidgey, "Do You Remember Olive Morris?"

27. Chidgey, "Do You Remember Olive Morris?"; Hazel V. Carby, *Race Men* (Cambridge, Mass.: Harvard University Press, 1998).

28. Chidgey, "Do You Remember Olive Morris?"

29. Olive Morris in "Responses to *Roots*," 94.

30. Purnima Mankekar, *Screening Culture, Viewing Politics: An Ethnography of Television, Womanhood, and Nation in Postcolonial India* (Durham, N.C.: Duke University Press, 1999).

31. Leila Kamali, "The Sweet Part and the Sad Part: Black Power and the Memory of Africa in African American and Black British Literature, " *Atlantic Studies* 6, no. 2 (2009): 213.

32. Kobena Mercer, *Welcome to the Jungle: New Positions in Black Cultural Studies* (London: Routledge, 1994), 100.

33. Robert McGill, "Goon Poets of the Black Atlantic: Linton Kwesi Johnson's Imagined Canon," *Textual Practice* 17, no. 3 (2003): 568, 572.

34. LKJ in "Responses to *Roots*," 84.

35. A. Sivanandan, *A Different Hunger* (London: Pluto Press, 1982), 89.

36. Linton Kwesi Johnson, "Reality Poem," on *Forces of Victory*, LP (Island, 1979).

37. LKJ in "Responses to *Roots*," 84.

38. Stuart Hall, Chas Critcher, Tony Jefferson, John Clarke, and Brian Roberts, *Policing the Crisis: Mugging, the State and Law and Order* (London: Macmillan, 1978).

39. Ashley Dawson, *Mongrel Nation: Diasporic Culture and the Making of Postcolonial Britain* (Ann Arbor: University of Michigan Press, 2007), 53.

40. Poet and the Roots, "It Dread Inna Inglan," on *Dread Beat an' Blood*, LP (Virgin, 1978).

41. Jayaben Desai quoted in Pratibha Parmar, "Gender, Race and Class: Asian Women in Resistance," in *The Empire Strikes Back: Race and Racism in 70s Britain*, Centre for Contemporary Cultural Studies (London: Routledge, 1992 [1982]), 267.

42. John Ellis, *Seeing Things: Television in the Age of Uncertainty* (London: I. B. Tauris, 2000).

43. For detailed discussion of my methodology, see Martin Stollery, "Methodology for Focused Interviews about Black British Reception of the Television Mini-Series *Roots*," accessed February 17, 2015, https://independent.academia.edu/martinstollery /Other.

44. See, for example, Kwame Kwei-Armah, "Going Back to My Roots," BBC News, March 23, 2007, accessed February 4, 2015, http://news.bbc.co.uk/1/hi/magazine/648 0995.stm.

45. Howard Becker, untitled contribution in Sarah Baker and Rosalind Edwards, *How Many Qualitative Interviews Is Enough?* (National Centre for Research Methods Review Paper, 2012), 15, accessed February 11, 2015, http://eprints.ncrm.ac.uk/2273/.

46. See Bayo Holsey, *Routes of Remembrance: Refashioning the Slave Trade in Ghana* (Chicago: University of Chicago Press, 2008): 122–148.

47. Howard Schuman and Jean Converse, "The Effect of Black and White Interviewers on Black Responses," *Public Opinion Quarterly* 35, no. 1 (1971): 44–68.

48. On "textual environment" see Nick Couldry, *Inside Culture: Re-imagining the Method of Cultural Studies* (London: Sage, 2000).

49. See Hannah Little, "Genealogy as Theatre of Self-Identity" (PhD diss., University of Glasgow, 2010), 193–195, accessed January 28, 2015, http://theses.gla.ac.uk/1434/.

50. Alison Donnell, ed., *Companion to Contemporary Black British Culture* (London: Routledge, 2002), xiv.

51. Toby Green, *The Rise of the Trans-Atlantic Slave Trade in Western Africa, 1300–1589* (Cambridge: Cambridge University Press, 2012), 20.

CHAPTER NINE

Re-Rooting *Roots*

The South African Perspective

NORVELLA P. CARTER, WARREN CHALKLEN,

AND BHEKUYISE ZUNGU

Africa has always called its diaspora home. The mass displacement caused by the East and West African slave trade in which millions of Africans were subjected to the cruelty of capture, imprisonment, and forced labor provokes their descendants to seek answers about their heritage, history, and personal identity. There are occasions in which an event ignites a noticeably compelling interest in the slave trade that took place on the continent of Africa. The miniseries *Roots* created such a spark as millions of Africans watched the series. Although most Americans may assume the viewing of *Roots* was as easy as selecting the appropriate television station, watching the 1977 premier of *Roots* in private homes was not convenient in South Africa. In fact, the miniseries was banned in South Africa until 1984.[1]

As interest in *Roots*, both as a book and as a miniseries, expanded throughout the world, the reception in South Africa may not have been anticipated by the global community. In apartheid South Africa, the book was mysteriously overlooked by the censorship bureau and became a best seller in 1977. According to the *Washington Post*, it was so popular in South Africa that an abbreviated version of the book was created expressly for the one million black residents in the African township of Soweto.[2] That version reduced the book's price from $15, which was too expensive for most Soweto residents, to a range of lower prices depending on location and demand. The soundtrack for the television version was scored by American Quincy Jones but featured South African singers Letta Mbuli and her husband, Katse Semenya. The LP soundtrack soared in sales to become a best seller among black South Africans.[3]

However popular the book and soundtrack, the Nationalist government declined to air the miniseries on South African television in 1978 in line with their apartheid segregationist, national policy.[4] Born in 1948 out of the colonial exploitation of South Africans of color, apartheid racially stratified the country in favor of the white minority until 1994. *Apartheid*, an Afrikaans word literally meaning "the state of being apart" or apart-hood, entrenched racial segregation through laws imposed by the white minority that restricted the social, economic, and political rights of the black majority. Apartheid classified people into four racial groups: black, referring to the indigenous African population; white, including those of European descent; colored, those of mixed ethnic origin with ancestry from Europe, Asia, and various African and Khoi San groups; and, finally, Indian, who were descended from indentured laborers brought from India to South Africa to work on sugar cane plantations in the late 1800s. Each group under the system of apartheid was organized hierarchically, with whites at the top and blacks at the bottom. Whites enjoyed maximum political, social, and economic freedoms, while the rights of all other groups were systematically restricted through violent suppression.

This oppressive system shaped the way South Africans interpreted *Roots* when the U.S. International Broadcasting Agency screened the series in five locations across the country in two marathon sittings of six hours each.[5] For black South African viewers, their lives under the oppressive system of apartheid was analogous to the experiences of men and women of African descent in *Roots*. Although separated by over a century, the similarities between South African apartheid and U.S. slavery have been well documented in the literature of both countries.[6] These points of convergence shaped the South African response to *Roots*, especially with respect to its critique of slavery and inequality, economic exploitation, the destruction of family relationships, and finally the creation of racial systems of superiority and inferiority.

Apartheid Censorship

To produce, maintain, and replicate racist ideology, the apartheid government utilized both hard and soft power. South Africans of color in their daily lives were relentlessly met with hard power, exemplified through state-sanctioned police brutality, harassment, and violent dispossession. Simultaneously, with the intention of controlling thought in the country, the Nationalist government utilized soft power to tightly control the flow of information through legislation. Information in the form of print media, academic freedom, radio, books, films, and theater productions contrary to the ideals of the apartheid government were banned and intensively censored, and its producers were often harassed or imprisoned.

While the apartheid regime initially utilized legislation to enforce censorship, eventually it resorted to state-sponsored violence. Scholar Christopher Merret argues that over one hundred laws inhibited the flow of information in South Africa.[7] Earnest control of information by the apartheid regime spanned forty years, beginning with the Public Safety Act of 1953. This act, instituted by the Department of Information, sought to disrupt internal communication and set the stage for the detention of journalists. Over time, attention turned to controlling expressionist forms of media with the Publications Act and the Internal Security Act of 1974, respectively. These acts banned specific titles, authors, and organizations that were deemed by the Department of Information to be contrary to the aims of the apartheid state. Merret calculates that 23,345 titles submitted to Publications Control Board between 1970 and 1990 were subsequently censored or banned.[8] The late 1980s also saw an increase in state-sponsored violence against intellectual "transgressors," as the government called them. Authorities were empowered to control individuals, proscribe publications, and declare war on any antiapartheid movement. The government tightened the ban on many titles through harassment, state-initiated death squads, and right-wing terror organizations.

Merret argues that apartheid controlled information for two broad reasons: tactical and ideological. As a tactic, enforcing strict control over information acted as an extension of white supremacy over the black majority.[9] Scholar Brian Bunting proposes that "apartheid [was] so resilient and sure of itself [that it] had a permanent intellectual and psychological need to control all forms of expression."[10] The desire for control stemmed from a racist ideological base that promoted division, exploitation, and authoritarianism through law, administrative process, and brute force. Efforts to assert complete control over South African society were not always fully effective. Indeed, one inconsistency was exemplified in the official state response to *Roots*. Although as already noted the novel evaded censorship to become the nation's top selling book in 1977, the miniseries was officially banned until 1984, when it was broadcast on Bop-TV, a station specifically set aside for the "homeland" of Bophuthatswana.[11] Kerry Bystrom and Sarah Nuttall argue that the miniseries was banned because it embraced ideals contrary to the apartheid government's larger aim, which was to erase black people literally and symbolically from the nation.[12] But banning *Roots* as a television series, but not as a novel, reveals the inefficiency of the system to fully implement the impractical policies and, in effect, validated the significance of the miniseries in visual form, sharpening its political message for black viewers living under the oppression of apartheid.

In 1976, the same year *Roots* was published in the United States, resistance against apartheid was reaching a peak. The first high schools for black students built in 1972 to perpetuate the Bantu Education—a policy designed to produce manual laborers for white industries—also became the galvanizing points for antiapartheid resistance across the country. Schoolchildren became aware of the gross inequalities and began to resist through various means. Seeing Bantu Education as the face of apartheid, students used their experience of inferior schooling to galvanize resistance to apartheid in the broader student body. These movements used the secondary schools as networks of resistance and began to resist through boycotting, peaceful protest, and intimidation of Nationalist government superintendents. This resistance peaked in June 1976, when black students from Soweto Township peacefully protested against the use of Afrikaans as a language of instruction and were met with police brutality. Scholar Sifiso Mxolisi Ndlovu notes that, although the official death toll was 575, this number has been disputed, with many scholars arguing it is higher.[13] Perhaps the most famous of these victims was Hector Pieterson, then aged twelve. One of the first students to be shot and killed by police, Hector became an icon for the 1976 Soweto resistance march in apartheid South Africa. A photograph circulated worldwide of a crying young girl hurriedly walking with a young male student who was carrying her fatally wounded brother. Hector's death became the battle cry for the dismantling of apartheid.[14]

Although the protest march began in Soweto, student resistance spread throughout the country and catalyzed increased police brutality, detention, and torture. It also led to deepened and more overt resistance as youths boldly protested and were subjected to violence and police cruelty for their role in reforming educational policy. Against this backdrop, *Roots* appeared in South Africa. The visual portrayal of slavery as a system of oppression and the impact of this system on individuals reflected very closely the lives of South Africans of color, posing both tactical and ideological threats to white minority control.

Roots and the Lives of Apartheid South Africans

Given *Roots'* portrayal of oppression of black people, the miniseries was banned by the South African government as undesirable. Although the miniseries remained unavailable through official avenues until 1984, in 1978 the U.S. International Communications Agency screened *Roots* in five venues across South Africa: Johannesburg, Pretoria, Durban, Cape Town, and the all-black township of Soweto. Requests to show the miniseries came from far and wide. The Kwazulu Legislative Assembly, the local governing body of South Africa's five million Zulus, formally requested permission to set up viewings for its people. According to journalist Caryle Murphy, multiracial audiences of three hundred people sat on the floor in Cape Town to watch the miniseries in two marathon screenings. In Durban, 1,400 people congregated in three rooms to watch the staggered, three-hour showings on four consecutive nights. At every site, people had to be turned away. In one case, a black projectionist had to be protected by the police because a group of black men were angry over being turned away from viewing rooms that had exceeded capacity.[15]

The intense interest in these screenings reflects the extent to which South

African viewers connected the position and status of blacks in U.S. society during slavery with the effects of the apartheid system under which they lived. *Roots* resonated with South Africans because of their similar experiences of racial exploitation and discrimination fueled by white supremacy. For example, one of the most powerful parallels between U.S. slavery and South African apartheid was the legal implementation of freedom and equality for white citizens alongside the legal prohibition of freedom and equality for black citizens. In *Roots*, black Americans could not move about freely and were legally defined as property, without the rights attendant to other human beings. Through chattel slavery, white authorities controlled the movements and interactions of slaves who worked and toiled, essentially livestock used for the owner's benefit. In apartheid South Africa, black Africans were totally segregated and confined under the rules and regulations of the minority white population. Black Africans worked for meager wages that kept them in poverty and oppressive living conditions. In contrast, whites in *Roots* and South Africa experienced freedom of movement, self-determination, travel, and engagement in the day-to-day operations in their communities.

Roots also revealed the material gulf between the enslaved and the owners. Several of the scenes in *Roots* showed the wealth that slave owners accumulated in their massive plantations, real estate holdings, businesses and properties, livestock, and carriages. The productive and reproductive labor of their slaves generated for their slave masters massive amounts of wealth. *Roots* also demonstrated how this wealth could impact their family members for generations, and that slave ownership could serve as a springboard for upward mobility. Meanwhile, black characters in *Roots* remained subject to violence and mired in poverty for generations.

South Africans engaged in an institutionalized system of racism that was very similar to slavery and used apartheid as a legal means of engaging in economic exploitation.[16] White South Africans designed the system of apartheid to ensure that black citizens could not participate in democracy, own property or businesses, work to earn livable wages, or accumulate earned wealth. They, too, accumulated wealth at the expense of their black citizens and continued to profit from economic exploits.[17]

In addition to portraying slavery as an economic institution, *Roots* contains poignant scenes showing men and women being forcibly taken from their homes, confined and violated in dungeon-like slave forts, shipped on deadly vessels to America, sold as pieces of property, and forced to work as slaves for the remainder of their lives. White South Africans reacted to *Roots* with anger and passion because they were perpetrating similar inhumane acts on black South Africans in the 1970s. The white South African government forcibly removed black men from their families and homes, putting them to work in the gold and diamond mines to bring wealth and luxuries to white families. Removing black men from their families and redirecting their labor to white benefit correspondingly impoverished and degraded the circumstances of black families.

Black women, meanwhile, were limited to employment as domestics in whites' homes while their own families were left in dire conditions. While white families lived in comfortable and affluent neighborhoods, black families were forced to live in shacks and subhuman conditions. White children were provided quality housing, health care, and schooling, whereas black children were denied adequate homes, medical attention, and education. Under the oppression of apartheid, black men and women were not able to provide for their families, and relationships suffered and often were shattered.

Roots also demonstrates the effect of slavery on interracial friendships in a storyline involving Kizzy and Master Reynolds's niece, Missy Anne. Kizzy is a slave-child who has fun and plays with Anne, who is her age. Decades after Kizzy is sold to another master, the women meet unexpectedly on the road as adults. Immediately, Kizzy recognizes and tries to speak to her former friend. Anne, however, denies ever knowing a "darkie named Kizzy." She treats her as a slave, demanding that Kizzy fetch her a cup of water. Kizzy surreptitiously spits into the cup before handing it to her unsuspecting former friend. The scene ends with Kizzy expressing bittersweet revenge as she realizes the impact of her status on a childhood relationship. It is now clear to Kizzy that she was merely a slave to a person she thought was her friend. As slavery is depicted in *Roots*, so was apartheid in South Africa a system capable of destroying friendships as children grew into adulthood and faced pressures to conform to societal norms.

Given the parallels between the historical context of the miniseries and the contemporary experiences of South Africans, viewers reacted strongly to the screenings. Throughout the viewings, Murphy interviewed white South Africans who were distraught over scenes in *Roots* and black South Africans in various audiences who expressed their sadness at seeing their own lives reflected in the enslaved African Americans on screen. Yet viewers also expressed optimism at the positive outcome experienced by Haley and his ancestors' long quest for freedom. A powerful and redeeming theme of *Roots* is the resilience of some black characters, their perseverance despite dire circumstances. They never give up on life, and their efforts are reflected in changes occurring during their lifetimes. This aspect of *Roots* ensured that South African viewers responded to the screenings with hope as well as sorrow.

When the miniseries was shown before an all-white audience in Pretoria, one woman had a visceral response during episode 5, when Miss Anne refuses to recognize her childhood friend Kizzy. The woman stormed out of the theater yelling, "What are they trying to do?" In a fury, she began to rip down the billboards and posters for the film. As reported by Murphy, the woman returned the next day to apologize to movie officials, even offering to pay for the damaged posters. She claimed to have been "incensed by the thought that the film was only being shown in South Africa, because of American disapproval of her country's racial policies."[18] The official informed her that the series was playing all around the world, not just in South Africa.

The same article reports that U.S. officials claimed one white South African was overheard to say that "we must get the 'Nats' [members of the ruling National Party] to see this before they kill us all." Murphy notes that although South Africa's all-white parliament was invited to screen the miniseries, virtually all members refused to see it. Colin Eglin, the leader of the opposition, was the only member who agreed to see *Roots*. Despite having read the book, one white legislator refused to see the movie "unless the U.S. government was prepared to also show films about all the 'Harlems' that exist in the United States." Fear and indignation were the greatest prevailing feelings among many white South Africans. When a mixed-race writer saw the film, he wondered, "If there is going to be a local version [of *Roots*], who will dare write it?"[19] South Africa was known for exiling, imprisoning, and even assassinating anyone—particularly artists, musicians, writers, and journalists—who threatened the apartheid regime. Rewriting a version of *Roots* for South Africa would be nearly impossible.

For some black South Africans, watching the series was an emotional experience because they internalized *Roots*. A middle-aged black woman, watching in an all-black audience, wept openly. She had just been released after being held without charge for five months in a detention center. Many of the responses by black South Africans opened old wounds and exposed the raw oppression they were currently facing. One black woman claimed, "It leaves you dazed.... I was depressed after I saw it." One of the viewers was Ellen Khuzwayo, a fifty-one-year-old social worker living in Soweto. Ellen was a leader in her community and affectionately known as the "grand old lady of Soweto." However, during apartheid she was arrested by the police and held in a detention center for over six months, then unceremoniously released without being charged. She noted that when she saw the scene in which Kunta Kinte is kidnapped, she was moved beyond expression. Many black South Africans could empathize with the *Roots* characters being captured and not knowing why or how long it would be until they were freed, because these were tragedies they had personally experienced. Most of the black South Africans who Murphy interviewed almost reflexively returned to their own personal encounters with apartheid and U.S. slavery. "People keep on saying we are freer than those slaves," said one black viewer. "But I see us in exactly the same situation. The white community here lives in a democratic atmosphere, but the black community lives in another world and in complete oppression."[20]

Other black South Africans found hope in *Roots*. Some cited that the miniseries was a lesson in perseverance. "We got a lot of encouragement from it," said one young black Soweto resident. "Kunta Kinte was striving to get his freedom and for us that meant that in spite of everything . . . we don't have to give up." Other black residents referenced the progress that black Americans had made in the United States, mentioning people like Andrew Young, a civil rights activist later appointed as ambassador to the United Nations by President Jimmy Carter in 1977 (the same year the miniseries debuted), as giving hope to black people all over the world.

Ultimately, the viewing experience for black South African audiences was something of a Greek tragedy and comedy. The *Johannesburg Post*, a black-oriented newspaper, ran a commentary on *Roots* that shrewdly observed, "*Roots* Wasn't Funny—But We Laughed." Journalist Ernest Shuenynane wrote, "whenever lines that degraded blacks were spoken, whenever action that displayed naked cruelty towards blacks was seen, the black audience reacted with laughter. But the laughter was not similar to that I usually hear at parties, night clubs, shows and functions. . . . It was empty, cold and creepy." A viewer from the Soweto audience, Zuko Tofile, explained exactly what Shuenynane was discussing. "It was not really a laughter of joy," Tofile said, "It was caustic. It's like when I don't want to cry openly. I want to show that I'm strong and I don't want to show my enemy that I'm hurt. . . . I laugh to keep from crying."[21] Thus, *Roots* was posed not as comedic relief but rather as a tragic mask behind which grunts of disgust and anguish were concealed. It was laughter without smiling.

Re-Rooting and the Reception of *Roots*

Re-rooting occurs when events connect African diaspora to their homeland (although "re-rooting" has been used to describe poverty, it also fits the diaspora context).[22] Taking multiple forms, re-rooting attempts to thread together African histories and voices within the complex realms of identity, race, and belonging. It is powerful in the sense that it describes and spurs Africans to action. Julius Nyerere, the first leader of Tanzania after independence in 1967, delivered the Arusha Declaration outlining his vision for the country.[23] The declaration embodies re-rooting by focusing on political, social, and economic emancipation, and affirming the belief that African dignity must be reclaimed by Africans themselves. While re-rooting is often exemplified in written form, it has also been exhibited through film and other media. The television series *Roots* exemplifies re-rooting because it encompasses the reality of slavery and prompted viewers to actively search for greater meaning; it spurred them to action.

Roots marked a significant shift from interest to insight into slavery and contributed to robust conversation about the lived and historical experience of slaves and colonized people worldwide. Spilling over from the epicenters of spaces with deeply rooted slave histories into the so-called periphery, descendants called for justice and challenged the foundation of slavery in their respective countries. Even as *Roots* aired, colonialism, slavery, and exploitation in Africa continued unabated. In 1978, Western Sahara, Seychelles, Djibouti, Zimbabwe, and Namibia remained firmly under the grip of European colonial powers. As already discussed, in South Africa the apartheid government was brutalizing black South Africans en masse.

Efforts to end oppression in these countries come from forces both internal and external. Internally, citizens rose up and continue to rise in an ongoing struggle to uproot colonialism and oppression. Externally, works of art such as *Roots* contribute tremendously to a global conversation about the end of colonialism in these countries through sanctions, boycotts, and civilian pressure. African American children growing up watching *Roots* would be spurred to support U.S. sanctions against South Africa a decade later. They provided the leaders of the antiapartheid struggle the necessary negotiation leverage to transition peacefully to a more peaceful, democratic South Africa.

Roots as a book and miniseries also prompted writers and artists in South Africa to use various media to express themselves about slavery and colonialism in the postapartheid era. While apartheid suppressed the opportunities for South Africans to trace their genealogy, there have been attempts to reverse this pattern since apartheid officially ended in 1994.[24] Postapartheid "*Roots* narratives" encompass the work of black Africans, Khoi and San, Chinese immigrants, Indian indentured laborers, Jewish settlers, and Afrikaners.[25] The broad range of narratives is reshaping the understanding of colonial history, dispossession, and belonging in the country.

For example, Botlhale Tema, a secretary general for the South African Commission to the United Nations Educational, Scientific and Cultural Organization (UNESCO), was involved in the South African chapter of the UNESCO Slave Route Project, which aimed to broadly explore slavery in South Africa. Tema wrote *The People of Welgeval*, a South African neo-slave narrative. Drawing on Haley's version of *Roots*, Tema reflects on the realization that she is descended from slaves, and she articulates the need to highlight the hidden forms of slavery that operate in South Africa.[26] Set against the backdrop of the Transvaal Republic's Sand River Convention of 1852, which outlawed slavery in the then republic, *The People of Welgeval* narrates the 1852 abduction of two children, Maja and Motumi, from their father, Chief Moloto, in the village of Moletji. The children are sold into slavery by the Boers as *inboekelinge* (black ivory), and the novel then traces the lives of these two siblings and their descendants over three generations.

Her book in a sense addresses the question posed by a *Roots* viewer years earlier: "If there is going to be a local version [of *Roots*], who will dare write it?" Indeed, a blurb for the book announces that "South Africa has been waiting for its Alex Haley, who traced his family back . . . and wrote the classic *Roots*."[27] Tema sees her work as the South African perspective. Thus, her book intertwines with *Roots* in a variety of ways. Like Haley's book and miniseries, *The People of Welgeval* uses a narrative style beginning with thick descriptions that became broader as time passes, with only a few pages about the author herself. Naming and sequence also references *Roots*; just as Kunta is renamed Toby in *Roots*, so Maja is renamed Christina. Christina marries a slave, Polomane, and gives birth to Stephanus, who in turn has a son named Davidson, who fathers the author, Tema. Finally, Tema like Haley pushes the history of slavery into the mainstream, breaking the silences that had prevailed in both countries. In particular, Tema's work for the first time forged strong links between slavery in the Cape and suffering of the black majority in South Africa.[28]

Like Haley and Tema, Diana Ferrus, a South African poet of mixed Khoi and slave ancestry, responded to the history of slavery through a written medium. Ferrus's 1998 poem "I've come to take you home" calls for the remains of Sarah Baartman, a South African slave, to be brought home for a dignified burial. Her poem provoked a nationwide campaign and brought worldwide attention to the remnants of slavery, much as *Roots* did two decades earlier.[29]

Sarah Baartman, a Khoi San slave born in 1789 in South Africa, was taken to London and Paris, where she was forced to perform in "freak show" exhibitions. Renamed the Hottentot Venus, which mixes the racist term for Khoi San people with Venus, the Roman goddess of love, Sarah Baartman was subjected to the worst forms of colonial oppression and gendered exploitation.[30] While alive, her body and bodily features were exhibited so as to perpetuate scientific racism. Throughout her life, she was forced by her owners to submit to physical examinations conducted by scientists and artists. This trend continued even after her death in 1815 at the age of twenty-five, when instead of being buried with dignity, her body was dissected by George Curvier. Her brain, skeleton, and genitalia would go on to be exhibited at French museums for more than a century, ending in 1974.[31]

Ferrus's poem, like *Roots*, brought the attention of the world back to the realities of slavery through the voices of their descendants. As *Roots* injected vigor into the public discourse of entrenched slave narratives, so Ferrus's poem galvanized the political momentum necessary to restore justice to Sarah Baartman. After the fall of apartheid in 1994, Nelson Mandela, then president of the republic of South Africa, wrote to French officials demanding the return of Sarah Baartman's remains for a dignified burial in her homeland. The request was met with resistance and legal debates that delayed the process. The French parliament contributed to the debate, stating that her remains were part of the French National Collection. Ferrus's poem, published in 1998, rallied a worldwide lobbying effort that resulted in Baartman's remains being returned in March 2002. The poem was so powerful that it was even entered into French law.[32]

Ultimately, re-rooting is perhaps best captured in the humanities and the arts. In the case of *Roots*, the media of poetry, film, and novels pushed the intertwining lives of slaves and their descendants together, resulting in a more revealing history. The depictions of the lives of slaves spurred people globally to action and demonstrated the power of artwork to deepen dialogue about meaning, often threatened by distortion, dilution, and deflection.

Reflections from Two South Africans

We believe that including here the personal reflections by coauthors Bhekuyise Zungu and Warren Chalklen as black and white South Africans will make the South African experience of *Roots* more real for readers. Regarding *Roots*, outside of their homeland one of the first questions they are confronted with as South Africans is, "What did you think of it?" Viewing the miniseries almost forty years after its initial broadcast provides a perspective that is personal, political, and relevant. So often our job as scholars is to interpret facts and to leave personal opinions out of it. However, this chapter represents a unique moment in which their opinions as scholars and citizens matter both for the impact *Roots* had on them and for the insight they provide on where change can go in the future.

An educator at the University of Witwatersrand in Johannesburg, South Africa, Bhekuyise Zungu also works as a community advocate. Having grown up under apartheid, he recalls that even childhood did not shield one from the oppression and violence of that system. While Zungu loves his hometown of Soweto, with its music, soccer, and community, he vividly recalls attending segregated schools and living in a constant state of policing. For example, when he was a middle school student, an Afrikaner patrolman holding an R4 rifle followed him and others throughout the day during even the most mundane activities. "He would follow me into the toilet and back to class," says Zungu. Although apartheid was an institutionalized norm, Zungu knew from a young age that it was wrong. However, he also was well aware that those who spoke out against the government paid for it dearly, usually with their lives. Attending school during the height of apartheid was fraught with fear, since everywhere Zungu went there were Afrikaners patrolling around in intimidating vehicles. "If you were black, you went to school or work and came home, and at each moment one was constantly under the threat," Zungu recalls. Conversely, "Black South Africans were not in the fields," he contends.

"But many of the men worked in the gold mine and the women as domestic servants. Black labor was relegated to menial or brutish work."

Accordingly, when Zungu watched *Roots* for the first time, he felt that it described exactly what most black South Africans were experiencing physically and psychologically then. For Zungu, history was repeating itself but evolving in its form. He witnessed firsthand the violence that wreaked havoc on the lives of black people. "In *Roots* it was clear the system was not a friend of black people, just like South Africa," Zungu claims. He recalled a neighbor who killed two blacks, for which he was imprisoned for just nine months, while another neighbor was imprisoned for five years for smacking a white person. In other words, violent black offenders with black victims were quickly returned to their communities and even the smallest of physical offenses against white bodies were treated with severity. During apartheid, Zungu personally witnessed the violent deaths of many people. Among these were children he went to school with who had been killed by state violence, children whose bodies he helped bury. The violence that African Americans experienced during the U.S. civil rights movement was no different from what Zungu and black South Africans experienced in their nation's struggles to end apartheid. For Zungu, the official ending of apartheid in 1994 was not in the distant past and its effects are ever present.

Zungu understands why *Roots* was banned: "*Roots* was banned because the regime did not want us to identify with anyone outside of South Africa. They used the education system to make us accept our situation and see things their way." He adds that, for many black South Africans, watching "*Roots* was like watching our own lives, describing on screen exactly what we were going through every day." Identifying with the struggles of others offers a powerful way to connect with people around the globe to discuss and hopefully dismantle the racist and colonial oppression that marginalized people experience daily. Zungu's school encouraged him and others to read the novel. For Zungu, having the book available was the best way to understand Haley's message and how it could influence the antiapartheid movement in South Africa.

As a white South African, Warren Chalklen's experiences with apartheid and *Roots* were quite different from Zungu's. Born in 1988 in Johannesburg, Chalklen grew up in a world on the cusp of change. He has a younger adopted sister who is of mixed race (referred to by South Africans as colored). This dynamic in his home shaped much of his understanding of the world and sensitized him to the needs of marginalized people. In many ways, Chalklen's upbringing was atypical. From a young age, he did things differently from his white counterparts. He studied isiZulu, majoring in both English and isiZulu in college. Few white South Africans speak Zulu, which they considered inferior to English or Dutch, but this did not dissuade him.

A group of U.S. students visiting South Africa mentioned *Roots*. "It was the first time I had heard *Roots* being spoken about as something important," said Chalklen. Although he had previously thought of it as just another Hollywood miniseries, he decided to research it and reflect on it.

Chalklen first learned about slavery in the United States in high school. Part of the lesson required learning about different forms of slavery around the world, in particular how colonization occurred in South Africa, and how that process led to apartheid. When it came to slavery in the United States, Chalklen states, "I remember my teacher calling it 'forced migration,' not slavery." His teacher added that, "What we saw in the Belgian Congo was slavery, what we saw in South Africa was slavery, but in the United States although it's called slavery, it was actually 'forced migration.'" Furthermore, in his predominantly white school, Chalklen's teacher attempted to sanitize slavery in the United States by reframing it. Chalklen was instructed that, when it came to African Americans, they were enslaved only in a specific period of history, and once slavery ended, there was no need for the class to continue further study of African Americans because the United States was a "first world country." Even his friends of color bore this sentiment: "I remember my black friend saying to me, 'African Americans complain about slavery, but they have no idea what it was like to live under apartheid because slavery is over, and it was almost over a hundred years ago, but we're still dealing with our parents who are illiterate today.'" For Chalklen, his interpretation of these responses from white and black friends and teachers framed his understanding of U.S. slavery as no longer relevant to contemporary conversations.

Only during his college years was Chalklen able to draw clear lines regarding the links between economics, politics, and the social inequality both in South Africa and abroad. In several courses, his professors explained the traditional, indigenous education systems that existed in South Africa before colonialism, and how colonialism in South Africa dismantled those systems to set up an apartheid-controlled education system, which then fostered a racial hierarchy of advantages and disadvantages based on skin color. Previously, slavery was presented to him as a social Darwinist approach. His college classes now challenged this notion, creating cognitive dissonance.

"Now, as I reflect," says Chalklen, "part of confronting this truth was an incredibly difficult process for me to understand because that white history was my own history." The white supremacist narrative he had been taught as a child did not match what he was learning in college and the reality he was living as a young white male in postapartheid South African society. For Chalklen, his college class was transformative because it was challenging the social, political, and economic systems. He claimed, the professor's class "was about fracturing myths ... myths I had built a lot of trust in during my youth."

When Chalklen first visited the United States, his transformation regarding race and racism continued. His most striking personal transformation was understanding how his white privilege operated in both South Africa and the United States. White privilege, in particular, was a useful framework for Chalklen to understand how the system of racism continues to reproduce itself unabated. He realized that, although South Africa has a white minority, white people in both South Africa and the United States enjoy the same amounts of privilege. "I enjoy privileges that American citizens of color do not enjoy at the hands of their own institutions, not because I am special," says Chalklen, "but because I am white, which amplifies for me that the system of white privilege is real and in many ways universal. It operates differently for each white person but holds true in different ways for all." Chalklen acknowledges that while living in the United States in a predominantly white town, his skin color allowed him to be able to walk down the street without fear of being racially profiled by the police. This was a reality that could not be said for many African American men or for black South African men, such as Zungu. For Chalklen, this is when the lessons of *Roots* hit home. *Roots* put faces to a system that continues to find ways to maintain its power through deception and discrimination.

Zungu, Chalklen, and the many South Africans who viewed the miniseries or read the book cannot escape the distinct parallels of their lived experiences. Whether stolen and shipped to a faraway land to be worked to death, or forced to work in mines and railways in one's homeland, the outcome was the same. Neither group profited from their own labor. According to Zungu, "All of us were enslaved in one way or the other." For these scholars and others, today's question lies in where communities go from here.

Certainly, each nation is past the days of slavery and apartheid, but the effects and the underlying infrastructure of racism in both countries remain. "In America, over hundred years after *Plessy v. Ferguson* [the U.S. Supreme Court case legalizing segregation] and in South Africa, over twenty years after apartheid, we are still living *Roots* now," contends Zungu. Chalklen agrees: "Being outside the country I began to see things more objectively and saw how colonization has continued despite the façade that things have changed. In *Roots* we see the bondage of slaves who are landless, controlled by the wills of their masters and stripped of human dignity. While political equality was achieved in our country, the social and economic sphere mirrors *Roots*. Black South Africans are not in physical bondage, but they continue to be excluded from social services and economic opportunity in much the same way they did under apartheid, which exemplifies a type of bondage."

Today white South Africans still control the majority of the land, continuing the 1913 Land Act that gave whites 87 percent of the land and reduced land ownership of black South Africans to less than 13 percent, despite their comprising more than 80 percent of the population. White South Africans, despite being less than a tenth of the population, still owned more than eight-tenths of the economy in 2015. Even within the white community, a small number of families continue to monopolize the wealth. Given the rise in economic opportunity for black South Africans, including a rising middle class and black billionaires, Chalklen argues that questions remain: Who are black South Africans really working for? Who reaps the profits at the end of the day? Unfortunately, there is less than a 15 percent chance that these profits are reaped by the black majority. Black South Africans are still working for white South Africans in the same way they have always done, although business is now conducted under different names or titles. Angered by white privilege, Chalklen believes change is impeded because "white South Africans hide the fact that they do very little or nothing at all to change the way society produces unequal outcomes by race to their advantage."

Conclusion: Unearthing and Deconstructing

Despite the initial miniseries ban, *Roots* made its way into popular South African visual and literary culture. The two main impacts *Roots* has had in South Africa fall into two distinct time periods: from 1994 to 2004, unearthing stories; and from 2004 until 2014, deconstructing deeper meanings. In the first period, which begins with the first democratic elections in South Africa, the country was focused on unearthing stories, particularly the immediate stories of postapartheid South Africans such as Sarah Baartman and other former slaves. *Roots* was largely responsible for this undertaking and the search for voices. Unbanned in 1984, ten years before the first democratic elections in South Africa, *Roots* provided a precedent for reclaiming lost voices and offered South Africans a new lens through which to scrutinize their own context. In the first ten years after apartheid ended, South African set about "unearthing" the lost and silenced histories of their country and its people.

In the second period, from 2004 until 2014, people's efforts shifted from "unearthing" to deconstructing deeper meanings. With a treasure trove of stories now at their disposal, South Africans spent this decade deconstructing black South African stories and voices, finding meaning, and tracing genealogy. Paul Faber, for example, compiled *Group Portrait South Africa: Nine Family Histories*, which traces the genealogies of nine South African families with slave histories all over the world, thereby extending the tradition of re-rooting. In this sense, *Roots* served as a springboard for further conversations about the impact of slavery not only on black South Africans, but on other populations, as well.

In the final analysis, the impact of *Roots* lies in what it means to be empowered and oppressed and empowered again. *Roots* emphasizes the importance of having a story and a voice in the midst of struggle. Too often the dominant narrative of white history and the counterhistory of postapartheid led by a black majority have excluded the voices of Khoi San, San, Chinese, and Indian South Africans who were also enslaved. Reflecting on their absence, *Roots* raises additional questions, such as where are their voices? Where are their histories? *Roots* becomes a catalyst for asking every culture not only about the foundations of its oppression, but about the development of its empowerment. Optimistically, the significance of its message will continue to serve as a catalyst for positive actions toward freedom and quality of life for people around the globe.

NOTES

1. Peter Macdonald, *The Literature Police: Apartheid, Censorship and Its Cultural Consequences* (Oxford: Oxford University Press, 2009).

2. Agence France-Presse, "*Roots*: A S. African Best Seller," *Washington Post*, May 30, 1977, D8.

3. Ibid.

4. Macdonald, *Literature Police*.

5. Caryle Murphy, "Rage, Tears Meet *Roots* in South Africa," *Washington Post*, May 27, 1978, A15.

6. Franz Fanon, *Black Skin, White Masks* (New York: Grove, 1967); George M. Fredickson, *A Comparative Study of American and South African History* (Oxford: Oxford University Press, 1982); William Gumede, "Centuries of Colonialism, Slavery and Apartheid: A Legacy of Institutional Racism." *Pambazuka News*, December 4, 2014, http://www.pambazuka.org/en/category/features/93555, accessed August 30, 2015; C. Rajab, *Zuma Out of Touch with Reality in South Africa* (Durban: Mercury, 2012); Fred Morton, "Slave-Raiding and Slavery in the Western Transvaal after the Sand River Convention," *African Economic History* 20 (1992): 99–118.

7. Christopher Merret, "A Tale of Two Paradoxes: Media Censorship in South Africa, Pre-Liberation and Post-Apartheid," *Critical Arts* 15, no. 1 (2001): 209.

8. Ibid.

9. Christopher Merret, *A Culture of Censorship: Secrecy and Intellectual Repression in South Africa* (Cape Town, South Africa: David Philip Press, 1994).

10. Brian Bunting, *The Rise of the South African Reich* (Harmondsworth, South Africa: Mayibuye Books, 1986 [1964]).

11. Kerry Bystrom, "Writing Roots in Post-Apartheid South Africa," *Safundi: Journal of South African and American Studies* 14, no. 1 (1998): 17–36.

12. Kerry Bystrom and Sarah Nuttall, introduction, in "Private Lives and Public Cultures in South Africa," edited by Kerry Bystrom and Sarah Nuttall, special issue, *Cultural Studies* 27, no. 3 (summer 2013): 307–332.

13. Sifiso Mxolisi Ndlovu, "The ANC's Diplomacy and International Relations," in *The Soweto Uprising: The Road to Democracy in South Africa*, vol. 2, *1970–1980* (Pretoria: University of South Africa, 2001), 615–668.

14. Lucille Davie, "Hector: The Famous Child Whose Face Is Unknown," *Joburg,*

June 14, 2002, http://www.joburg.org.za/index.php?option=com_content&do_pdf=1 &id=880, accessed July 31, 2015.

15. Murphy, "Rage, Tears Meet *Roots* in South Africa."

16. George. M. Fredickson, *A Comparative Study of American and South African History* (Oxford: Oxford University Press, 1982).

17. William Gumede, "Centuries of Colonialism, Slavery and Apartheid: A Legacy of Institutional Racism," *Pambazuka News*, December 4, 2014, http://www.pambazuka .org/en/category/features/93555, accessed July 31, 2015.

18. Murphy, "Rage, Tears Meet *Roots* in South Africa."

19. Ibid.

20. Ibid.

21. Ibid.

22. Ashwin Desai, *Uprooting or Re-Rooting Poverty in Post-Apartheid South Africa? A Literature Review* (Durban, South Africa: South Africa-Netherlands Research Programme on Alternatives in Development, 2005).

23. Julius Nyerere, "The Arusha Declaration and TAMU's Policy on Socialism and Self-Reliance" (Dar es Salaam, Tanzania: Tanganyika African Nation Union, 1967).

24. Bystrom and Nuttall, introduction.

25. Ibid., 319.

26. Botlhale Tema, *The People of Welgeval* (Cape Town, South Africa: Zebra Press, 2005).

27. Fred Morton quoted in ibid., back cover.

28. Bystrom, "Writing Roots in Post-Apartheid South Africa."

29. Diana Ferrus, "I've Come to Take You Home," reprinted in *I've Come to Take You Home* (Kuils River, South Africa: Xibris Press, 2011), 15–16.

30. Pamela Scully and Cliffton Crais, *Sarah Baartman and the Hottentot Venus: A Ghost Story and a Biography* (Princeton, N.J.: Princeton University Press, 2009).

31. Sadiah Qureshi, *Peoples on Parade: Exhibitions, Empire, and Anthropology in Nineteenth-Century Britain* (Chicago: University of Chicago Press, 2011).

32. Ferrus, "I've Come to Take You Home."

CHAPTER TEN

One Man's Quest
Chiang Ssu-chang, *Roots*, and the Mainlander Homebound Movement in Taiwan

DOMINIC MENG-HSUAN YANG

On May 10, 1987, Mother's Day, in the scorching heat of Taiwan's thriving capital and commercial center, Taipei, a small group of men in their fifties and early sixties gathered to protest in silence. Under the vigilant gaze of plainclothes police observing nearby, these lone seniors stood tall with sadness and determination, unfazed by the prospect of arrest and persecution. They distributed leaflets to passersby and raised signboards covered with passionate messages for their mothers and relatives in mainland China, whom they have not seen or heard from for decades. They wore matching white shirts printed with two large Chinese characters *xiangjia* (missing home) in front, and had poems, verses, and songs of nostalgia written on their backs (*figs. 2 and 3*). Numbering only about a dozen, the protestors formed a thin but solemn picket line on the western edge of Sun Yat-sen Memorial Hall. The hall was a prominent public monument in Taipei built by the island's exiled Nationalist dictator, Generalissimo Chiang Kai-shek, to commemorate his mentor and the founding father of the republic, Dr. Sun Yat-sen.

By staging a demonstration outside the hall, this tiny band of elderly men challenged openly the anticommunist ideology of the Nationalist Party, which had prohibited hundreds of thousands of Chinese civil war exiles, also known as mainlanders, in Taiwan from returning home to China since they relocated to the island in the mid-twentieth century.[1] Held on the cusp of Taiwan's steady march toward democracy, the Mother's Day demonstration was intended to pressure the Nationalist authorities to allow the aging mainlanders to go home and see their relatives, from whom they had long been separated. Spearheaded by this small group of retired soldiers, the campaign came to be known as the Mainlander Homebound Movement (MHM).[2] By that autumn, the MHM had gained so much momentum and generated so much public sympathy that it compelled the generalissimo's eldest son and successor Chiang Ching-kuo to lift nearly four decades of travel prohibition to the "communist bandit territory" of mainland China.

FIGURE 2. At the MHM Mother's Day demonstration in 1987, Chiang Ssu-chang (far left, in sunglasses) holds a sign that reads "Do you miss home?" Courtesy of Digital Archives for Memories and Narratives of Taiwan Waishengren.

FIGURE 3. Police harass the MHM protestors in Taipei, May 1987. Courtesy of Digital Archive for Memories and Narratives of Taiwan Waishengren.

In less than a year, more than two hundred thousand homesick mainlanders in Taiwan rushed back to China in desperate search for lost homes
and relatives.[3] More would follow in the next few years. The success of MHM
also paved the way for the return of Taiwanese political dissidents in North
America and Japan, as well as Taiwanese civil war captives stranded in mainland China since the great divide in 1949. The movement also provided the
legal basis for displaced aboriginal populations on the island to go back to
their tribal homelands. More importantly, the MHM ended the decades-long
military standoff in the Taiwan Strait and opened the door to contemporary cross-strait interactions and negotiations. Scholars have lauded Chiang Ching-kuo and his counterpart in the People's Republic of China (PRC),
Deng Xiaoping, for reaching this historical compromise.[4] Yet, little is known
about the instrumental role played by a few ordinary veterans who found the
strength and courage to stand up to the authoritarian party state that oppressed them and, in doing so, changed the course of history in East Asia.

A key individual who helped orchestrate the MHM—in particular designing slogans and messages that won over the conservative public in Taiwan
and ultimately forced the hand of the generalissimo's son—was fifty-one-year-
old Chiang Ssu-chang, a retired Nationalist veteran who had become a high
school music teacher. In 1950, at just thirteen years old, Chiang was abducted
at gunpoint by a retreating Nationalist army unit passing through his tran-
quil fishing village on a coastal island in South China. Countless young men
and teenage boys were pressed into military service during the Chinese civil
war and Communist Revolution (1946–1950) and the earlier Anti-Japanese
War (1937–1945). Those who stood in solidarity with Chiang in 1987, including the vocal spokesman for the group, the truculent and intractable veteran
from Hubei Province, Ho Wen-teh, were among the hundreds of thousands
of mainland soldiers forcibly displaced to Taiwan.[5] They were not allowed
to return home or to have any contact with their families on the mainland,
as these attempts were considered high treason or espionage, punishable
by death under the martial law imposed by the generalissimo's authoritarian regime. Richard Nixon's historic 1972 visit to China and Sino-U.S. détente
brought new hope to homesick mainlanders on the island. In the early 1980s,
Deng Xiaoping's reform reopened China to outside visitors. Yet the Nationalists continued to prohibit contact from Taiwan until this courageous group of
retired soldiers led by Ho and Chiang finally cracked open the door.

Unlike his comrades, who were fighting for their right to return, Chiang
had already entered mainland China secretly via Hong Kong and reunited
with his family in 1982 prior to launching the MHM. Although most clandestine returnees wisely kept a low profile, Chiang not only helped forward letters he brought back from China but also encouraged others to go home in
defiance of the martial law.[6] Chiang's homebound journey and his social ac-

tivism were profoundly influenced by *Roots*, which aired in Taiwan in early March 1978, just over a year after the miniseries premiered in the United States.[7] In 1984, Chiang authored an article on the topic of return that was published in his native place association magazine (native place associations are civil organizations for mutual assistance formed by migrant populations from the same province or region in China). He used Alex Haley's determination to search for his African ancestry as an example to encourage fellow natives to take immediate action and find ways to go home.[8]

I first read about Chiang's source of inspiration in his published memoir in 2010 when conducting my dissertation research in Taiwan.[9] The memoir, *Xiangchou* (Nostalgia), was published in 2008. Fascinated by the effect of *Roots* on this retired Nationalist veteran who had little prior knowledge of African American history, I decided to pursue a separate project on him. This chapter is based on my personal interview with Chiang in July 2014, his published memoir, videotaped interviews of other MHM participants stored in the digital archives of Academia Sinica (Taipei), newspaper reports, and other documentary sources.

Chiang's story demonstrates the transnational political efficacy of *Roots* in a single but nonetheless extraordinary case of cross-cultural referencing and resonance of trauma. Several chapters in this book identify the political limitations of *Roots* in the United States. The following narrative illustrates how Haley's novel and the TV miniseries inspired one traumatized and oppressed yet determined individual in a distant land to take action against structures of power. And the action not only made a difference but helped alter the course of history. Chiang's case offers a new vantage point for us to reconsider the global influence and political potentials of *Roots*.

The Airing and Reception of *Roots* in Taiwan

The political, intellectual, and cultural tremors generated by Alex Haley's best-selling *Roots: The Saga of an American Family*—and its enormously popular TV miniseries adaptation, *Roots*—in the United States have been well documented.[10] However, there has hitherto been little research on the influence of *Roots* in East Asia, particularly in countries where the TV drama also became popular and was viewed by many audiences. These societies might not possess intimate knowledge of the Atlantic slave trade and racial discrimination in the United States, but their lifestyles, cultural trends, and literary productions came under heavy U.S. influence during the Cold War.

Taiwan was one such society. The island became a U.S. outpost in the West Pacific against the spread of communism in Asia following the outbreak of the Korean War in June 1950, when the Truman administration resumed support of the Nationalist regime—reversing its earlier policy of trying to establish a relationship with Mao's new government in China in order to split the socialist camp.[11] For the next decade and a half or so, U.S. aid and the presence of U.S. military, intelligence, and technical personnel helped sustain militarily and economically Chiang Kai-shek's island bastion of what was then called Free China, which transformed Taiwan's culture and lifestyle.

By the early 1970s, the winds of the Cold War had shifted. The U.S.-Taiwan alliance was on shaky ground in the wake of Nixon's visit to Beijing in search of an escape from the Vietnam quagmire. Yet, around the same time, the island's export-oriented industrialization developed rapidly under U.S. and Japanese investments and ample business opportunities created by the demands for the war in Indochina in what was later described as the Taiwan miracle.[12] As an increasing number of islanders began to enjoy abundant material wealth and an affluent lifestyle, they started consuming U.S. cultural products with great enthusiasm. People in Taiwan loved American novels, pop songs, TV shows, and movies. Even the islanders' deep sense of betrayal—following Nixon's visit to China in 1972 and the Carter administration's formal recognition of Beijing in 1979—did not stop them from assiduously following the media and cultural trends on the other side of the Pacific.

Roots aired to eager audiences in Taiwan on March 7, 1978. The anticipation started in early 1977, when the island's press began reporting on the extraordinary success of the African American TV drama in the United States.[13] Shortly after, two unauthorized Chinese translations of Alex Haley's book appeared on the market. Both pirated copies sold briskly.[14] In April 1977, the *China Tide*, a popular left-leaning literary magazine in Taiwan, reviewed Haley's book. The article explained the socioeconomic history of slavery as well as its cruelty and lasting influence in the United States.[15] Eager to follow the latest trends and the most talked-about series in the United States, the Taiwanese were impatient to see the epic African American family saga. In November 1977, China Television Company (CTV) purchased the miniseries from ABC and immediately started announcing the coming of *Roots* to their network.[16] A few months later, CTV broadcast *Roots* to viewers in Taiwan.

The island media reported that CTV paid a handsome copyright fee for the show.[17] Initially, CTV executives were ambivalent about purchasing *Roots* due to its high cost and their lingering doubts about whether the story could resonate with average viewers in Taiwan, who lacked a deep understanding of slavery in U.S. history. Yet, after witnessing the tremendous success of the show in the United States, CTV executives decided that it was "worth the risk to give it a try."[18]

They apparently made the right decision. The broadcasting of *Roots* caused a sensation in Taiwan. A local journalist described it as "a viewing frenzy." Although the ratings numbers and the profits generated by the show have never been disclosed, the venture was lucrative enough for CTV executives to purchase immediately the sequel, *Roots: The Next Generations*. On September 4, 1979, CTV began running the original series once again, followed by the sequel.[19]

The popularity of *Roots* was also evident in the island's warm reception when Cicely Tyson, one of the show's leading actresses, visited Taiwan in late June 1978. Approximately three months after the finale of the original series, the Emmy nominee for her role as Binta, young Kunta Kinte's mother in the Gambia, attended the Asia-Pacific Film Festival in Taipei. During the three-day event she became a media darling. Folks in Taiwan adored her, immediately forgiving her for coming on stage shouting in broken Mandarin *ni-ma-hao*? (How's your mother?) rather than *ni-hao-ma*? (How are you?).[20]

Although *Roots* resonated with viewers in Taiwan, when the show was over, people wiped their tears away and mostly forgot about it. The miniseries became just another television sensation imported from the West, having no apparent social impact. Nonetheless, years later *Roots* influenced Taiwan indirectly through an extraordinary individual. Chiang Ssu-chang, the retired Nationalist soldier and schoolteacher mentioned earlier, was so inspired by the story that three years after watching *Roots* he overcame tremendous obstacles to sneak back to China to see his family. Returning to Taiwan, he helped orchestrate the Mainlander Homebound Movement.

One Man's Quest to Return to China: Chiang Ssu-chang and *Roots*

I met Chiang on the early morning of Sunday, July 27, 2014, at the main gate of Academia Sinica, Taiwan's premier state-funded research institute. I established the initial contact in late 2013 through Mau-kuei Chang, a research fellow in the Institute of Sociology, Academia Sinica, who spent years collecting, preserving, and digitizing documents, images, and videotaped testimonies of MHM participants. The septuagenarian former soldier was an amicable and soft-spoken man of medium height and build. He walked and moved about briskly, full of life and energy despite his poor hearing. Chiang arrived with a translated copy of Alex Haley's *Roots* in his hand. In a previous phone conversation, he told me that he was excited to learn that a researcher from the United States was interested in knowing how *Roots* affected his life. As a leader of the MHM, Chiang was interviewed by many local journalists and scholars. There were even several made-for-television short documentaries about his life in 2007, when the entire Taiwanese society collectively looked back on two decades of cross-strait relations.[21] Yet, no one had ever asked him about Haley's book and the TV drama. The book he brought to the interview was one of the hard-bound pirated copies from early 1978, still in mint condition from his careful handling of the book. Before the taped interview began, Chiang remarked, "It's no longer easy to find one of these in Taiwan, even in secondhand bookstores. I lent the very first Chinese copy I bought after watching the TV show to a friend. But he never returned it!" Briefly, this congenial man seemed rather perturbed, perhaps because this important piece of his personal history was gone. He then went on to say, "I read the book and watched the show many times. I know every little detail."[22]

Chiang wasn't exaggerating. I had already read his 1984 article, in which he describes his experience watching *Roots* on television: "When this lengthy twenty-two day miniseries played on CTV, I left everything behind. I was glued to the television every night when it was on. Tears streaming down my face after I finished watching every episode. Following the TV series, a translated version of the book in Chinese became available. I bought one immediately and read every word carefully. The book shook my heart deeply. It strengthened my resolve to take action to 'repair the severed umbilical cord' [between me and my native land]."[23] Greatly touched by the story of Kunta Kinte, the retired veteran even purchased an English copy of the book. Not having much training in English, he labored over Haley's thick text with a dictionary. After reading the original version, he reports, "I was moved even more profoundly. There were things I could not describe. It's like [a fishbone] stuck in the throat."[24]

During the interview, I asked Chiang what exactly he saw in *Roots* that moved him so profoundly. Before I even finished the question, he pointed to the Chinese book he brought with him. The cover featured one of the most iconic images of the TV miniseries—young Kunta Kinte (LeVar Burton) locked in chains, an iron collar around his neck. Kunta was about to be sold on the slave market in Annapolis, Maryland (fig. 4). Mr. Chiang said this scene impressed him the most, and as he was speaking was visibly welling up with strong emotions. "You just look at this expression of helplessness and disorientation. I have this picture of me as a child soldier arriving in Taiwan. I didn't know what to do. I couldn't handle the situation. . . . We have the same look!"[25] Chiang emailed me a number of photos and personal documents two weeks before our scheduled meeting. I had these with me at the interview. Among the materials he sent was a black and white picture of a young boy wearing a rough cotton uniform. The boy stares blankly into the camera, just as Kunta Kinte stares blankly at the auctioneers and buyers in episode 1 of the TV series (fig. 5). This Nationalist veteran felt strongly connected to a teenage African slave from a distant time and a distant culture. Like Kunta, he was abducted at a young age and was put through a grueling sea passage and made to endure a life of servitude.

Chiang Ssu-chang was born and raised in a small fishing village on the coastal island of Daishan in South China in July 1936, a year before the Anti-Japanese War broke out. His birth name was Chiang Wen-piao. Ssu-chang

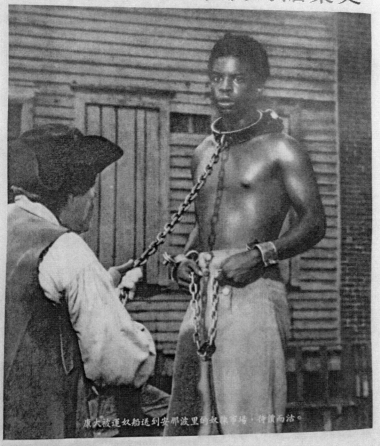

根

一個美國黑人家族的滄桑史

康大被運奴船送到安那波里倒奴隸市場，傷慎而沽。

FIGURE 4. The front cover of the 1978 Chinese edition of *Roots* that Chiang brought to our 2014 interview in Taipei.

Figure 5. Chiang Ssu-chang, age fourteen, circa 1951, after his induction into the Nationalist army. Courtesy of Chiang Ssu-chang.

was a pseudonym he made up to hide his identity in Taiwan from Chiang Kai-shek's military police when he absconded from the army unit that kidnapped him and his school friends in China.[26] For this reason, Ssu-chang became the name under which he was legally registered. Like Kunta Kinte, Chiang was forced by circumstances to change his name. Nevertheless, he was able to choose his own name instead of being forcibly given one by his oppressor. *Ssu* means "missing" or "thinking about." *Chang*, according to Chiang, was the name of a female middle school classmate he secretly admired back in Daishan.[27] Combined, these two characters represented his enduring but suppressed nostalgia for home.

Chiang's home island, Daishan, is the second largest landmass among some 1,390 isles, shoals, and rocks that comprise the Zhoushan Islands. These islands lie just off the coast of northern Zhejiang Province, outside the busy port city of Ningbo. They are known for their scenic natural beauty, abundant fishery, and rich religious and cultural heritage. Although China and the Gambia are nations far apart on different continents, the pastoral scene in Juffure, Kunta Kinte's home village, in episode 1 of *Roots* must have left a deep impression on Chiang. Like Kunta, Chiang spent his early childhood in a relatively secure and carefree environment. He was the eldest son of a well-to-do fisherman. The Japanese invasion in 1937 had little effect on his home island, as the war quickly moved inland. Chiang had fond memories of his childhood in Daishan. During our interview, he reflected on how his grandmother doted on him. His father paid well for him to be educated in the island's county seat, a privilege few could afford at the time. The victory over Japan in August 1945 brought little change to life in Daishan, although Chiang does recall that Japanese was suddenly no longer taught in school.[28] Notwithstanding Daishan's relative peace through the Japanese invasion in World War II, the ensuing civil war between China's two revolutionary parties would turn the island upside down and ultimately change the boy's life.

In early 1949, the Nationalist government in China began to crumble after its army suffered devastating losses at the hands of the Chinese Communists. Peace and tranquility in Daishan were shattered when hundreds of thousands of routed troops and refugees from the mainland poured into Zhoushan.[29] The Nationalists mobilized the local population to build barracks, roads, and an airbase in Daishan. Fishing, farming, and the salt trade were severely disrupted. The islanders were driven from their homes by troops and refugees seeking shelter or wood for fuel. The military confiscated their food and soldiers assaulted local women.[30] Before the Nationalists left Zhoushan for Taiwan, they pressed thirteen thousand male islanders, both young and old, into military service out of a total population of half a million.[31] Chiang was among this sea of human misery.

In the early afternoon of May 15, 1950, thirteen-year-old Chiang Ssu-chang was taking the long walk home from the county's middle school with his two classmates from the same village. The three boys were in jovial moods. They sang, giggled, and shoved one another as they strolled down the road, relishing a reprieve from their studies. On the previous night, the three had returned to their living quarters to find their middle school completely abandoned. At the otherwise empty school, they met an older student who was packing up to leave and who warned them to "go home or lay low because the army is pulling out," but the boys were too young to understand the implications.[32] It was common practice for many army units in China to press-gang civilians into service when they had to replace deserters or they were retreating from their enemies. Like the trading of human cargo in West Africa, a large number of innocent people were abducted, although in this case not for profit but for military service.

On that fateful day, after walking an open road for several hours, the three jolly young teenagers were less than a mile from their village. They came upon a company of Nationalist soldiers, who seized them at gunpoint. The terrified youngsters cried and screamed loudly, begging to be released. The young lieutenant commanding the company felt sorry for the boys and did

set them free. He even had a corporal escort the boys to hide in a small nunnery nearby. They were told not to show their faces until dark. However, the
three were too frightened and anxious to get home to heed this admonition.[33]
Slipping out of the nunnery, Chiang and his friends soon met another band
of troops on the same road. This time the youngsters' pleading and weeping were met with bone-crushing blows from rifle butts. Chiang received a
heavy whack to the waist. He could still remember how much it hurt as he
had trouble standing up straight for days.[34] Moments after being captured, an
older draftee in the group attempted to escape. He was immediately chased
down and shot dead by one of the soldiers. Witnessing the atrocity, the boys
huddled together, quivering in absolute horror. From that moment onward,
they followed every command given by the soldiers and did not dare to think
otherwise.[35]

Chiang's group was first locked in a makeshift dormitory for the construction workers who were building the Nationalist airbase in Daishan. They were
then forced to march all night with little food or water to the island's main
wharf, to be shipped off to Taiwan. Chiang remembers seeing female relatives
of fellow draftees weeping and kneeling along the road leading to the waterfront. They beseeched the soldiers not to take their loved ones away, but to no
avail. Scared, exhausted, and confused, Chiang and his friends kept quiet and
tried to hold back their tears, since every time they cried, the soldiers would
beat them.[36] Upon reaching the wharf, which was cordoned off by a battalion
of heavily armed troops, Chiang's group and hundreds of other draftees were
forced to strip and don military uniforms. They were herded onto a dozen
small boats, and then onto a transport ship anchored farther out. The an-
guished families on shore began to wail and scream loudly in desperation, a
scene that left an indelible mark on young Chiang. On the departing vessel,
the traumatized boy could no longer hold back his tears. He did not identify
familiar faces on the shore, but he later learned that his mother, then pregnant with his younger sister, was among the frantic crowd.[37]

The voyage from the Zhoushan Islands to Taiwan was short in comparison to the Middle Passage across the Atlantic. Nonetheless, it was harsh
and grueling. Chiang remembers boarding the ship on May 16 and arriving
at the Keelung Harbor in northern Taiwan three days later. According to
Chiang, the transport ship was packed with thousands of troops and draftees like him. Those onboard were only offered one meal (a piece of flatbread)
on the entire voyage and had to fight for water. Many people fell overboard
and drowned due to the crowding when they lined up on the deck to receive
water. Just as Kunta Kinte and his fellow captives experienced brutality and
coercion, there was constant violence meted out to those on board. Chiang
recalls: "There was a squad of military police from the division headquarters
with long sticks patrolling the lines. They smacked people around to main-

tain order. My friend and I were short because of our age. When we felt the sticks coming, we just ducked. The adults standing around us would get hit."[38]

Chiang's unit was assigned to the lower decks. They were commanded to sit on the floor with their legs tucked under for days on end, except for the short intervals they were allowed above decks to get water. "It was hot and smothering.... It was so crowded down there that every time someone tried to stretch his legs, he would kick the person in front," Chiang recalls.[39] Insufficient space accompanied by inadequate toilets meant that the floor was awash with urine, vomit, and feces. The filth and stench were unbearable. Asked whether he drew a parallel between this unpleasant journey and the slave ship scene in *Roots*, Chiang nodded and said, "certainly." He later remarked, "Of course they [Kunta and his fellow captives] had it worse than we did. Yet I thought we were just like them, only without the shackles."[40]

Not long after reaching Taiwan, Chiang and one of his friends escaped from the machine gun company that had kidnapped them. The two teens could no longer endure the daily physical abuse from the officers and soldiers in that unit. As a deserter, Chiang changed his name around this time to avoid capture by the Nationalist military police.[41] However, to survive physically in Taiwan, where he had no relatives or friends and did not speak the local dialects, Chiang later joined a unit in the Nationalist Air Force and served on the ground crew at an airbase. A relatively easier life in the air force did not alleviate Chiang's pain or nostalgia about being torn from his home, however, nor did it change his ill will toward the Nationalist military. As Chiang grew older, he became indignant and rebellious. He considered conscription to amount to bondage. This was why Kunta Kinte's rage, defiance, and impulse to escape in the novel and also depicted in the miniseries resonated with Chiang. Unlike other draftees who were afraid to speak out, Chiang spoke openly about being abducted by the army in mainland China, a taboo subject before Taiwan became a democracy. He refused to sign a "volunteer" form to extend his military service, which the Nationalist authorities compelled many of the mainland conscripts to submit in the late 1950s. Chiang also came under suspicion as a Chinese Communist spy because he told other recruits he had written to his father in China twice shortly after reaching Taiwan, before 1951, when the Nationalists clamped down on correspondence via Hong Kong.[42] When his superiors tried to bully him into submission, Chiang deserted again. This time, he got as far as the bus station outside the barracks. The internal security squad of the air force had already put him under surveillance. Chiang was apprehended immediately and sentenced to three years in a military prison.[43]

Chiang's incarceration became a major turning point in his life. Most of the time he was imprisoned, his cellmate was Jen Hsin-chu, a handsome and suave Nationalist fighter pilot from Guangdong Province. Jen was sentenced to death for attempting to fly an army aircraft across the Taiwan Strait back to China.[44] Well educated and sophisticated, Jen discussed Chinese history and literature with Chiang. He taught him the Latin alphabet and ballroom dancing. Shortly before the two bade their teary farewell before Jen's execution, he told Chiang not to put up futile resistance against an unjust system, throwing away his life as he had done, but instead encouraged Chiang to "build up your strength and wait for a chance [to strike back]."[45] Chiang followed Jen's advice after serving out his sentence. He convinced the Nationalist authorities that he had repented and reformed. Chiang took exams to enroll in a military academy. He received a postsecondary education and became a commissioned officer. When he retired from the military, he became a high school music teacher. He appeared to be a model citizen. Yet Chiang never stopped missing home, and he never stopped thinking about striking back at the Nationalists.

Watching *Roots* on television in early 1978, two decades after his imprisonment, reignited the fire inside Chiang. The African American TV drama became a catalyst for another major turning point in his life. It made him take action to embark on the journey home. During our interview, Chiang described a particular scene from the miniseries that motivated him. This was when young Kunta Kinte is flogged repeatedly but refuses to take the name "Toby" given by his owner. Chiang reminisced: "The scene was so moving.... I thought if this uneducated and powerless young African could be so bent on preserving his name and memory of home, I need to make a much stronger effort to go home no matter how great the obstacles were."[46]

In the next few years, he did just that. Chiang's memoir details his efforts to reestablish contact with his family in Daishan via intermediaries in the United States and Hong Kong.[47] Deng Xiaoping's reform in China in 1979 and a more tolerant political atmosphere in Taiwan during the late 1970s and early 1980s came at an opportune time for Chiang. Yet, planning a clandestine trip to China from Taiwan was still daunting because of the constant intimidation and bureaucratic obstructions.[48] Chiang was certainly not the only one who sneaked back to the mainland from Taiwan before the government lifted the ban in late 1987; thousands or even tens of thousands might have already made the trip by the mid-1980s (due to the secrecy of these undertakings, the exact figure remains unclear).[49] Yet, Chiang was among the first few who tested the limits of official tolerance by daring to cross the line in the early years.

On August 11, 1982, after overcoming tremendous obstacles and risking imprisonment, Chiang forged a fake identity with the help of a friend in Hong Kong and entered mainland China via Hong Kong and Macao.[50] More than thirty years had passed since his abduction. His family members were overjoyed to see him. At the dock of Ningbo, Chiang hugged tightly his three

FIGURE 6. Chiang reunited with his parents on Daishan Island, Zhejiang Province, China, August 1982. Courtesy of Chiang Ssu-chang.

siblings who came to receive him. The four adults huddled together and wept, ignoring the curious gazes of other passengers. They immediately took a boat to meet their mother, who was receiving medical treatment on the main island of Zhoushan. As the boat approached the dock, his second sister pointed out his mother and another younger sister among the crowd waiting ashore. Chiang yelled and waved at his mother hysterically. Before the boat came to a complete stop at the pier, he jumped on land, kneeled in front of the old woman, and began to cry loudly. With tears streaming down her own face, his mother held him tightly and caressed his forehead gently. Other family members formed a circle around the two. Everyone wept.[51] When the group reached the wharf at Daishan several days later, his anxious father was already waiting at the waterfront. Chiang fell to his kneels once again. His father sobbed and held him up. Tears came in a torrent. Chiang writes in his memoir: "I really couldn't stop crying. I cried on the walk to register with the local Chinese authorities from the wharf. I cried on the car ride home to Dongsha Village from Gaoting. I only stopped when it was time to pay ritual respect to our ancestors. I gave vent to more than thirty years of separation, resentment, and suffering"[52] (fig. 6). In *Roots*, Alex Haley gives vent to similar emotions at his ancestral village in the Gambia when the villagers greet him and cry out together, shouting his African family name: "A sob hit me somewhere around my ankles; it came surging upward, and flinging my hands over my face, I was just bawling, as I hadn't since I was a baby."[53]

Notwithstanding the joyful reunion with his family, Chiang was sur-rounded and pestered daily by Daishan residents. People came from all cor-ners of the island when they heard that someone had returned from Taiwan. They were eager to learn if Chiang had news of their relatives who had also been taken away by the Nationalists in 1950. They wanted him to forward let-ters and messages to loved ones. People camped outside the family home and waited for hours to see him. Chiang was overwhelmed by all the requests, but he made a promise to his fellow Daishan natives that he would do his best to locate their loved ones on Taiwan.[54]

The Mainlander Homebound Movement

Arriving back in Taiwan several days later, Chiang immediately contacted his friends and native place association. Over the next many months or so, he spent countless hours and went through a great deal of trouble to find the relatives of those who had asked for his help in Daishan. However, he got only lukewarm responses when he privately told these people, "I have already gone back. You should do the same. Your parents and family really miss you."[55] A majority of his fellow natives in Taiwan were cautious and even feigned in-difference. Although they privately wanted to return home just as much as Chiang, they feared reprisal from the Nationalist authorities. Chiang was will-ing to risk his own freedom and career to help others, but very few had the courage to act on this help, which made him feel frustrated and lonely. His article in his native place magazine was his attempt to use Alex Haley and the story of *Roots* to motivate his fellow expatriates.[56] But his words had no apparent effect.

In early 1987, Chiang received a telephone call from his friend Fan Hsun-lu, a political activist affiliated with the island's newly established political op-position, the Democratic Progress Party (DPP). Fan told Chiang that the DPP had been approached by several retired Nationalist veterans seeking the party's assistance in organizing a social movement to help them go home.[57] Although the Nationalists relaxed their political control considerably in the 1980s, partly due to growing strength of the political opposition, an over-whelming number of civil war exiles were government employees, teachers, and military personnel who feared losing their jobs and pensions by dis-obeying the law. Moreover, impoverished low-ranking retirees from the army lacked the financial means and overseas connections to establish contact with family on mainland China. Knowing this and still very passionate about assisting others to return, Chiang decided to help lead the movement. He met Ho Wen-teh and other veterans through Fan and her group of political and social activists who were running *Progress Weekly*, a magazine sponsored by the political opposition. Together they organized the MHM, which demanded that the Nationalists authorities lift the ban immediately on the grounds of reuniting families and social justice.[58] Ho, Chiang, and other retired soldiers would lead the charge by protesting in the streets and distributing leaflets in veterans' homes and other public places. The DPP and *Progress Weekly* would offer financial and logistics support behind the scenes.

The movement faced tremendous obstacles at first. Chiang and his comrades were not only continuously monitored by plainclothes police, they were also harangued by hostile spectators and, on one occasion, physically beaten by other retired soldiers, the very people they were trying to help.[59] The intrepid and headstrong Ho Wen-teh, who acted as spokesperson for the group, was ready to go to jail.[60] Another veteran, Hsia Tzu-hsun, even sold his house to establish an emergency fund for his family in case he was incarcerated.[61] The tiny movement was David facing the state Goliath. Although the government could have easily squashed the dozen members, the participants knew that the key to success hinged on whether their demand could find a sympathetic audience among the general public in Taiwan, especially the hundreds of thousands of retired soldiers and civil servants who had hitherto been staunch supporters of an authoritarian regime that prohibited them from contact with their loved ones in China. According to Chiang, the various essays he wrote in the five MHM leaflets were an important factor in gradually stirring up support for the movement, in particular from mainlanders. Rather than attacking the Nationalist regime outright in the leaflets, Chiang's essays argue that everyone has the right to go home to see their parents. This longing for one's "roots" is not only universal but also a cornerstone of Chinese culture. Chiang pointed out that ordinary soldiers had sacrificed a great deal for the nation, remaining silent for nearly forty years. Their parents in China were already quite elderly, if they were still alive, so the government should lift the ban without further delay. The message was simple but powerful.[62] In designing the message, Chiang drew from his personal return experience and from the motivation and inspiration he received from Alex Haley's *Roots*.[63]

The leaflets were effective. The Mother's Day demonstration at Sun Yat-sen Memorial Hall was followed by a massive rally at Chin-hua Junior High School in late June 1987. The meeting was attended by over twenty thousand people, including prominent university professors, social activists, the DPP politicians, and most important of all, a substantial crowd of retired Nationalist military personnel. As the rally was wrapping up, Chiang took the stage with his veteran comrades and Yang Tsu-chun, the cofounder of *Progress Weekly*, who was also a popular folk song singer. Together they asked the crowd to sing a 1930s Chinese song, "Mother, Where Are You?" From reading Haley's book and from his own homebound trip, Chiang knew the transcending power of searching for one's roots and belonging. He knew that affection for separated loved ones could overcome any external obstructions and in-

FIGURE 7. At the MHM rally at Chin-hua Junior High School on June 28, 1987, Chiang Ssu-chang and Yang Tsu-chun engaged the crowd in singing "Mother, Where Are You?" Courtesy of Chiang Ssu-chang.

timidations. This song drove these points home. The huge crowd of grown men wept openly during the sing-along (fig. 7). The event was soon reported to the Nationalist Party. It shocked the high authorities deeply, in particular Chiang Ching-kuo, who was gravely ill and near the end of his life. Facing a political opposition growing in strength, the Nationalists could not afford to lose their most loyal supporters. The ban was lifted later that year.[64]

Conclusion

Chiang's story illustrates the ways in which representations of African American cultural trauma resonated with a devastated and suppressed expatriate and motivated him to fight against an oppressive and unjust system, not only for himself but also for others. The case may be exceptional, but it offers a new perspective to reassess the influence and political efficacy of Alex Haley's work beyond U.S. borders.

Sadly, Chiang's reconnection with his "roots" did not end as happily as did Alex Haley's own search. Despite the intense and tearful reunion with his family early on, Chiang was heartbroken later to realize that he had become a stranger in Daishan and that his native village no longer felt like home. His relationship with his homeland and with relatives in China is similar to what

Saidiya Hartman describes in *Lose Your Mother*.[65] Although Chiang did not share this part of his personal story during our interview, his memoir reveals this sorrow.[66] Hundreds of thousands who followed his footsteps years later would experience the same reverse culture shock.

NOTES

1. See also Joshua Fan, *China's Homeless Generation: Voices from the Veterans of the Chinese Civil War, 1940s–1990s* (New York: Routledge, 2011); Mahlon Meyer, *Remembering China from Taiwan: Divided Families and Bittersweet Reunions after the Chinese Civil War* (Hong Kong: Hong Kong University Press, 2012).

2. For more on the MHM, see Chiang Ssu-chang, *Xiangchou*—yige *waishengren de liuli wu youshang* [Nostalgia—the exile and grief of a "mainlander"] (Taipei: Wenjin-tang, 2008), 180, 216–218; Zhongyang yanjiuyuan shehuixue yanjiusuo, "Xiangjia (fan-xiang yundong)" [Missing home (homebound movement)], in *Taiwan waishengren shengming jiyi yu xushi* [The life stories and memories of mainlander Taiwanese], Academia Sinica Digital Resources http://ndweb.iis.sinica.edu.tw/TWM/Public/content /story/hometown/gohome.html (accessed August 26, 2014).

3. Chiu Hei-yuan et al., *Dalu tanqin ji fangwen de yingxiang* [The effects of visiting relatives in mainland China] (Taipei: Caituan faren Zhang Rongfa jijinhui guojia zhengce yanjiu ziliao zhongxin, 1989), 41.

4. Jay Taylor, *The Generalissimo's Son: Chiang Ching-kuo and the Revolutions in China and Taiwan* (Cambridge, Mass.: Harvard University Press, 2000), 416–417; Ezra F. Vogel, *Deng Xiaoping and the Transformation of China* (Cambridge, Mass.: Belknap Press of Harvard University Press, 2011), 479–488.

5. See also Joshua Fan, *China's Homeless Generation*, 19–48.

6. Chiang Ssu-chang, interviewed by the author, July 27, 2014, Institute of Sociology, Academia Sinica, Taipei.

7. "Dianshi yingji gen zhongshi xiayue bochu" [TV miniseries *Roots* will begin next month], *Lianhe bao*, February 19, 1978, 9.

8. Chiang Ssu-chang, "Yige you zunyan de feizhouren: zaidu meiguo heiren zuojia aili kesi halei mingzhu 'Gen' zhihou zhi ganxiang" [An African with dignity: thoughts after reading again the masterpiece by American black novelist Alex Haley], *Zhoushan tongxiang* 188 (March 1984): 26.

9. Chiang Ssu-chang, *Xiangchou*, 212–215.

10. See William L. Van Deburg, *Slavery and Race in American Popular Culture* (Madison: University of Wisconsin Press, 1984), 155–157; David Chioni Moore, "Routes: Alex Haley's *Roots* and the Rhetoric of Genealogy," *Transition* 64 (1994): 4–21.

11. See Nancy Bernkopf Tucker, *Patterns in the Dust: Chinese-American Relations and the Recognition Controversy, 1949–1950* (New York: Columbia University Press, 1983).

12. See Thomas B. Gold, *State and Society in the Taiwan Miracle* (Armonk, N.Y.: M. E. Sharpe, 1986).

13. See Ying Hsiao-tuan, "Meiguoren zhengkan 'miyuantou' yibu hongdong de dianshi yingji" [Americans are rushing to see *Roots*, a sensational TV drama], *Lianhe bao*, February 13, 1977, 9.

14. Halei Ailikesi (Alex Haley), *Gen* [*Roots*], translated by Chang Yan (Taipei: Hao-shinian chubanshe, 1978), 7.

15. Su Wen-cheng, "Gen he yigen—heinu xueleishi" [*Roots* and "uprooting"—black slave's history of blood and tears], *Xiachao* [China tide] 2, no. 4 (April 1977): 86–88.

16. "Zhongshi jinqi tuichu 'gen'" [*Roots* is coming to CTV soon], *Lianhebao*, November 23, 1977, 9.

17. Huang Pei-lang, "Zhongshi jiemu xinchangshi huangjin shijian bo yingji yi 'gen' da qianfeng shitan guanzhong de fanying" [New CTV programming schedule tests the waters by first putting *Roots* on prime time to gain feedback from the audience], *Lianhe bao*, December 4, 1977, 9.

18. Ibid., 9.

19. Wang Yu-po, "'Gen' de xuji gengshang cenglou" [The sequel of *Roots* is even better], *Lianhe bao*, September 3, 1979, 9.

20. "'Gen' yingji nuzhujiao xixiliya lai baodao" [Cicely Tyson, the leading lady for *Roots*], *Lianhe bao*, June 29, 1978, 3.

21. Chiang Ssu-chang, *Xiangchou*, 180–189.

22. Chiang interview.

23. Chiang Ssu-chang, "Yige you zunyan de feizhouren," 26.

24. Ibid., 26.

25. Chiang Ssu-chang interview.

26. Chiang Ssu-chang, *Xiangchou*, 4.

27. Ibid., 294.

28. Chiang Ssu-chang interview.

29. See Chang Hsing-chou, *Yinghai tongzhou* [On the same boat at sea] (Taipei: Minzhu chubanshe, 1972), 33–40.

30. See Chen Ling, *Zhoushan chetui jimi dangan: liushi nianqian de yiye cansang* [Secret files of the Zhousan retreat: a piece of history from 60 years ago] (Taipei: Shiying, 2010), 41–46.

31. Ibid., 95.

32. Chiang Ssu-chang interview.

33. Chiang Ssu-chang, *Xiangchou*, 186–187.

34. Chiang Ssu-chang interview.

35. Chiang Ssu-chang, *Xiangchou*, 4.

36. Chiang Ssu-chang interview.

37. Chiang Ssu-chang, *Xiangchou*, 185.

38. Chiang Ssu-chang interview.

39. Ibid.

40. Ibid.

41. Chiang Ssu-chang, *Xiangchou*, 294.

42. Ibid., 5; Chiang Ssu-chang interview.

43. Chiang Ssu-chang, *Xiangchou*, 207.

44. See Kongjun zongsiling bu, "Jen Hsin-chu weifa an" [The case of Jen Hsin-chu], National Archives Administration, Hsinchuang District, New Taipei City, A305000000C/0045/013.1/2221/1/001.

45. Chiang Ssu-chang, *Xiangchou*, 208.

46. Chiang Ssu-chang interview.

47. See Chiang Ssu-chang, *Xiangchou*, 7–10.

48. Chiang Ssu-chang interview; Chiang Ssu-chang, *Xiangchou*, 10–11.

49. See Yin Ping, "Guixiang jie" [Return-home complex], *Yuanjian zazhi* [Global views monthly] 12 (June 1987): 16.

50. Chiang Ssu-chang, *Xiangchou*, 12.

51. Ibid., 15–16.

52. Ibid., 17.

53. Alex Haley, *Roots: The Saga of an American Family*, 30th anniv. ed. (New York: Vanguard Press, 2007), 879.

54. Chiang Ssu-chang interview.

55. Ibid.

56. Chiang Ssu-chang, *Xiangchou*, 18.

57. Fan Hsun-lu, "Fan Hsun-lu tan waishengren fanxiang yundong" [Fan Hsun-lu reflects on the Mainlander Homebound Movement], in *Taiwan waishengren shengming jiyi yu xushi* http://ndweb.iis.sinica.edu.tw/TWM/Public/content/story/collectable .jsp?pk=178 (accessed September 11, 2014).

58. Chiang Ssu-chang, "Chiang Ssu-chang tan waishengren fanxiang yundong."

59. Hsia Tzu-hsun, "Hsia Tzu-hsun tan waishengren fanxiang yundong" [Hsia Tzu-hsun reflects on the Mainlander Homebound Movement], in *Taiwan waishengren shengming jiyi yu xushi* http://ndweb.iis.sinica.edu.tw/TWM/Public/content/story/ collectable.jsp?pk=182 (accessed September 13, 2014).

60. Ho Wen-teh, "Ho Wen-teh tan waishengren fanxiang yundong" [Ho Wen-teh reflects on the Mainlander Homebound Movement], in *Taiwan waishengren shengming jiyi yu xushi* http://ndweb.iis.sinica.edu.tw/TWM/Public/content/story/collectable .jsp?pk=179 (accessed September 13, 2014).

61. Hsia Tzu-hsun, "Hsia Tzu-hsun tan waishengren fanxiang yundong."

62. See "Women yijing chenmo le sishinian" [We have kept silent for forty years], Mainlander Homebound Movement leaflet, unpaginated, April 1987.

63. Chiang Ssu-chang interview.

64. Wang Hsiao-po, "Wang Hsiao-po tan waishengren fanxiang yundong" [Wang Hsiao-po reflects on the Mainlander Homebound Movement], in *Taiwan waishengren shengming jiyi yu xushi* http://ndweb.iis.sinica.edu.tw/TWM/Public/content/story /collectable.jsp?pk=181 (accessed September 14, 2014).

65. Saidiya Hartman, *Lose Your Mother: A Journey Along the Atlantic Slave Route* (New York: Farrar, Straus and Giroux, 2007).

66. Chiang Ssu-chang, *Xiangchou*, 383.

CONTRIBUTORS

ERICA L. BALL is a professor of American studies at Occidental College. Her work interrogates the connections between African American expressive culture, gender, class formation, and popular representations of slavery. She is the author *To Live an Antislavery Life: Personal Politics and the Antebellum Black Middle Class* (University of Georgia Press, 2012). Her latest project explores slavery in the American imagination.

NORVELLA P. CARTER is a professor of education and endowed chair in urban education in the Department of Teaching, Learning and Culture at Texas A&M University. She is the author of numerous publications and the editor of the *National Journal for Urban Education and Practice*. As an urban specialist, she has presented her work in the United States and internationally in Canada, England, France, Mexico, Niger, and South Africa, among other countries.

WARREN CHALKLEN is an adjunct professor in the Department of Teaching, Learning and Culture at Texas A&M University. A former high school teacher and policy analyst, he earned his doctorate in curriculum and instruction from Texas A&M University and a master's degree in public administration from the Bush School of Government and Public Service. His research examines the intersection of Ubuntu philosophy, critical race theory, and the capabilities approach in South African education policy.

ELISE CHATELAIN earned her doctorate in cultural studies in 2012 from the University of California, Davis, and now teaches sociology at the University of New Orleans. Her academic work focuses on the representational politics of labor on film and television. Other research and teaching interests include domesticity and the family, youth culture, and style-fashion as entry points for examining the production and negotiation of meaning, subjectivity, and power in popular culture.

ROBERT K. CHESTER completed his undergraduate studies in England before coming to the United States in 2001. He teaches in the American Studies Department at the University of Maryland, College Park, where he obtained his doctorate in 2011. His research focuses on remembrances of war in U.S. culture, with particular attention to representations of World War II, race, and national identity in Hollywood cinema. His work has appeared in *American Quarterly* and *War and Society*.

CLARE CORBOULD is the author of *Becoming African Americans* (2009) and coeditor of *Remembering the Revolution* (2013). An Australian Research Council Future Fellow in Monash University's History program in Melbourne, she is working on a book about interviews with former slaves conducted in the 1920s, 1930s, and 1940s. With Michael McDonnell she is also writing an account of the memory and legacy of the American Revolution among African Americans.

HENRY LOUIS GATES JR. is the Alphonse Fletcher University Professor and founding director of the Hutchins Center for African and African American Research at Harvard University. He is an Emmy Award–winning filmmaker, literary scholar, journalist, cultural critic, and institution builder. He has authored or coauthored twenty books and created fifteen documentary films. He hosts the PBS TV series *Finding Your Roots—with Henry Louis Gates Jr.*

KELLIE CARTER JACKSON is an assistant professor in the Department of History at Hunter College, CUNY. Her research focuses on slavery and abolition, historical film, and black women's history. Her manuscript "Force and Freedom: Black Abolitionists and the Politics of Violence" is the first book-length project to address the politics of violence and black leadership before the American Civil War.

C. RICHARD KING, a professor of comparative ethnic studies at Washington State University, has written extensively on the racial politics of culture, indigeneity, race and representation, and white power. Among the books he has authored or edited are *Animating Difference: Race, Gender and Sexuality in Contemporary Films for Children*, *Beyond Hate: White Power and Popular Culture*, and *Redskins: Insult and Brand*.

DAVID J. LEONARD is a professor at Washington State University, Pullman. He is the author of *After Artest: The NBA and the Assault on Blackness* (2012).

DELIA MELLIS holds a doctorate in U.S. history from the Graduate Center, CUNY. She teaches U.S. history for the Bard Prison Initiative, where she is the director of College Writing and Academic Resources. Her research focuses on the role of violence in sustaining ideologies of race and gender and attendant structures of inequity in U.S. society. She is working on a book, "'The Monsters We Defy': Washington, D.C. in the Red Summer of 1919."

FRANCESCA MORGAN is an associate professor of history at Northeastern Illinois University in Chicago. She is the author of *Women and Patriotism in Jim Crow America* (2005). She has received an outside grant from the New England Regional Fellowship Consortium for her book project, "Nation of Descendants: Genealogy and the Self in America." She has also published in the *New England Quarterly* (2010).

TYLER D. PARRY is an assistant professor of African American studies at California State University, Fullerton. He received his bachelor's degree in history at the University of Nevada Las Vegas in 2008, graduating summa cum laude. Parry obtained his master's degree in 2011 and his doctorate in 2014 at the University of South Carolina. His research examines slave marriage and violence in the African Diaspora.

MARTIN STOLLERY is the author of *Alternative Empires: European Modernist Cinemas and Cultures of Imperialism* (2000). He has published numerous essays on various aspects of film and television history and on representations of the non-Western world. He remembers watching *Roots* when it was first screened on British television.

DOMINIC MENG-HSUAN YANG is an assistant professor in the Department of History, University of Missouri–Columbia. His research examines the mass exodus from China when Mao Zedong's Chinese Communist Party came to power in 1949. He is working on a book-length study of that exodus, which constituted one of the largest human migrations in East Asia following World War II. He has published related works in *China Perspectives* and *Journal of Chinese Overseas*.

BHEKUYISE ZUNGU has native proficiency in many South African languages. He holds master's degrees in social science education and in continuing and lifelong education from the University of Georgia. A doctoral student at the University of the Witwatersrand, he is also a lecturer in the School of Education at Wits University in South Africa.

INDEX

Nation of Islam, 9, 66, 132. See also
  Autobiography of Malcolm X; Malcolm X
National Party (South Africa), 171
Nazi(s), 64, 131, 139; American Nazi Party,
  140–141
NBC (National Broadcasting Company), 102,
  115, 129
Negro History Bulletin, 66
Neo-slave narratives, 50, 173–174
New social history, 63, 97–98, 100, 101–102,
  110
New York Times, 5, 7, 8, 71
Nixon, Richard M., 184, 186
Northup, Solomon, 9
Nostalgia culture, 97; fiction, 51–52; in *Roots*,
  110–111
Notting Hill Carnival, 157

Obama, Barack, 109
Oral history, 65
Oral History Review, 68

Parkinson (TV show), 148
Pascall, Alex, 158
PBS (Public Broadcasting Service), xiv, 4, 99
People of Welgeval, The (Tema), 173–174
Pieterson, Hector, 168
Pioneers of Television (TV series), 99
Plagiarism, 47, 57–59. See also *Roots* (Haley);
  Walker, Margaret
Playboy magazine, 139–140
Plessy v. Ferguson, 178
Progress Weekly, 196–197
Proud Shoes (Murray), 67–68
Public Safety Act of 1953 (South Africa), 166
Pulitzer Prize, xi, 12

Queen (Haley), 114

Race and Class (journal), 150–157
Race relations, U.S., 26–27
Racial triumphalism, 130–132. *See also* World
  War II
Racism, U.S., 27, 34–37, 39–40, 158. *See also*
  White supremacy
Raintree County (film), 117–118
Rape, 86, 89, 91–93
Reader's Digest, 7, 8;
Reagan, Ronald, 36–37

Reconstruction, 14, 40, 50, 67, 87, 92, 97, 102,
  121, 129
Red Ball Express (film), 131
Reed, Robert, 4, 83
Reggae, 157–159
Revolutionary War, 65, 130
Rich Man, Poor Man (TV miniseries), 29, 115
Richards, Lloyd, 129, 139
Rockwell, George Lincoln, 140
Rogers (Parks), Lillian, 98, 102
Rogers, Maggie, 98, 102
Roosevelt, Franklin Delano, 103
Roots (Haley), 67, 116; cultural impact of,
  2–3; plagiarism charges, 47–59; scholarly
  critique of, 11–14, 71–72; success of, 2
Roots (TV miniseries): Africa in, 116, 119;
  black actors in, 115–116; black American
  responses, 3, 8, 11–12, 37–41, 72, 126–
  127; Black British response, 152–156;
  black families in, xii, 10, 100–102;
  black masculinity in, 89–93; Black
  Power and, 92–95; censorship (South
  Africa), 165; class dynamics in, 84–86;
  commercialization of, 3; cultural impact,
  xiii, 2–5, 114–115; freedom in, 87, 102–103;
  in Great Britain, 147–152; immigrant
  story, 6–7, 105, 121; labor relations in, 102;
  memory of, 159–161, 175–179, 187–189; new
  social history and, 100–103; paternalism
  in, 107–108; ratings, 2; scholarly critique
  of, 11–14, 71–72, 130; slaveholders in, 83–87;
  soundtrack, 157, 165; Taiwan broadcast,
  185, 186–187; violence in, 81–82, 85–86,
  91–95, 120; whipping scenes, 81, 84–85, 88,
  100, 123–124; white American responses,
  28–37, 126–127; white characters in, 4–5,
  83, 113, 121–124; white masculinity in,
  83–89
Roots: The Next Generations (TV miniseries),
  16–17, 102, 114–115, 121, 129, 133; ratings, 129;
  response to, 140–141; World War I in, 135–
  138; World War II in, 138–140
Rottenberg, Dan, 71
Roundtree, Richard, 90, 96n9, 115

Schomburg Center for Research in Black
  Culture, 68
Senate Resolution on *Roots*, 32
Shabazz, Betty, 33, 69–70

Since 1970: Histories of Contemporary America

Jimmy Carter, the Politics of Family, and
the Rise of the Religious Right
        by J. Brooks Flippen
Rumor, Repression, and Racial Politics: How the Harassment
of Black Elected Officials Shaped Post–Civil Rights America
        by George Derek Musgrove
Doing Recent History: On Privacy, Copyright,
Video Games, Institutional Review Boards, Activist
Scholarship, and History That Talks Back
        edited by Claire Bond Potter and Renee C. Romano
The Dinner Party: Judy Chicago and the Power
of Popular Feminism, 1970–2007
        by Jane F. Gerhard
Reconsidering Roots: Race, Politics, and Memory
        edited by Erica L. Ball and Kellie Carter Jackson

36/ 548 - 59 00

CPSIA information can be obtained
at www.ICGtesting.com
Printed in the USA
LVOW12s0840120218
566199LV00002B/287/P